THE SAXON CHURCHES OF SUSSEX

Uniform with this book

Anglo-Saxon Towers: An Architectural and Historical Study by E. A. Fisher, MA, DSc

THE
SAXON CHURCHES
OF SUSSEX

by

E. A. FISHER, MA, DSc

DAVID & CHARLES : NEWTON ABBOT

ISBN 0 7153 4946 5

Set in eleven on thirteen point Juliana
and printed in Great Britain
by Clarke Doble & Brendon Limited Plymouth
for David & Charles (Publishers) Limited
South Devon House Newton Abbot Devon

Contents

6 *Contents*

List of Illustrations

PLATES

7

Page

(Unless otherwise acknowledged, the photographs are reproduced by kind permission of the National Monuments Record and the National Buildings Record)

FIGURES IN TEXT

Preface

The comparative isolation of Saxon Sussex and the lack of easy communication between Sussex masons and those in other parts of the country had a marked influence on the architecture of the area. Many churches were primitive in appearance and lacked typically Saxon features, so it is difficult to date them or to be sure of their Saxon or post-Saxon origin. Among such doubtful churches are Aldingbourne, Bignor, Horsted Keynes, Ovingdean, Slaugham, North and South Stoke, Stopham, Tangmere and West Hoathly. Saxon masons too continued to work, and their sons and grandsons after them, using their traditional methods, for much longer after the Conquest than was the case elsewhere.

Churches of Saxon type were built in Sussex as late as the mid-twelfth century, eg Bishopstone tower dated to 1100–1150 (see pp 46–8), Southease Church and the two south doorways at Lyminster. If Saxon architecture, like Norman, is a way or manner of building then these churches should be regarded as Saxon, and are so regarded in this book.

Very many Saxon churches have disappeared, some from general neglect, some through the disappearance of the village as at Botolphs and Warning Camp, some through encroachment of the sea as at Addington, Middleton-on-Sea and Selsey Cathedral.

Some writers (eg, Prof D. Knowles, *The Tablet*, Dec 1962 and Feb 1963) are of the opinion that most Saxon churches were built for poor communities in rural, rustic, out-of-the-way areas, especially in the more backward parts of the country, and that this explains the disappearance of so many through general neglect. This theory has been discussed and controverted elsewhere (E. A. Fisher (c) pp 11–13). Here it is sufficient to say that most disappearances are more likely to have been due to the growth of towns: the churches were replaced by larger buildings required by increases of population in urban areas.

In this book the four sections on Bosham, Jevington, Singleton and Sompting have been reprinted with only minor alterations from the author's earlier book *The Greater Anglo-Saxon Churches,* and the section on Eastdean from his book *Anglo-Saxon Towers.* It would have been unfair to readers to refer them to other publications for five churches, including two of the most interesting in the county, Bosham and Sompting.

At the foot of each section is given a list of authors, details of whose publications are in the bibliography, to whom readers may refer for more detailed information. References concerning particular features are given in the text in bracketed inserts. The numerals in the text refer to notes collected at the end of the book.

The church plans given are drawn, purely for convenience, of closely similar sizes, ie they are not to scale with respect to one another. Each plan, however, is strictly to scale with respect to its various features.

E. A. FISHER

November 1969

Introduction

Up till late Saxon times Sussex was rather isolated from the rest of England, and backward. There were the almost impenetrable forest of the Andredesweald (The Weald) to the north and impassable extensive swamps and marshes between Sussex and Kent. Only from the west and the sea was there reasonable access. During the first Iron Age C Belgic invasion and colonisation of Kent and Hertfordshire (c 75 BC), the early Iron Age A inhabitants of Sussex remained uninfluenced by the new and more advanced Belgic culture of Kent and the Thames valley. The later Belgic invasion of c 50 BC was via Hampshire, probably through Southampton, and it spread northwards to Berkshire and eastwards into Sussex, but did not penetrate further than about Worthing. The eastern part of Sussex remained primitive. Under the Roman domination of Claudius, AD 43 to c 50, the semi-independent, highly Romanised Belgic tribe of the Regnenses held west Sussex under their king Cogidubnus, who built in his capital city, Noviomagus (Chichester) a temple to Neptune and Minerva; the dedicatory inscription still survives in the Chichester museum.

This area from about Worthing westwards into south-east Hampshire and then northwards into Berkshire was dotted thickly with Roman[1] villas and settlements. There was easy road access from the west along the Roman road from London, via Silchester (Calleva) and Winchester (Venta Belgarum) to Chichester. This road was nearly twice as long as the direct Roman road, Stane Street, from Chichester to London. The latter ran through the almost uninhabited district of the Weald; in the early third century Roman official instructions for travellers from London to Chichester were to use the longer route.

The later Saxon settlements were predominantly in the same area. Though they penetrated further east as far as or beyond Hastings, the eastern part of Sussex and the area north of the South Downs remained lightly inhabited right up to Norman times, as is sufficiently evident from the distribution of manors shown in any Domesday Book map of the area (see map on pp 232–3).

As a result of this partial geographical isolation, and in spite of the earlier relatively high Romano-British culture of the western part, Saxon Sussex for long remained economically and culturally backward, and it was the last of the Anglo-Saxon kingdoms to accept Christianity. Its first Christian king, Aethel-wahl, c 660–86, appears to have made little impression on his country's paganism until the energetic Wilfrid appeared to spend five years, 681–6, of his second exile from Northumbria in Sussex, evangelising the area. The success of his mission, not only in Sussex but in south-east Hampshire and Wight, was remarkable and permanent. There appears to be no record of any return to paganism, or of a pagan king in Sussex after his return to Northumbria. In Sussex he must have built many churches (as he had done in north-east Mercia during an earlier exile), and a monastic cathedral at Selsey.

The Saxons did not occupy the Romano-British villas but preferred to build their own timber houses on new sites. The Roman villas became derelict and in the succeeding centuries provided much building material for Saxon churches, which developed on a surprisingly wide scale for so relatively sparsely populated an area. Domesday Book mentions 111 then existing churches, but the actual number in 1086 must have been far more. Domesday Book was an economic survey; its interest in churches was purely economic, and perhaps mentioned only those possessing endowments of economic value, such as land. It is known from early charters that there were at least nine churches in the borough of Lewes in 1086, not one of which is mentioned in Domesday Book; nor is there any mention of a church at Selsey though the see had been transferred to Chichester only about ten years before.

Besides those mentioned in Domesday Book there are about forty churches which the writer considers Saxon, in whole or in part, or probably or possibly Saxon, and which are discussed below. These make a total of more, perhaps many more, than 150 Saxon churches in the county of which about sixty remain entire or in fragmentary condition.

SOME CHARACTERISTICS OF SUSSEX SAXON CHURCHES

General

Sussex is poor in native building stone. The chalk of the South Downs is too soft, though it is occasionally to be found as dressings of openings and in walling mixed with flint rubble. For this reason Sussex did not develop schools of stonecraft like those which grew up near famous quarries elsewhere, as at Barnack (Northants). Sussex masons were not so highly skilled and this may account for the severely plain, rather primitive looking churches, almost if not quite free from ornament. Many of these churches show few specifically Saxon features or details. Genuine 'long and short' or 'upright and flat' quoining or pilaster work is almost absent from Sussex, except at Sompting, Woolbeding and Worth. It is this comparative rarity of Saxon features which makes dating difficult, so much so that some writers describe as early Norman churches which show no specifically Saxon features even though they may have no Norman features either. Thus, Baldwin Brown (op cit pp 456–7) refers to a group of such churches which he was unable to regard as Saxon because they have no 'distinctive Saxon features, but may all be reckoned to date within about a half-century after the Conquest.' He agreed however that some churches 'of essentially the same general character', such as Poling, may have, say a double-splayed window and therefore must be regarded as Saxon. Among these excluded churches were: Eastdean, Eastergate, Ford, Friston, Hangleton, Lyminster, Ovingdean, Rottingdean, Rumboldswyke, Tangmere, Walberton, Westhampnett. All these the present writer considers to be Saxon.

In some cases, though specific Saxon details may be absent, the presence of less specific features may at least indicate strongly a church's Saxon origin; for example, very high and thin (not more than 2ft 6in) walls and a ratio of nave length to breadth of three or more to one.

There are a few highly finished churches in Sussex of an advanced and elaborate type, such as Bosham, Sompting, Worth, which must be the work of highly competent and experienced masons. Possibly these masons were imported from other parts of the country or from overseas. Access from the sea was easy through such ports as Bosham, Lyminster or Ford at the head of the Arun estuary, Westdean (the river Cuckmere, now a mere streamlet, was navigable for small ships to Westdean), and Steyning, Bramber and Buncton close together on the River Adur. Caen stone was imported from Normandy, usually in exchange for wheat, long before the Conquest, though importation increased greatly after the Conquest. This early importation of Caen stone is important historically: its presence, often in small quantities only, in walls (mixed with rubble) and in quoining or as dressings to openings cannot be used legitimately as an argument for a Norman date for a church, an argument which has been used by some writers.

These early relations with France may have had some influence on the type of church building in Sussex. Apart from the possible importation of masons, many French abbeys held land and some had cells in Sussex; among them were Almanesches, a nunnery, St Martin of Séez, Fécamp, Greistein, St Florent at Saumur. There may also have been communication with Flanders and the Rhineland. Such influences may perhaps be seen in the Rhenish helm roof of Sompting tower, and the apses (apses were not popular in Saxon England) at Worth, Exceat and Eastdean.

Proportions

Early Northumbrian churches were long, narrow and high with nave length-breadth ratios of more than 3:1. Kentish churches had ratios of less than 2:1. The high northern ratios spread south, but not significantly, to south of the Thames, except to Sussex where there are about twelve at Aldingbourne, Barcombe (not Saxon but apparently built on Saxon foundations), Botolphs, Easebourne, Lyminster, Rottingdean and perhaps Sompting (see p 175). All other churches in this county have ratios of 1½ to 1¾:1, except Southease, Coombes (which has been shortened, see p 93), Westdean, Bosham and Kingston Buci which have ratios of 2¾, 2¾ or 2⅓, 2⅓, 2½ and 2½:1 respectively.

Towers were not numerous in Saxon Sussex; only nine 'square' ones: Bexhill, Bishopstone, Bosham, Guestling, Jevington, Singleton, Sompting, Sullington and Eastdean (a turriform church). There are also three round towers but only one of these—Southease—the writer would consider to be Saxon.

Of the 'square' towers two only are strictly square, Jevington and Sullington; three others, Guestling, Sompting, Singleton, are wider north-south than east-west; three, Bexhill, Bishopstone, Bosham, are longer east-west than north-south, measurements characteristic of 'porch' towers though neither tower is. At least one tower, Sompting, is axial.

Tower wall thicknesses range from 2ft to 4ft, averaging about 3ft 4in, about the average (3ft 6in) as a whole.

There is an attached staircase tower at Guestling.

Some Sussex churches also have very high walls of, say, 20 to 30ft; among these are Bexhill, Clayton, Guestling, Lyminster, North Stoke, Stoughton. Other high, but not so high walls are at Bishopstone, Chithurst, Kingston Buci, Ovingdean, Poling,

Selham, Stopham, Sullington, West Stoke. Most walls, too, are thin, rarely more than 2ft 8in, a typically Saxon characteristic.

Doorways

In the earliest Saxon churches, those of Augustine and Benedict Biscop and Wilfrid, the main or only entrance was a portal in the west wall. Later, when parish churches, as distinct from monastic or communal minsters, began to multiply, the single western portal gave place to a pair of doorways, opposite each other in the north and south walls, usually near the west end but often centrally placed and occasionally in other positions east or west of central. In towered churches however the western portal was retained, except when the tower had no external entrance (being built perhaps partly for defence or as a refuge against raiders). A great majority of Sussex churches have north and south doorways. In some churches there was only one doorway, north or south, or only one doorway now remains, the other having been destroyed during later rebuilding. In other churches both doorways may have been destroyed and one or both replaced by later openings. Even so, thirty-nine Sussex churches have or had north or south, or north and south, doorways recognisable as certainly or probably Saxon. Only four towerless churches have or had western portals: Bishopstone (originally towerless), Walberton and perhaps Aldingbourne and Cocking.

North and south doorways are of two types as regards size. Some are very tall and relatively narrow, a northern characteristic which again conceivably may be due to Wilfrid's influence, with a height-breadth ratio of $2\frac{1}{2}$ or more to 1. Among these are: Bolney, Chichester, Easebourne, Selham with ratios of 3:1; Worth, two doorways with ratios of 4:1; Lurgashall, Lyminster, Patcham, Wivelsfield with ratios of $2\frac{1}{2}$:1. The other twenty-nine doorways have ratios ranging from $1\frac{1}{2}$ to 2:1.

There is no doubt of the Saxon character of the tall door-

Page 17 : Bishopstone, church from south-west.

Page 18: (left) Bishopstone, south porch and sundial; (right) Arlington, Saxon window.

ways. It is more difficult to assess the age, or whether Saxon or
Norman, of the shorter ones. Some writers regard many as
Norman as they lack specifically Saxon details. This reason for
rejection seems unsatisfactory for the doorways show no Norman
details either, so as they are undoubtedly ancient they are as
likely to be Saxon as Norman. Thus Baldwin Brown writes of
the two ornamented doorways at Bolney and Wivelsfield that
'the design is of Norman character' and that 'as a whole they
have nothing Saxon about them' (op cit pp 488, 370). This
question is discussed below (pp 52–6) where doubt is expressed
concerning the Norman character of the ornament.

Doorways show considerable variety in constructional details.
Only one, Burpham, has a flat lintel; one, at Bignor, seems to be
an arched lintel of two stones; one, at Eastdean, has a flatly
segmentally arched lintel. Six have flat lintels with semi-circular
or segmental arches above them, either as relieving arches (which
are not really needed with lintels) or to enclose plain tympana;
these are at Buncton (2), Hangleton (2), Hardham (1), Patcham
(1, on exterior face only). Thirty have or had round, including
a few segmental, heads; these are Bignor, Bolney, Chichester,
Clayton, Coombes, Easebourne, Elstead, Friston (2), Horsted
Keynes, Lewes, Lyminster (2), North Stoke (2), Ovingdean,
Patcham, Rumboldswyke, Selham, Slaugham, South Stoke (2),
Stopham (2), West Dean (2), West Stoke, Wivelsfield, Worth
(2). Fourteen are of unknown type as remains are fragmentary,
or they have been replaced by later types: Botolphs, Exceat (2),
Ford perhaps (2), Rottingdean, Southease (2), Storrington,
Stoughton (2), Treyford, Woolbeding, West Stoke. Among the
30 round-headed doorways 13 have imposts, including 2 (Stopham, both doorways) which have angle shafts and capitals,
and 16 have neither imposts nor capitals. Five are richly ornamented: Bolney, Lewes, Stopham (2), Wivelsfield; the remainder
are plain. All except three are of one order, Bolney, Ovingdean,
Wivelsfield which are slightly recessed.

Seven towered churches—Bexhill, Bosham, Guestling, Jevington, Singleton, Sompting, Sullington—have or had nave western

portals. These were open arches, not doorways, and of one order. Only Bexhill and Jevington appear to have had openings in the tower west wall.

Chancels

These are normally small and approximately square. Sixteen out of about 27 are square on the exterior, the interior therefore being longer east-west, than north-south by the thickness of one wall, say about 2½ft. Seven are of greater size and proportions. Only 3 have or had apses: Eastdean (a turriform church), Exceat and Worth.

Chancel Arches

Among these may be considered also 4 tower arches and 2 side arches leading to north and south porticus, making a total of 25 arches. Of these, 22 (16 chancel arches and the 4 tower and 2 side arches) are of one order; one at Buncton is of two orders on the west face only and of one on the east; 2, at Bosham and Stoughton, are of two orders on each face. One, at Up Marden, is gable headed. One, the tower arch at Stopham, is of unique design: a curved gable of seven stones. All others are round-headed. Of these, one, the chancel arch at Worth, has half-round reveals and half-round strip work on the jambs on one face, and square strip work on the other face and round the head on both faces; one, Botolphs, has soffit roll to head only; Selham has rolls down the jamb reveals only; Sompting has soffit rolls round the heads and down the jamb reveals; three, Bosham, Clayton and Stoughton, have rolls on soffits and down jamb reveals, and round the heads and down the jambs on both faces (see pp 65–6). Others without soffit rolls but with square strip work round the heads on one face, and down the jambs on both faces, are the two side (porticus) arches at Worth. Four, the chancel arches at Bosham, Selham, Stoughton and Buncton, have capitals and bases ornamented or moulded; one, Sompting tower arch, has ornamented capitals only with no bases. Of these five, the two at Selham and Sompting have imposts or abaci as well as capitals. One, the altar recess at Stopham has neither capitals nor imposts. The remaining twenty have imposts only, of which those at Buncton are elaborately ornamented.

Windows

Little need be said of these. All are small, usually short and narrow, of the 'loop' kind. There are some circular ones at Bosham and Bishopstone. Most are single-splayed; double-splayed are found in some of the later churches. Arched lintels are very common. A few openings narrow upwards, an early feature. Some have sills turned up at the ends, a Norman feature indicating a late date when not merely replacements. Some are very primitive, with no dressings, mere openings cut through or left in the walls, as at Arlington.

Only four towers—Bishopstone, Guestling, Jevington, Sompting—have or had the characteristic Saxon belfry double lights. One church, Worth, is unique in England in having such 'belfry double lights' as its nave lighting.

Porticus

Four churches only have or had porticus or transepts: Bishopstone (exceptionally at the west end), Rottingdean, South-ease and Worth.

Building Materials

Flints are the commonest building material in Sussex. They occur in great profusion covering the chalk and in the fields of the river valleys which have cut through the South Downs. On the surface of the Downs, a few inches below the turf, there occurs a layer of almost unmixed flints below which the actual chalk rock sets in. Flints were also used, and still are, for road making. Flints are common in the churches of west and central Sussex and of the seaboard. In the last named area occur also beach pebbles in churches—and cobbles in houses and pavements. Pebbles and cobbles differ only in size, pebbles being usually less than 2½in in diameter while cobbles may vary in dimensions between 2½ and 9 or 10in.

Flints are usually knapped (split) in church walls, though up to the fourteenth century usually unknapped in secular buildings. Pebbles and cobbles were normally unknapped. Flints were usually uncoursed, though in some churches attempts at rough coursing are evident. Owing to their irregular size and shape, much mortar was necessary; the 'joints' were of necessity wide and in some church walls there is as much mortar as flints.

Chalk. Though this is too soft for normal walling, two hard kinds of chalk found under the surface chalk, known as chalk rag and clunch, are used in walling, the former at Easebourne, Elstead, Treyford and in some other churches in the north-west corner of the county, and the latter for dressings at North and South Stoke and Burpham and in quoins at Hangleton and, alternating with a green calcareous sandstone, in the walls at Aldingbourne.

Limestone and sandstone. When these are used in walling they are usually un-dressed, ie rough, natural stones broken up into pieces of varied shapes and sizes, more or less 'thrown together' with much mortar (though occasionally with some attempt at coursing). This is called rubble or stone rubble—in the Middle Ages *roghwalle*. Only in some late buildings and in post-conquest and Norman (or later) repair work occur smooth, carefully dressed blocks with fine mortar joints producing a smooth surface. This is the so-called ashlar. Only occasionally are very thin walls built of ashlar, for it is generally used as comparatively thin slabs of stone to face rubble or brick. Stone used for ashlar is commonly called freestone due to it being easily and freely worked by freemasons. Rubble stone is not necessarily freestone; it may be and usually is any hard, coarse textured stone that is not a freestone; such stone is often called rag or ragstone.

Of the two types of building stone common in the Midlands and southern England—limestone and sandstone—the former is less common in Sussex than the latter.

A freshwater limestone is found at the Bracklesham beds of the Selsey peninsula. It is sponge-like in appearance, filled with small holes rather like tufa or travertine[2]. It is not good for carvings or mouldings but it weathers well. It occurs in some churches in the south-west of the county, as in the pre-Conquest work at Bosham, Singleton and at Sompting, in the last example especially in the 'long and short' pilasters and pilaster-buttresses of the tower.

Binstead stone is another hard white stone which may have come from the Isle of Wight. It is close grained, rather like Portland stone but coarser and slightly greener than Caen stone. This occurs in some churches of the south-west, as at Eastergate and Singleton.

Quarr Abbey stone is another type, formerly found in Wight and elsewhere on the Sussex coast; the quarries have long since been worked out or covered by the sea. It is a freshwater stone and occurs as dressings in most pre-Conquest churches of west Sussex near the sea: at Bosham, Ford, Lyminster, Poling, Singleton, Sompting, Walberton, and in a few in east Sussex as at St John-sub-Castro, Lewes, and in some early Norman work.

Sandstones come from the geological layer or stratum called the Greensand which encircles the central Weald of clay; it lies between the Weald and the North and South Downs and ends at the sea coast near Dover in the east and at Eastbourne in the south. Sandstone consists of sand or quartz particles held together by a kind of natural cement of silica, or calcite or dolomite (which chemically are carbonates of lime (calcium) and magnesium respectively), or oxide of iron, or just clay, or mixtures of these. These types are described as siliceous, calcareous, ferruginous, and argillaceous. The firestone and Bargate stone of Surrey, found in some Sussex churches, are ferruginous; their brownish colour, which may become very dark on weathering, is due to iron.

Some local sandstones are:

Pulborough sandstone, used locally and also at Lyminster. The carved relief at Tangmere is made of it. It shows various shades of brown, yellow, greyish green, even orange. It weathers well but has a rough striated appearance due to its uneven composition and is suitable only for plain work.

Horsted Keynes sandstone is fairly hard and of even texture. It is quarried at Horsted Keynes and used locally in the church there and at nearby West Hoathly.

Eastbourne rock is a hard greenish-white sandstone of even texture. It is found on the coast near and in the hills behind Eastbourne. It is used at Arlington, Eastdean, Westdean, Friston, Jevington.

Horsham slabs, known as 'stone healing' in Sussex, were widely used for roofing—and paving—and are almost indestructible. But they are very heavy and require exceptionally massive roof timbers for support. As a consequence when they do need renewal they are generally replaced by lighter materials. Those still existing are good to look at from both exterior and interior —on account of the fine timbers of the interior roofings. Horsham slabs are used at Clayton, Coombes, Lyminster, Old Shoreham, Sompting, Southease, Stopham, and in many manor houses and even cottages in the Horsham and Lewes area. They turn brownish on exposure, and are very subject to moss which should be removed.

Roman bricks or tiles occur widely in the round heads of windows, as at Arlington, in the chancel arch heads formerly at Westhampnett and Rumboldswyke, and mixed with other materials in walling at Arlington, Buncton, Chichester, Eastergate, Ford, Hardham, Jevington, Rumboldswyke, Sompting, Stoughton, Tangmere, Walberton, Westhampnett. Some of this Roman tile work—at Eastergate, Rumboldswyke, Westhampnett —is in herring-boning without spines. Herring-boning was a well know structural feature in Romano-British work and was probably copied by the Sussex masons from the derelict villas from which they looted the bricks. There is some herring-boning in flint work at Hangleton, Jevington and Ovingdean, and in thin shaly rubble at Bosham, Bexhill, Elsted, Lurgashall, Selham. This feature may be of direct Romano-British lineage. In other parts of the country herring-boning is regarded by most authorities as a Norman feature only rarely used in very late eleventh-century Saxon buildings, and therefore an indication of late dating. This however may not apply to Sussex in view of the Romano-British examples. Here it would be dangerous to use it even as merely suggestive of a late date.

Roman bricks vary considerably in size. Typically they are about 12in by 6 by 1¼, but may be as large as 18in by 12 by 1½; some at Brixworth are even larger. They may also be square, and sometimes as thin as one inch or less, as at Hardham and Stoughton, but rarely as thick as two inches. In Roman times they were frequently used as bonding courses in flint walls.

In dressing stones the Saxon mason's tool was the axe, and in view of the surprisingly good dressing of much of the work in quoins and interior arches he was expert in the use of this tool. The chisel did not come into general use until the second half of the twelfth century, but Salzman is of the opinion that it was probably used earlier than this for finishing carvings.

Tooling, whether Saxon or Norman earlier than c 1150, was also done with the axe. Broadly speaking, Saxon tooling was rough and indiscriminate; often there was none at all. Norman tooling was diagonal on flat surfaces and vertical on rounded surfaces of columns, capitals, fonts etc.

Saxon mortar was excellent, very hard, being comparable with Roman in this respect. According to Salzman, Roman mortar varied considerably in quality being on the whole neither better nor worse than later kinds. The admitted hardness of existing Romano-British mortar is due to the characteristic of well made mortar that it hardens progressively with progress of time. Presumably Saxon mortar is hard for the same reason.

It was used for flooring, some of which remains today at Barnack and Peterborough. Roman mortar and plaster were often mixed with powdered brick—hence its pink colour—especially when used for the outer facings of walls; the addition was supposed to render it less permeable to rain. Saxon plaster was also good and hard. Much remains today on exterior walls though much has peeled or is peeling off.

Further reading: H. Braun; A. Clifton-Taylor; A. D. Hall and E. J. Russell; P. M. Johnston (l); L. F. Salzman (b).

Churches

ALDINGBOURNE: *Church of the Virgin Mary*

The dedication is modern; the earlier one is not known. The place is situated about 6 miles south-west of Arundel and about 5 miles south-east of Chichester.

The village is an ancient place, Caedwalla, King of Wessex, granted[3] in 683, 87 hides of land at Aldingbourne, Lidsey, Selsey and elsewhere to Wilfrid to found a monastery at Selsey (Selsige). Bede (p 223) records that 87 hides were granted to Wilfrid by King Aethelwahl; this appears to be the same grant; Aethelwahl signed it as under-king to Caedwalla. At that date Caedwalla was in exile from Wessex living in the Andredesweald forest and carrying on intermittent fighting against Aethelwahl. For a period he was in control of Sussex, with Aethelwahl as sub-king, but was later thrown out. During this period he was converted to Christianity by Wilfrid. After becoming king of Wessex in 685 he again fought, and killed, Aethelwahl in 686. He died in 688.

Later, in 692, King Nothelm of the South Saxons granted land[4] in the same place to his sister Notgitha to found a monastery at Lidsay (Lydsige); she immediately re-granted[5] the land to Bishop Wilfrid,[6] a grant later confirmed by the over-king Offa of Mercia.

It is difficult to reconcile these two grants of apparently the same lands, to found two different monasteries, to the same person, by two successive kings within less than ten years. Many Anglo-Saxon charters have come down to us in unsound condition, and close scrutiny of them reveals many problems. However, such niceties of historical scholarship and criticism are not strictly relevant here. The charters are quoted only as evidence of the early dates of the places mentioned, which were active communities centuries before Edward the Confessor.

Later, apparently, these lands reverted to the crown for Alfred the Great in his will[7] left 'the ham of Ealdingburnam' to his nephew Ethelm. The place is mentioned in Domesday Book as Aldingborne. There was a church and priest here in King Edward's time. It was held later by the bishop of Chichester (the see was transferred from Selsey in 1075).

The west wall and the western half of the nave north wall may be Saxon, ie part of the Domesday Book church. The west wall is only 2ft 7in thick (or according to Poole 2ft 4in), which is a Saxon thickness. On the other hand, the top seven stones only of the north-west quoin are visible above the old but later buttress; these are of small stone work in side-alternate arrangement, suggestive of a post-Saxon date. The Victoria County History gives an early twelfth-century date on the plan, but in the text writes 'the oldest recognisable work, probably part of the Domesday Book church, consists of the three western arches of the arcade formerly opening into the north aisle, since destroyed.' This wording is ambiguous: it may mean the walling through which the arcading was (later) cut. Aisles in parish churches were unusual in Saxon times. All other writers regard the arcading as later; Tristram c 1200.[8]

Two of the arches are blocked and no longer visible. The western one was opened out in 1905 and now leads into a modern vestry. Only the plain, square-cut, single-ordered roundhead of 17 voussoirs is original. The piers between the arches were oblong in plan, probably pieces of walling. On the arch soffit are the remains of coeval painting which Johnston dated to c 1080–1100, and Poole not earlier than 1100. Tristram, our main authority on early English wall paintings, dated them to c 1200 which he considered to be the probable date of the arcading and former aisle. The paintings consist of brownish-red geometrical patterns in an orderly arrangement: plain v's, concentric circles, four-petalled saltire-like heads, and series of single inverted v's below two inverted U's.

The eastern half of the nave north wall is modern rebuilding, as are also the two north windows and the west window above the thirteenth- or fourteenth-century west doorway. The tower, projecting north from the east end of the nave is late thirteenth or early fourteenth century.

The south aisle is late twelfth or early thirteenth century, as is the chancel. There is painting on the south arcade dated by Tristram to c 1250, rather later than the painting on the north arcade.

The walls of the nave are of white clunch alternating with a brownish calcareous sandstone rubble, much like Surrey firestone. In the later chancel is a considerable admixture of flints. The nave is plastered on the exterior; old, but not necessarily original, plaster covers the west wall interior. The nave is very long and narrow: 63ft by 16ft 3in, a length-breadth ratio of 4:1. It is possible that it may originally have been a single-celled church with no structural division between nave and chancel, the present chancel being built on later. Alternatively, the nave may have been lengthened westwards, as suggested by the small-stone work of the quoins; if so this must have been done not later than the building of the north arcade and aisle. That the need for increased accommodation grew rapidly is further suggested by the erection of a south aisle so soon, only about fifty years, after the north aisle. This of course is conjecture, though some explanation seems required for so unusually great nave length-breadth ratio.

In the church is a tiny font bowl stated to be the original font of 'the ancient chapelry' of Lydsey. This chapel may well have been part of the late seventh-century monastery founded by Notgitha (or Wilfrid). Lydsey, or Lydsige, was closely associated with Aldingbourne in Anglo-Saxon charters. The manorial overlordship remained with the bishops of Chichester. Part of Lydsey constituted the hide in Aldingbourne held in 1086 (Domesday Book) by one Ausfrid, a Saxon name.

The font is of very crude rough workmanship, approximating to a shallow, circular tub-shape, though the widest diameter is at the top. It is 20in across the top, only 10in high and its lip 2½in thick. There are four small lugs at the top which once extended downwards to the base; the lower parts of the lugs have been broken away. It has no base and now stands on a short portion of a tree trunk. The font is not in use; there is a large hole in the bottom.

Further reading: P. M. Johnston (l), pp 362–7, (k); H. Poole; E. W. Tristram (a), p 97, (b) pp 315, 501; VCH IV, pp 136–8 plan.

ARLINGTON: *St Pancras Church*

The dedication suggests a possible connection with Lewes Priory which had the same dedication. The village is about 8 miles north-west of Eastbourne. The place appears in Domesday Book as Herlintone, but no church is mentioned.

The walls are largely of flints of various sizes, mainly knapped and only roughly coursed. There are many large blocks of stone interspersed in the walls, and bits of Roman bricks here and there.

The Saxon parts are all the nave quoins and immediately adjacent walling, much of the nave south wall and the nave east wall to the north and south of the chancel arch, which is four-teenth century. The church was originally of nave and chancel only. The chancel was almost entirely rebuilt at the same time as the arch, though some of the eastern (interior) quoins may be earlier. The chapel to the north at the west end of the chancel is early Norman. The north arcade and aisle and tower were Norman Transitional. The tower was not bonded into the nave west wall. The tower arch is fourteenth century and may have replaced an earlier, perhaps Saxon, doorway though there is no direct evidence for this. The present and only entrance to the church is the fourteenth-century south porch and doorway. There is no evidence of early north and south doorways.

The fourteenth-century rebuilding was probably after a fire traces of which were found during a general restoration of 1892 about 6in below the then floor (which was about 1ft below the existing one). Burnt stones of the twelfth–thirteenth century were found in the debris and lying on top were mason's chips and stone dust. Some burnt stones, worked and moulded, were

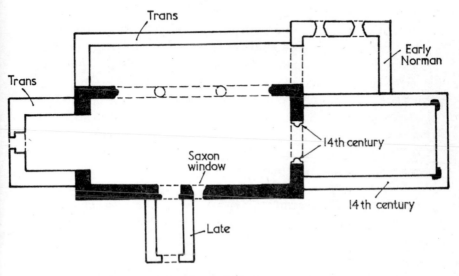

Fig 1. Arlington

built into the existing fourteenth-century work. This fourteenth-century re-building brought the church to its present form. There had been an earlier fire, traces of which were found 3in below those of the later fire. Some Roman bricks and pottery were found in the lower debris which led Powell to think the church had been built on a Roman site, a conclusion which by no means follows, and is not now accepted.

The nave walls are 2ft 6in thick and have no plinth. The nave north-east quoin is hidden by the north aisle. The other quoins are all similar: some modern brick replacements at the base, then to about half way up large upright and flat slabs, the upper halves being of face-alternate slabs. The chancel quoins are visible on the exterior above the later corner buttresses; they are of irregular upright and flat arrangement. All are visible on the interior; here they are of smaller stones than those of the nave.

In the nave there were originally three windows in each—north and south—wall; only the middle one in the south wall remains (plate p 18) just to the east of the south porch gabled roof. It is double-splayed, including the 'sill'; the round head is of Roman bricks and of poor construction; the jambs and sill are of flints, with some Roman bricks—just walling. There are some remains of old plaster on the exterior. On the interior all is plastered, like the walls, with modern plaster. The outer edges of the interior jambs, but not the aperture, taper slightly upwards and then die into the head; there are no imposts. It is relatively short and wide for so early a window. It is 9ft 4in above the modern tiled floor.

On the interior nave walls were scanty remains of fourteenth-century paintings overlaid with some seventeenth–eighteenth-century paintings.[9] There may be more under the plaster.

There are no original openings in the chancel.

In the early Norman north-west chapel are two original windows with early features. One is 8¾in wide at the aperture. It has a double-arched lintel, jambs mainly of short uprights on end, and sill turned up at the ends in Norman fashion. It has a double splay of complex type, evidently designed for a light shutter (drawing and section in Powell).

Further reading: P. M. Johnston (l); C. E. Powell, plans; H. Poole.

BEXHILL: *St Peter's Church*

Before and up to the Reformation the dedication was to SS Peter and Paul.

The place is called Bexelei in Domesday Book. It was held by

Bishop Alric of Selsey of King Edward. It was held under the Conqueror by the Count of Eu. It was assessed at 20 hides of which Bishop Osbern held 10 and two clerks (clerics), Geoffrey and Roger, held one hide as a benefice *(in prebenda)* under the Count.[10] Two churches are mentioned, one of which is certainly St Peter's.

An alleged grant of land[11] 'in the place which is called Bixlea' was made in 772 by King Offa to Oswald, bishop of Selsey, for life with reversion to the see for ever for the building of a minster *(monasterium)* to augment the cathedral *(basilicam)*. According to VCH no such bishop is known. His name does not appear in Walcott's list of the bishops of Selsey and Chichester. His bishop Bosa or Bosy, the fifth in succession after Wilfrid, no date given, may be the same man. In W. G. Searle's list of Anglo-Saxon bishops the fifth bishop of Selsey after Wilfrid is given as Osa, or Bosa, or Osweald for whom he gives the following dates: earliest and latest mention in any charter 765 and 772 respectively; dates of consecration and of death (or translation) any date between 747–65 and 772–80 respectively. Evidently this is the same bishop as Oswald of the charter of Offa, so there seems no reason to doubt the authenticity of the charter. Apart from this charter nothing is known of so early a church on this site. That the land was used as a burial ground is suggested by a child's coped coffin-lid or grave slab, 2ft 9in long, and elaborately ornamented, dug up in 1878 about 6in below the nave floor close to the first Norman pier of the south arcade. J. Romilly Allen (op cit, p 274–7, good drawing), stated that the particular interlacement ornament in the central square (eg a square divided diagonally into four triangles, each of which is filled with a similar piece of knotwork) of the stone occurs in England only at two places—Bexhill and Yarm (Yorks, NR)—though it is fairly common in Scotland; he refers to fifteen examples there. It also occurs in two MSS in the British Museum, one an English eighth-century psalter (Vesp A1). The ornament may therefore be Hiberno-Saxon. Interlacement ornament occurs also on an imported, ie not local, stone at Ford church (see p 115), and on abaci at Selham church (see p 172). Johnston was of opinion that these are the only examples of interlacement ornament in Sussex. However, later writers, especially A. W. Clapham and T. D. Kendrick, consider the Bexhill grave slab to be early eleventh century. Kendrick indeed considered it 'certainly eleventh century work' and as a 'solitary archaizing sculpture' difficult to explain. D. Talbot Rice thought it to be ninth century. In view of these conflicting opinions the slab cannot safely be quoted as evidence of an early graveyard, though it must be earlier than the Norman arcade (1150–60) and probably contemporary with the Saxon nave, say a century earlier than 1150.

The church has had a complicated building history as a result of which the Saxon parts still incorporated in the fabric were not recognised as such until 1907 when J. E. Ray was able to examine early work during the re-building of that date. A short account of this history is necessary for a clear idea of the Saxon portions of the church.

There is Saxon work of two periods, the earlier of the eleventh century and pre-Conquest, the later post-Conquest of c 1070–85. The pre-Conquest nave appears to have been small and is represented by the existing west wall and the north and south walling above the existing Norman two-bay arcades. It was about 26ft long by about 16ft wide. Nothing is known of an early chancel. The shortness of the nave suggests that it is unlikely to have been a single-celled church with the east end used as a chancel, and it seems a reasonable presumption that there was a small chancel, which may perhaps have been as wide as the nave and very short.

In 1070–85 a western tower of at least two stages was built, the ground stage of which still exists. Possibly the old chancel, if there was one, remained, or it may have been rebuilt, or a new one erected, again conjecturally as wide as the nave, say, 16ft wide by about 11ft long.

In 1150–60 Norman arcades of two bays and of two orders were cut through the north and south walls and narrow

Page 35 : *(above)* Bosham, tower base from south-west; *(below)* Coombes, west wall exterior.

Page 36: Bosham:
(*left*) chancel interior
from south-west;
(*right*) nave west
wall interior.

north and south aisles built, 9ft 3in and 9ft 9in wide respectively.

In 1230–40 the nave was extended eastwards by about 13ft and a third bay was added to the arcade in the contemporary Early English pointed style. Either the old chancel was demolished, or only the east and west walls were removed, the north and south walls being retained to form the nave extension. Bits of walling appear to have been left on the east sides of the early Norman responds, between them and the new arches. The old chancel was replaced by a new and larger one, about 37ft long by about 17ft wide, further east. The north and south aisles were extended eastwards as far as the new chancel, and the original arch or doorway, leading to the tower from the nave, was replaced by a pointed arch similar to the new chancel arch and arcade eastern arches.

Various additions and alterations were made in the fifteenth and sixteenth centuries, and a drastic rebuilding was carried out in 1878 under R. Blomfield. The old thirteenth-century chancel was partly incorporated into the nave which was thereby extended in length by about 23ft, ie by two bays, to its existing length of 62ft.

The present nave therefore is of five bays of three different dates: two western Norman ones, the centre one of mid-thirteenth century, and the two eastern bays of the south arcade (the north wall here is open to a fifteenth-century chantry) of 1878 date. A new chancel of similar dimensions to the old was erected further east. The old thirteenth-century chancel arch was re-erected in its new position, 23ft further east. A new, wider and higher south aisle was built, a south porch added and repairs made to the north aisle. The tower above the ground stage was removed and rebuilt.

Curiously the south wall of the nave, but not the north, was made to diverge slightly towards the south from about the point of the middle Norman south pier, the width of nave in consequence being 16ft at the west end and 17ft 9in at the eastern (interior measurements). This resulted presumably from the

C

Saxon south wall beginning to lean outwards before the erection of the Norman arcade. The first member of the arch, built round the centring is normal but the second or upper member laid upon it follows the slant of the wall. The result is that in the second, or eastern, arch on the south the upper member projects 5¾in on each side of the lower where it leaves the capital, but when it reaches the top of the arch head, the projection is only 4in on the north side and 7½in on the south, the difference of 1¾in representing the divergence of the wall from the vertical at that point. This slanting of the wall was continued in the later walling.

In 1907 the last restoration was carried out: the north aisle was re-built and widened and the south extended westwards nearly as far as the west wall of the tower. It was during this restoration that J. E. Ray was able to establish the early date of the earliest parts of the church by examination of the exposed portions of the nave north wall. This wall, built of stone rubble, had been raised 16in, probably when the aisle was built in 1150–60. Below this later upper part the wall was clearly of a different date. Below this lower earlier walling the Norman bays had been cut through, for a narrow strip of walling around the arch heads was less compact, of looser structure, than the eleventh-century wall above. The rector of that time, Rev L. S. Clarke,[12] wrote that when the plaster was removed he found the wall 'to be very hard and strong, and it was evident that the Norman builder had cut away the wall and erected the arches under the superstructure of the old Saxon wall, and just filled in the slight interval with loose rubble'.[13] The eastern—thirteenth century—part of the wall was separated from the older western part by a narrow stretch of walling approximating to ashlar which seemed to mark the east end of the old Saxon wall. This narrow stretch corresponded to the similar narrow stretch left attached to the eastern Norman responds when the thirteenth-century extension was made (see p 37). The height of this old wall was over 20ft and it was only 23in thick. It also had some rough herring-bone courses. There were continuous sleeper walls below the north and south arcades which indicated continuous earlier walling before the arcades were cut.

The tower is 15ft wide and 18ft 6in long (E–W) internally. The walls are 3ft 6in thick except the north wall which is 3ft 8½in. Internally the tower is about a foot narrower than the nave, but externally it would originally have projected on north and south about a foot beyond the nave walls. The ground stage is 18ft high and there was a slight off-set between it and the stage above, indications of which are visible on the interior of the north wall. The upper stage, or stages, were removed and rebuilt in 1878. There were, and are, plain one-ordered round-headed arches in the north and south walls, 6ft wide and 4ft 11in high above the modern floor to the 4in imposts. Each head is of two rings, an outer and an inner. The north one has ten voussoirs on the south, the springers being rather longer than the others, and fifteen on the north. The south arch head has ten voussoirs on the north and ten on the south; they vary considerably in lengths, the longer ones being cut to appropriate curved shape. The arch faces are flush with the wall faces, and are not rebated for doors. They are original for they differ from the Norman arcades in being of a different kind of stone, and having no chamfers as the lower members of the arcade arches have, though they have chamfered imposts. The arches were built up at some time but were opened out in 1907. Their object is not known. They did not lead into aisles—there were none. No foundations of lateral outbuildings were discovered when the ground was trenched in 1907 for the western extension of the south aisle. But they do indicate that the tower was not built for defensive purposes. The original tower eastern arch or doorway (replaced by the present pointed arch in the thirteenth century) may have been similar for its original chamfered imposts of Caen stone, still in the later arch (though 5ft higher up than those in the other arches), are similar. The western doorway and the window above are fifteenth century but the tracery of the window and the facings of the doorway are of

1907 date. Nothing is known of an original western doorway. It seems likely that the tower had arched openings in all four walls, as at Monkwearmouth.

Further reading: C. Earwaker; P. M. Johnston (h); W. H. Mullens; H. Poole; J. E. Ray, plans; VCH, IX, pp 121–2.

BIGNOR: St Cross Church

The village is about 4½ miles south-west of Pulborough. A manor and church are mentioned in Domesday Book as Bigneure. Some parts of the existing church may be Saxon. Poole dated them to the Overlap as they show 'some definite Norman features'; the only definite ones appear to be the chamfers of the jambs of both north and south doorways. These doorways, chancel arch, font and parts at least of the walling may well be Saxon.

The walls are of squared stone rubble. All nave quoins are hidden by later buttresses. The chancel quoins are of large and long stones arranged face alternately. The wall at the chancel arch (jamb width) is 2ft 8½in and at the south doorway 2ft 11in thick. The nave is 42ft long by about 18ft wide. The very long chancel is 29ft by 18ft but the original length is uncertain; it may have been lengthened at some time.

The chancel arch is fine. The head is of two thin (outer and inner) rings of voussoirs, square-cut of one order, slightly horse-shoed, with 17 voussoirs on east and west face, all very roughly axe dressed. The jambs also are roughly and irregularly tooled with one stone only with diagonal tooling. Each jamb is of five stones on each face, all very thin like the voussoirs; the top stone is small, the others tall—12 to 24in long—on end. Between the thin east and west faces are two to three large slabs per course. The imposts, also roughly dressed, are duplicated laterally; ie each is of one eastern slab 2ft long and one western one 8in long. The western ones only have diagonal tooling, and may be renewals. They have no chamfers and are not returned along the wall faces. The opening is 8ft 9in wide and 6ft 10½in high to the under-side of the 12in imposts, and about 12ft 2in to the crown of the arch.

The north doorway is blocked. It is about 10ft from the west wall but is not in its original position, being now in the later aisle. On the interior its jambs look old, with later chamfers. The head is a very flat segment of voussoirs. The doorway is 7ft ½in high from the aisle floor and 3ft 5in wide. The exterior face is later; the head is pointed.

The south doorway is 4ft 3in from the west wall. It is in the nave, probably in its original position (the south aisle is short and to the east of the south porch). It also has a flat segmental head but of two stones only; it is really a flatly arched lintel of two stones. The jambs have eight stones on the east, four being on end, the others side-alternate, and nine on the west all side-alternate. They are chamfered but the tooling is rough. There are no imposts. The opening is 4ft wide and 6ft 5in high to the 'springing'.

The font has very rough tooling and finish. It is circular; the bowl is 20in high, on a modern stem which stands on a modern base. It is 2ft 2in across the top, tapering and rounded downwards to about 18in. The lip has no fillet and is two inches thick.

Further reading: P. M. Johnston (l); H. Poole.

BISHOPSTONE: St Andrew's Church

The village is midway between Seaford and Newhaven. The manor, but not the church, is mentioned in Domesday Book as Biscopestone. It was held by the bishop of Chichester, hence its name.

The church is very beautiful and more elaborate than many early churches both in plan and details; it is a three-celled church with a western tower attached. It is not known whether the elaboration was intended by the Saxon builders, or was due to Bishop Seffrid II (1180–1215) who rebuilt the eastern part of the church. It consists now of Saxon nave and south-west porch;

the western tower, north aisle, choir and gabled shallow projecting outer doorway of the porch with corresponding inner doorway to the nave are of Norman date; the chancel or sanctuary
is of the Norman–Transitional period.

The original church of nave, chancel and south porch was
dated by Baldwin Brown to probably 900–950 or later, though
he also suggested the end of the eighth century as conjecturally
possible. W. H. Godfrey thought it might be as early as the
ninth and not later than the tenth century. Jackson and Fletcher
thought the early eighth century possible on account of similarities of its original plan and other features to the church at
Bradford-on-Avon (Wilts) which they showed was Aldhelm's
original church of c 700 up to as far as the string courses. Poole
called it simply pre-Conquest. Any date between the early eighth
and mid-tenth century would be consistent with the monumental evidence. It was recognised as Saxon by Rickman.

The Nave. The south-west quoin is of one long stone on end
(3ft 3in by 15in by 17in), one long flat (2ft 9in by 12in by 18in)
and then small irregular slabs of mixed face and side-alternate
arrangement. The south-east quoin is no longer visible. The
north-east quoin is not visible as it has been integrated into the
north aisle wall. The aisle west wall was largely integrated with
the nave west wall, but four quoin stones were left and are
still in situ: two long flats separated by one long upright, and
one cubical block below, all much worn, and all of yellow sandstone. The walls are of knapped flints. They are high and stated
to be less than 2ft 6in thick. Actually at the south doorway the
wall appears to be only 2ft 2in thick, and at the tower arch
2ft 1in.

The Porch (plate p 17). The quoins like those of the nave are
of sandstone, but more massive—almost megalithic. The south-
west quoin is of four tall slabs on end (pillar quoins) of diminish-
ing heights; the bottom one is 4ft 4in by 18in by 12in; then
come two long flats in face alternate arrangement. All are
roughly dressed. The south-east quoin has one very long stone,
then one very short, then one very long all on end, then one

long tall flat, one long, one flat. The porch is 12ft 5in deep and 9ft 2in wide internally, and 21ft high. The outer doorway is centrally placed, as is usual. The inner doorway, 3ft 3in wide, of Norman date, is close to the west wall to allow room for an altar against the east wall; it is 5ft from the east wall and only 9½in from the west. The thin gabled porch-like projection to the outer south doorway is contemporary with the inner doorway, built at the same time or perhaps a little earlier than the north aisle—early twelfth century. This porch, originally a porticus, must have been lighted. At present the only window is in the west wall. It is rather widely single-splayed. The sill is of one thin stone, also splayed. The exterior jambs are of two rough upright slabs each. On the interior the jambs are of four rough slabs each, with plaster fillings between the outer and inner jambs, and a modern timber flat lintel just above the level of the outer lintel which is arched in a curious way, rather thirteenth century than Saxon. This opening may have replaced an earlier one though there is no evidence of this. There is a recess in the east wall, 5ft above floor level, of unknown date; it now has ornate Gothic filling. It is above where the altar would have been.

According to Jackson and Fletcher the porch was originally a porticus, the main entrance to the nave being a western portal. The later tower has no external entrance. This necessitated another portal, hence the conversion of the south porticus into a porch. The altar was presumably removed and a through-way made by cutting a doorway through the south wall and a reconstruction, and possible widening, of the interior south doorway to the nave; this interior doorway was originally the entrance to the porticus and may have been a narrow open archway.

Baldwin Brown and Clapham thought that some porches were given altars, to be dual purpose porches-cum-side chapel, as are the chapel of St Gregory under the south porch tower at Canterbury, and the porch at Bradford-on-Avon. Clapham op cit (*a*), pp 120–2 considered the porch to be a successor to and of later date than the porticus: a porch was a porticus with an outer doorway; a true porticus had no through-way. He is not clear whether the earliest porches were converted porticus, ie converted to dual purpose, but implies that this is so, or at least that the use as porch was secondary. This is denied by Jackson and Fletcher: porches were not a development from porticus, nor were there dual purpose porticus used both as lateral chapels, with altars, and as porches. The two adjuncts developed independently.[14] Early porches were always at the west end, as at Monkwearmouth (Co Durham), Titchfield (Hants) and Bradwell-juxta-Mare (Essex). Supposed dual purpose porticus are survivals of porticus later converted to porches of entry, superseding the earlier usage after removal of the altars. At Bishopstone the later outer south doorway was centrally placed. Curiously at Bradford-on-Avon the inner door, leading into the porticus, was centrally placed, the outer one being displaced towards the west, to avoid the altar; it may be that the altar here was retained for some time after the conversion to porch.

There may have been a corresponding north porticus; one would expect one. No excavations have been made and there is no direct evidence. But a considerable number of large stones (one at least is over 4ft long), similar to the megalithic quoin stones of the south porticus, are to be found in the later north buttress and as base courses under the corners of the extended chancel. Where did these come from? They were possibly rejected by the Norman builders (who disliked large stones) when, or if, they pulled down the supposed north porticus and built the north aisle, and may have lain about for centuries until re-used for their present purpose, probably in the 1849 restoration.

Saxon sundial (plate p 18). This is in the porch south wall immediately above the outer gabled Norman doorway. It is inscribed with the donor's or mason's name, Eadric. The style hole and thirteen lines, five with crossbars which are longer than the others. These mark the four Saxon tides of the day and each tide is divided into three parts thus marking the times from 6am to 6pm in Roman hours. It is 10 or 11ft above ground and faces roughly S + 15°W. There was an earl or ealdorman Edric, who is known to have signed various documents as 'dux' between 932 and 949. He was a brother of Earl Aethelstan of Essex[15] and of Earl Aethelwold, a landowner in Sussex. The latter in his will, made in the reign of King Edred, 946–55, left an estate at Washington 'to my brother Eadric'. If this Eadric is the donor of the sundial, which is in situ, this is evidence of the latest possible date of the porch, say, mid-tenth century.

After the Saxon period there were four, or possibly five, building periods in the twelfth century; the first three (or four), perhaps close together in time, were of Norman date (say, 1100–80), the last Norman Transitional of c 1180–1200.

The earliest Norman work was the erection of the western tower; the second was the replacement of the Saxon chancel by the existing choir (then the chancel); the third was the cutting of a two-bayed arcade through the north wall and the erection of an aisle; of about this time or perhaps a little earlier were the gabled south doorway to the south porch and the reconstruction of the inner doorway to the nave. The last work was the building of the beautiful little sanctuary, lower and narrower than the choir and not much more than 10ft square; this was probably carried out by Bishop Seffrid II (1180–1215).

The Choir. The second Norman work was the replacement of the Saxon chancel with what is now the choir. This was built contrary to the usual custom as wide and as high as the nave. The reason for this is not known. It may have been built on the same plan and foundations as the earlier chancel as is suggested by the fact that the walls are no thicker than those of the Saxon nave; or, a further extension eastwards was contemplated, in which case it was intended to be eventually a presbyterial space between nave and chancel as at Brixworth, Deerhurst and early Glastonbury.[16] It has a blind arcade of two arches on the south wall, and originally on the north wall too but the latter was cut through later to the north aisle when this was made. The eastern arch of each is decorated with chevron patterns, the western ones moulded. The more elaborate ornament of the eastern arch was due probably to its being more easily seen by the congregation in the nave.[17]

The windows, two in each north and south wall, were originally round-headed; those in the north are now blocked, those in the south[18] were replaced by lancets in the thirteenth century. Originally there were two ranges of windows (at least in the south wall), the lower ones were within the arcades[19] and in Sharpe's day one was blocked and one half-built up; above these were two windows, one round-headed Norman, blocked, similar to those in the sanctuary, and one thirteenth century lancet to the west. Figg's elevation of 1849 showed two lancets above, as at present and none below; hence in the 1849 restoration the lower range must have been blocked and the flint walling made good (no remains of the windows are visible now) and the Norman window above replaced by another lancet to make the existing pair. These windows are higher up than the similar thirteenth-century south lancet windows of the nave; between the two sets the junction of choir and nave wall is marked by three large stone slabs in the flint wall—perhaps the remains of the original nave south-east quoin. The eastern quoins of the choir are of Norman small stone work of mixed face and side-alternate arrangement.

In the east wall, above the later sanctuary roof and below the choir ceiling and so visible from both interior and exterior, are two occuli; small on the exterior and single but not widely splayed towards the interior. Each is cut from three stones. Similar occuli occur in a number of Sussex and Surrey churches. Where the chancel roof is lower than that of the nave the occuli are in the nave east gable. They may have lighted an inter-roof space.

The Tower. This was the earliest work here of Norman date. Though chronologically Norman it is most un-Norman in its proportions and details though there is some Norman 'feeling' in the belfry windows and perhaps in the moulded western quoins of the upper stages. Architecturally it is more Saxon than Norman (plate p 17). Its tall slender proportions and its

four receding stages separated by string courses, and its double-
light belfry windows are those of a typical English–Carolingian
tower, very different from the low, squat, relatively wide and
heavy-looking towers so commonly met with in small Norman
parish churches. The thickness of its walls, about 4ft or a little
less, is hardly typical. If its date were not known no one could
mistake it for a Norman tower. It would seem unreasonable and
even misleading to omit such a tower from consideration in a
book on Saxon churches: to the writer it is simply twelfth-
century Saxon.

The tower is 45ft high to the corbel table; the interior of the
ground floor is 13ft east-west by 11ft north-south. It is of fine
proportions; the stages are 14ft 6in, 10ft 6in, 11ft 6in and 8ft
6in in height. The four receding stages are separated by string
courses. The two lower strings are plain chamfered above, the
top string square-cut. The walls, like those of the nave, are of
flint, originally plastered. The ground stage had, and has, no
external entrance, a not uncommon Saxon feature. The ground
floor round-headed windows, one in each wall, are modern. The
second stage windows, one in each wall, very narrow and tall
(loop variety) rest on the strings; they have arched lintels, jambs
of four slabs each, side-alternate, and are chamfered all round.
On the interior the jambs are of small slab work with some
renewals, and have flint rubble fillings behind the shallow
jambs. The single splays are narrower than those of the ground
floor windows, not the usual wide Norman type. Immediately
above the lintel exterior of the west opening is a corbel with
worn animal head, reminiscent of those at Barnack and Deerhurst.

The third stage windows on the north and south are similar
to those in the second stage but are above the strings and so
have separate sills, of single slabs; jambs are of side-alternate
slabs of about equal heights; heads and jambs and sills are chamfered. In the west wall is a circular window, touching the string,
with supposed ball ornament.

The fourth stage is the belfry. The north, south and west

openings are similar, of the usual Saxon double type but have rather wide mullions, instead of shafts (a Norman feature), which, with the arch heads, end in simple roll mouldings. The eastern opening has a shaft with cushion capital and base, the faces of which are flush with the outer wall face.

The east wall of the tower (originally the thin Saxon west wall of the nave) was strengthened, thickened by a very tall round-headed arch, supported on hollow chamfered imposts, or corbels, high up in the north and south walls. This is visible from the tower interior; its head is on a level with the sills of the third stage windows. This arch cuts across the remains of two single-splayed original windows (Jackson and Fletcher (d), pl II) side by side, as at Monkwearmouth, in the nave west wall. These are blocked and invisible from the nave, but plain from within the tower. Below these windows there is no evidence of an original western portal, though there must have been one. The existing entrance to the tower from the nave, cut through the Saxon west wall, is necessarily narrow (the tower interior width being only 11ft) but wide enough to have obliterated any sign of an earlier doorway. The existing arch is round-headed, of one order, square-cut on the west but with a three-quarter round facing on the east to head and jambs. The head is of short slabs cut to curved shape, 19 on the east, 17 on the west, with rubble or flint filling between the two rings. Jambs are of short slabs (8–9in) on end. The imposts have a quirk and lower chamfer on the east, but on the west are cut off flush with the wall face. They are not returned along the wall face beyond the arch head.

The tower quoins, mostly of Caen stone, are of slabs irregular in heights and dispositions, though of mixed face and side-alternate arrangement in the ground stage. Stones are duplicated in places, especially in the top two stages 'where each angle is cut to form an external angle shaft'; that is, a three-quarter round moulding up the edges of the top two stages.

North Aisle. This also has some Saxon features: windows, and thin walls no thicker than those of the nave. There are five small round-headed windows in the north wall; the eastern and western ones are modern, whether replacements is not known. The three older ones have arched lintels on the exterior, pillar monolithic jambs, and sills turned up at the ends in Norman fashion. They are chamfered all round. The interior single splays are rather wider than those of the tower openings. The heads are of fourteen small very irregular stones, the jambs of three pillar stones each with no imposts (on interior or exterior). On the exterior the openings are 20in by about 7in, on the interior the splays are 3ft 9in high. The aisle roof is continuous with the nave roof but brought down at a different angle. Roofs are of red tiles, except the tower which is shingled.

Further reading: G. Baldwin Brown; W. H. Figg; W. H. Godfrey (b) and (c), plans; E. D. C. Jackson and E. G. M. Fletcher (c) and (d); H. Poole; T. Rickman.

BOLNEY: St Mary Magdalen's Church

The village is 11 miles north of Brighton and 7 south-east of Horsham. Neither church nor place is mentioned in Domesday Book. Baldwin Brown considered the church to be definitely Norman mainly on account of what he thought to be Norman ornament on the south doorway. VCH dated nave, chancel and south doorway to c 1100, a reasonable date in view of the evidence. Poole called the doorway 'a typical Norman doorway'; the present writer cannot agree.

The walls are of rather large but irregular stone rubble, fairly well coursed but with wide joints. The nave south-east quoin is of smallish rectangular slabs, side-alternate; some stones, especially upper ones, have diagonal tooling, but the rest are roughly dressed with no tooling. On the fifth stone from the base is a small circular sundial, only 4in in diameter, with hour lines all round, which is unusual. The south-west quoin stones are of rougher shapes and finish, mainly of greyish stones with some yellow and brown here and there. Some groups of slabs have their longer sides pointing east, not alternately; the west face of the quoin is hidden by a buttress. Here also is an exactly similar sundial on the fifth stone from the base. The north-west and north-east quoins are hidden by the tower and aisle. The chancel south-east and north-east quoins are similar to the nave south-east quoin, side-alternate with some diagonal tooling.

The nave is 42ft 6in long by 20ft 6in wide; the chancel is about 23ft 6in by 18ft. The chancel walls are about 3ft thick. At the south doorway the nave wall appears to be about 3ft 3in thick, a Norman rather than a Saxon thickness.

The Chancel. This is deflected on its axis to the north. It has two original windows, one in the north and one in the south wall, rather east of centre. The south window on the exterior has an arched lintel, the jambs are of two slabs each, the lower one being more massive than the upper, a short sill not turned up at the ends, and a slight chamfer all round. The opening is 2ft 4in high by 8½in, splayed on the interior to 4ft 9in by 3ft. The splay appears less wide than is customary with Norman windows. The interior head is of eight voussoirs of fairly uniform breadth and thickness, though rather thin, and of variable length. The jambs are of four slabs each, side-alternate. There is some diagonal tooling though it is mainly indiscriminate. The north window is similar. Dale stated that during the restoration of 1853 he found slight indications of similar windows to the north and south of the existing thirteenth-century east window; there are no indications now. Dale (who was vicar from 1849) also reported that a very few years before he took over 'a fine old *zigzagged* chancel arch, flanked by two smaller ones, was taken down, replaced by a tall staring pointed arch *plain to ugliness*' (his italics). It was altered to its present smaller form by Dale in 1853. Such a zigzagged arch suggests a Norman date for it and perhaps also for the church, though the arch might be later, as at Coombes. The chevron ornament was introduced into England between 1110 and 1120 and may not have reached Sussex till much later. It is possible that Dale's zigzag ornament on the arch may not have been chevron, but the same V-ornament as on the south doorway. High up in the chancel east gable is a circular opening cut from four stones on the exterior. It has very slight single splay on the interior. Both nave and chancel have very sharp gables; the chancel ridge is only about a foot below that of the nave.

According to Dale all the windows in the nave were originally similar to those of the chancel, but were blocked before the then recent (1853) rebuilding, when the arcade and north aisle were built and a new chancel arch inserted. He found remains of one in the nave south wall (indicated in VCH plan, to the east of the doorway). There is little indication now of this except perhaps three stones near to and west of the modern two-light south window: one, which might be a small impost, with diagonal tooling, and two smaller ones above with indiscriminate tooling.

The South Doorway. This is about centrally placed; it is now within an eighteenth-century (1718) porch. It is stated that the jambs at some time were re-cut to make a wider opening. This is more than doubtful: the inner arch is splayed (a rather useless splay would surely have been removed in a desired widening of the opening); a widening of the outer opening would be evident (and it is not) from the resulting setting back of the cut jambs behind the arch head, instead of the more usual setting back of the arch head behind the jambs. The imposts however have been cut back flush with the reveals and the western, but not the eastern one, flush also with the wall face.

The arch seems to have been made in three sections. The inner opening is plain, of one order, square-cut, and may be regarded as a deep rebate for the door which shut flat against the narrower outer opening. The head is of nine voussoirs and the jambs of nine slabs each, some with rough diagonal tooling, some without. There are no imposts or through-stones. The opening is 3ft 10in wide on the interior and 3ft 6½in on the exterior, ie where it meets the outer opening. It is 7ft 7in high to the springing, that is about 9ft 6in to the crown of the arch. It is 2ft 7in deep from the nave interior wall face. As the outer opening is only 8in thick this gives a thickness of 3ft 3in for the wall here. The outer opening is 6in narrower than the interior, ie 3ft wide in the clear. It is 8ft 1in high above the nave floor (and 8ft 11in above the later porch floor) to the crown of the arch; that is, the outer head is 1ft 5in lower than the inner.

The imposts are plain chamfered on their outer edges and perhaps originally on their reveals too before they were cut back. The eastern one projects about 1½in. They are just long enough to cover the two orders of the arch head. The jambs, like the imposts, are chamfered and are of large slabs of up to about 14in long.

The outer arch head is of two very slightly recessed, about 2in, orders on the exterior and of one plain order on the interior. Each order is of eight voussoirs each, about 12in long in the outer order but rather shorter in the inner order (the fourth from the east in the outer order is very narrow). The two orders were cut separately as the joints do not run through both orders. The outer order is 7½in wide and the inner one 9½in. The arch head appears to have been built in two sections, a plain inner one and the outer ornamented one built flat against the inner one with a straight joint, which is visible all round the soffit. The joint is 3 to 4in from the inner face and 4 to 5in from the outer. Curiously however the voussoir joints run straight through the two layers; that is, the inner and outer voussoirs were of identical sizes. The imposts were built similarly, but there is too much repair work in cement patching for it to be seen whether the jambs were constructed similarly.

The ornamentation of the outer arch face is extremely interesting. It is identical in all respects with that on the arch face at Wivelsfield, only 5 miles east-south-east of Bolney; both must have been cut by the same mason. The outer ornament consists of three V-shaped grooves round the head with their points facing inwards. The inner is of two V-shaped grooves above, then a half-round, and one-and-a-half V-shaped grooves below, the V-points facing outwards (Poole, pl III; also drawing in Dale, p 60).

Page 53: (above)
Bosham, chancel arch
north column base;
(left) Lyminster, Saxon
(above) and Norman
(below) blocked south
doorways.

Page 54: (above) Clayton, chancel arch from west; *(below)* Lyminster, chancel arch from west.

Baldwin Brown regarded this ornament as a distinctively Norman feature: an alternation of half-rounds and angles similar to that on the piers of the south transept at Ely (1081–93), and the north transept at Winchester (1079–93) cathedrals. To the present writer this seems an unduly imaginative, even far-fetched comparison between the plan of a complex Romanesque pier and a piece of pure decoration on a flat surface. The Winchester piers[20] are rectangular, with a flat pilaster on each face and a half-round column on each pilaster, each pilaster and each half-round supporting something above. In plan therefore there would be an alternation of one half-round, three angles, one half-round, three angles and so on round the four faces. This fundamental plan is further complicated by additional half-rounds on two faces—on each side of the pilaster strip—and angle shafts on another face. To unroll, in imagination, this plan of a complex functional feature, to see what it looks like in the flat, and then apply it as pure decoration to a flat arch face does not strike one as psychologically likely. A little more likely perhaps, but still rather improbable, would be to grasp by direct insight that such a complex pier plan, with no intentional decoration on it, might form a basis for the decoration of a flat surface. The difficulty seems greater when it is seen that there is no alternation in the Bolney or Wivelsfield ornament: two adjacent sets of V-shaped half-rings with a single half-round in the middle of one set cannot meaningfully be called an alternation, as it is called by Baldwin Brown. The basis of any real comparison, or relationship, or influence between two such different features seems to the writer to be just not there.

It should be pointed out, too, that this V-shaped grooving has no resemblance to the characteristically Norman chevron ornament. A better comparison would be with rather similar, and undoubtedly Saxon, decorated window heads at Swalcliffe (Oxon) and doorways at Somerford Keynes (Glos), and St Patrick's chapel, Heysham (Lancs).[21] These form an interesting and comparable group. Heysham and Somerford Keynes are ancient, possibly late eighth century. Both have arched lintels

D

and are of similar construction with height-breadth ratios of more than 3:1. Heysham however has three sunk flutings round the lintel while Somerford Keynes has three raised cable mouldings. Swalcliffe has groovings though it is probably later than the other two. Bolney and Wivelsfield have heads of voussoirs, not lintels, though the ornament can hardly be regarded as more sophisticated than Somerford Keynes.

The slight recessing of the two orders is not Norman, still less is it characteristically Norman. Norman recessing was usually deep; the inner order would be built on centring, the outer order on the inner order with considerable projection on both faces. Slight recessing, of but one or two inches, on one or both faces, was by no means uncommon in late Saxon times. It occurs in the (old) chancel arch and tower west doorway at Kirk Hammerton (Yorks, WR), in the tower west doorway and lower east arch at Old Clee (Lincs), in the fine tower arch at St Mary the Younger in Bishop Hill Junior (York), in the tower east arch at Langford (Oxon)—all dated to c 1040 or perhaps later. Two definitely post-Conquest, ie Overlap, examples occur at Pattishall church (Northants) in the chancel arch and blocked north doorway.

The exterior wall face around the Bolney doorway up to the height of the imposts and within the porch has been refaced with very large slabs, well dressed to ashlar appearance, similar to those of the porch walls; some of the slabs are up to about 17in by 12in, larger than the jamb stones. This refacing appears contemporary with the porch (1718). Above impost level the walling is original rubble.

Further reading: G. Baldwin Brown; J. Dale; P. M. Johnston (1); H. Poole; VCH, VII, pp 139–40, plan, pl of church from SE facing p 137.

BOSHAM: Holy Trinity Church

The original dedication is not known. According to an Episcopal Visitation of 1281 it had no dedication. The first mention of a dedication was in a Patent Roll of 1330. But the church had several altars each dedicated to a different saint.

The village is situated on Bosham Channel or Creek in the area known officially as Chichester Harbour. It is an ancient place, of some importance in Roman days. There were Roman settlements at Bosham and round about. Roman pottery and sculptures have been dug up in the district, one large head from the churchyard. But the suggestion of some early writers that there was a Romano-British basilican church on the site of the present church is mere conjecture. The place was a port of considerable importance in Saxon times. It was from here that Earl Harold, later King Harold, sailed on his unfortunate trip to Normandy. His departure and Bosham church are depicted in the Bayeux tapestry. Bosham was a royal manor belonging to Edward the Confessor and may have been a royal manor of Canute's. There is a centuries' old tradition that a small grave at the east end of the nave, near the chancel steps, is that of a young daughter of Canute. The grave was opened in 1865 and found to contain the skeleton of a young girl of about eight years of age, but there was nothing in the coffin, not even grave clothes, to serve as means of identification. There may be some truth in the tradition. It would carry the origin of the church back at least to the period of Canute, a likely date and consistent with the architectural details. Baldwin Brown dated it to the reign of Edward the Confessor (1042–66). It was certainly in existence in Edward's time for he granted it to his kinsman, Osbern, later second bishop of Exeter (1072–1103), a gift confirmed by William the Conqueror. It was a particularly rich church. In Domesday Book it is recorded that in Edward's time it was worth £300 and owned 112 hides of land. The precise size of a hide of land is not known; it certainly varied widely in different parts of the country. Stenton thought it approximated to 40 acres in Wilts and Dorset (it was 120 acres in Cambridgeshire). The commonest church endowment recorded in Domesday Book is about one hide. With 112 hides, equal to perhaps 4,500 acres or more, Bosham's endowment must have been one of the richest in

Saxon England. Surely such a large estate must have developed over a considerable period of time by accretion of numerous gifts. Either the church is earlier than Edward the Confessor or even than Canute, or the existing church must have replaced an earlier one of which we know nothing.

The tower, much of the nave and the western third of the chancel are pre-Conquest. The timber spire shingled with oak is later. The church is badly set out, in true Saxon manner: none of the corners is a right angle, no two walls are parallel or of equal length and the (lengthened) chancel diverges to the south from the axis of the nave by 3ft 4½in. All walls are thin and of the same thickness everywhere: 2ft 6in. They are built of fairly large rubble with wide joints. The tower quoins are of rather irregular sized upright and flat slabs. One upright in the south-west quoin is more than 3ft tall and has rough tooling, probably by axe, not chisel. Some flats run far into the wall, one for about 3ft and another for 5ft 9in. There is no plinth. The tower has four stages with string courses between the lower three stages. The west wall is 20ft 4½in wide; the interior width is about 15ft 4in at the west and about 16ft at the east. It is about 3ft longer east-west than north-south. This and the thin walls might suggest a porch tower, but there is no evidence for this; the tower is in fact not a porch tower. Though unusual there are some Saxon non-porch towers with their longer axes east-west, as at Ledsham, Middleton-by-Pickering and Wharram-le-Street (Yorks).

In the ground stage there is a round-headed single-splayed window in each north and south wall; each head is of seven voussoirs, the jambs of three slabs each—flat, upright, flat, the top flat serving as impost. There is no western doorway or other opening in the west wall of this stage. In the second stage are single-splayed round-headed windows in the north, west and south walls, similar to but taller and narrower than those below in the north and south. In the third stage in the west wall is a single tall blocked round-headed opening, badly worn. On the south and north were originally double round-headed openings of the usual Saxon belfry type. The heads were of ten real voussoirs each, with the centre voussoir common to both heads. Each jamb is of three flats and two very tall uprights, the top flats serving as imposts. They were the original belfry openings; they are now blocked and modern neo-Gothic double windows inserted in the blockings. In the fourth stage in the west is an original double opening of belfry type. It has four voussoirs to each half-head, central straight shaft with a capital brought to roughly circular form below by means of chamfered edges, and plain necking below the capital. The central and jamb imposts are thin square slabs. The base to the shaft is like the capital reversed and stands on a thin square stone like the impost above. The jambs are of roughly square slabs in no particular arrangement. The openings in the north, south and east walls are of modern neo-Gothic.

The tower arch (plate p 36) is fine but dwarfed by the truly magnificent chancel arch. Its head is of voussoirs in two rings with rubble filling between the rings. The lowest three arch stones on each side are not voussoirs but flat stones running further into the walls than the very even voussoirs above, and cut to appropriate shape on their soffit ends. The sloping of the joints to a common centre only begins at the fourth stone above the imposts. The head is thus slightly stilted and set back slightly behind the jamb reveal faces. The jambs are of six upright and very long flat slabs each, the top flat being immediately below the impost. The uprights are through-stones, the flats are three per course. The imposts are hollow chamfered on their soffit ends only and are not returned along the walls. The arch is 6ft 11in wide and 8ft 8in high to the lower side of the imposts.

Above the tower arch about 18ft above floor level is a large gable-headed opening (plate p 36) cut straight through the wall, ie with no splay. It now contains glass but was originally a doorway opening from the second stage of the tower to a gallery across the west end of the nave, as a similar opening did at Deerhurst. This gallery was removed in the mid-nineteenth century. Whether this was the original reason for the doorway is not known; but it is likely that it was intended as a means of ingress to the second stage of the tower, perhaps by ladder from the nave, as was the case in many other Saxon churches. To the south of this doorway is a small rectangular opening made of four stones: a massive lintel and sill and two thinner upright stones as jambs. Above and slightly to the north of the gable-headed doorway is a fairly large round-headed opening with no dressings. Its sill is 29ft above floor level and on a level with the top of the nave walls. It was probably an ingress to an inter-roof space or chamber above the nave.

The nave is 56ft long and about 23ft wide. It is high, 29ft to the eaves. The quoins are rather different from those of the tower; they are of large square slabs in no particular arrangement. There are three circular single-splayed original windows high up in the north wall.

The chancel is nearly as high as the nave and about 18ft wide. It is not built centrally against the nave but about 3ft to the south of centre. Only the western third, about 15ft, is of Saxon date; the next third or slightly more is Norman and the eastern third is late twelfth century. The Saxon and Norman parts are stated to have ended apsidally. The three parts are plainly evident on the interior through slight differences in the walling (plate p 35). The Norman middle section also differs from the Saxon part in having some herring-boning in its walls. In the north wall of the Saxon part are the remains of an original single-splayed window, blocked and cut into by a later twelfth-century window. It had a round head of selected stones, not voussoirs, and jambs of selected rubble and no imposts.

The chancel arch is magnificent, one of the finest in the country. It is centrally placed in the chancel west wall and therefore a little to the south of centre viewed from the nave. It is taller and wider than the tower arch. It is of very late Saxon design, and not necessarily of the same date as the main fabric. It has soffit rolls and normal angle shafts running up the jambs and round the head. The complicated bases and capitals are alike though the members of the capitals are thinner than those of the bases (plate p 53). The jambs stand on two huge slabs or plinths; the lower one, square-cut, measures 4ft east-west and rather less north-south and is 8in thick; the upper one is a circular disc 3ft 6in in diameter and 8in high with a half-round edge. They have been stated to be re-used Roman stones but there is no evidence for a Roman origin and Baldwin Brown considered them to be characteristically Saxon. Massive stones in quoins and bases are indeed characteristic Saxon features. On these two stones stand the actual bases of the columns, a tall circular chamfered base 8in high with two quirks, and above that a flat faced band (a kind of complex wide necking) 6in high, chamfered above and below between two quirks. The capitals are similar to the bases, though of course reversed, with a similar round-edged disc and square-cut abacus above. There is a half-round, or rather segmental, strip-work hood mould round the arch head on both east and west faces. Unlike many other chancel and tower arches, both faces are similar.

The distance between the two massive plinths is 9ft 5in. The plinths protrude from the walls about 2ft 6in so the width of the opening behind the dressings would be about 14ft 5in. It is 20ft high to the square abaci.

Further reading: G. Baldwin Brown; A. W. Clapham (a) and (b); K. H. Macdermott; H. Mitchell.

BOTOLPHS: St Botolph's Church

The manor is not mentioned in Domesday Book, but Annington, as Haningdune, is. Annington appears to have been the manor served probably by this church. The village was prosperous. The river Adur was navigable as far as Bramber (near Steyning), about a mile up-stream from Botolphs, and Annington shared in the sea trade, possibly having its own wharf. The sea began to recede c 1350 and the village to decay in consequence; it is now 3 miles from the sea. By 1536 the village was so impoverished and reduced in size that it was incorporated in the parish of St Nicholas of Bramber, as it is today, the combined parish being designated Bramber-cum-Botolphs. There is now no village of Botolphs; it is a mere hamlet of a few houses (including one called Annington Manor House) and mounds where farm buildings and villagers' houses once stood. The church is isolated on the east side of an unimportant road roughly parallel with the main road from Steyning to Shoreham.

Bramber and Steyning, only about a mile apart, were the two main towns of the Rape of Bramber, and Bramber castle was the seat of W. de Braose who was tenant-in-chief of Bramber Rape under the Conqueror. Between Bramber and Annington was Beeding, called Beddinges in Domesday Book and reported therein to have two churches. According to VCH one of these was probably the church or chapel *de Veteri Ponte* (of the old bridge), the bridge across the Adur between Beeding and Bramber. The remains of this bridge, with the remains of a chapel on it, were discovered in 1839 about 250yd from the existing Bramber stone bridge (E. Turner (*a*); W. H. Godfrey (*b*)). From literary sources it is known that this chapel was dedicated to St Mary. There was another 'old bridge' associated with a church of St Peter, which apparently gave its name to a parish called St Peter de Veteri Ponte (A. H. Allcroft (*c*)). This church was given to the French abbey of St Florent at Saumur by W. de Braose when he handed over Beeding Priory together with St Nicholas, Bramber (Brambria), and St Nicholas, Shoreham (Sorham) to the Abbey c 1080.[22] Salzman makes out a strong case for locating this church and bridge at Annington (or Botolphs), ie equating the parish of St Peter de Veteri Ponte with that of Annington. The evidence seems convincing. Thus, in a lease dated 1469 of 'the rectory of St Peter de Veteri Ponte' it was stated that the rectory was 'in Annington and Botolphs'. There is however a difficulty in accepting Salzman's thesis without some qualification. Salzman identified Botolphs with Annington[23] presumably because the latter was mentioned in Domesday Book and the former was not. He also identified Annington with St Peter de Veteri Ponte at Beeding. The inference is that there were only two churches, whereas Domesday mentions three: one at Annington and two under Beeding. This difficulty would be removed if Salzman's identification of Botolphs with Annington was wrong, and there really were two churches at Annington: St Peter de Veteri Ponte and nearby Botolphs. If this were so, Salzman's identification of Annington with St Peter de Veteri Ponte would be convincing. It would also explain some other historical points. The bridge was old in 1086, hence its name, and perhaps already out of use. It and its church may have deteriorated further in the next century or so and the congregation transferred to nearby Botolphs. This would explain the addition of a north aisle to Botolphs c 1250 and the association of St Peter with St Botolphs in the dedication. After c 1440 there is no further record of this bridge; it seems to have disappeared, and the church too, and its site is unknown. About the same time or later, St Peter was dropped from the dual dedication of Botolphs, St Botolphs becoming again the sole dedication, as it is today.

The nave and chancel arch are undoubtedly Saxon, possibly late, though their date is not known. Poole thought the nave pre-Conquest; the chancel arch probably is post-Conquest for it has soffit rolls, a late Saxon feature. Baldwin Brown regarded this nave as post-1040, that is, in the Confessor's period or the Overlap. The chancel is later, probably c mid-fourteenth century, the same date as the tower. It has been stated that the chancel replaced an apsidal one but there is no evidence for this.

The church is built of knapped flints and was plastered on the exterior; some plaster remains. The roof is of Horsham slabs, though the interior timber roof is modern. The nave is long and narrow, about 55ft 6in long by 17ft 6in wide, interior measurements, a length-breadth ratio of slightly more than 3 : 1, an Early Saxon proportion. Such a high ratio is of great interest, especially in Sussex where there are twelve churches (including two perhaps rather doubtful) with similar high ratios.

The earliest architectural developments in Saxon England took place, in very different styles, at the two extreme ends of the country: in Kent, under Augustine, from c 600, and in Northumbria from c 670 under Wilfrid of Ripon and Benedict Biscop. One of the more striking differences between the two styles was dimensional: the ratio of nave length to breadth in Kent was about 1½ or 1¾ to 1; in the North it was rarely less than 3:1. As the two styles spread northwards and southwards respectively so the ratio also spread. To avoid undue precision it may be taken that a ratio of 2 or less than 2 to 1 is typical of the south, and 2, 3, 4 or more to 1 of the north. From available data there appear to be about 14 such ratios north of the Humber, 39 between Humber and Thames (ie in greater Mercia, including Lincolnshire, East Anglia and Essex), 1 in Wessex, 1 in Kent and 10 or 12 in Sussex. The spread south apparently accompanied the spread of Northumbrian culture after the political hegemony passed from Northumbria to Mercia. Apparently too this culture did not spread significantly south of the Thames even when Wessex was dominated by Mercia in the time of Offa. Why was Sussex an apparent exception? This may well have been due to Wilfrid who spent five years, 681–6, of his second exile from Northumbria in Sussex evangelising the area. Here he must have built many churches (as he had done in north-east Mercia during an earlier exile), and a monastic cathedral at Selsey. The success of his mission was remarkable and permanent. There appears to be no record of any return to paganism, or of a pagan king, in Sussex after his return to Northumbria. His influence persisted.

The chancel is 20ft 4in long by 15ft 8in wide, exterior measurements. On the interior the chancel is about 16ft by 10ft; this agrees with north and south wall thicknesses of about 2ft 10in but makes the east wall over 4ft thick which it might well be in a fourteenth-century wall. The nave walls are 2ft 7in at the south door, and 2ft 8½in at the chancel arch.

The south-west quoin has tall stones, up to 20in by 18in, on end below; the upper ones are of modest sized slabs, side-alternate. The north-west quoin is largely of modern brick replacements but has some almost cubical blocks on end. The south-east and north-east quoins are of small slabs side-alternate, with some renewals; the chancel quoins are similar. There is some diagonal tooling here and there, but mostly none.

A north aisle was cut through the wall c 1250. Some centuries later, when the village had deteriorated, the aisle was removed and the wall built up again. The three wide pointed arches are still plainly visible in the outer wall face, with round-headed windows, one in each arch, built in the blockings.

In the nave south wall, near the west end, is a small original window, now partly a modern replacement on the exterior: the round head is of cement, perhaps very badly worn and cemented over. The exterior jambs are of two stones each, a massive cubical one above a smaller narrower stone in the west jamb; in the east the lower stone is massive. On the interior it is round-headed and rather widely splayed. The head is of eight very small and very roughly dressed and worn stones. The interior jambs are of five stones each; the top one in each is tall and on end, the others small and side-alternate. There are no imposts. Godfrey described the window as Norman, but apart from the not very wide splay it looks more Saxon than Norman in workmanship. A blocked window above the later south-east window appears to be Saxon.

The south doorway, about centrally placed, is not Saxon, but seventeenth century; the porch is modern. There is no north doorway; if there was one it would have been destroyed when the north arcade was cut.

The chancel arch. This is of great interest. It is of one order and has a soffit roll, ie a roll round the soffit of the arch head but not down the jamb reveals. Soffit rolls are a late, perhaps a very late, Saxon feature, not a Norman feature. They occur at Bernay Abbey (1017–40 or 45) and a few other Norman buildings of the first half of the eleventh century, but after c 1050 they disappear from the Duchy being replaced by multi-ordered arches with rolls on their edges.

H.M. and J. Taylor, in their monumental descriptive catalogue of Saxon churches, call Botolphs soffit roll 'an unusual feature'. In this context the phrase may be misleading. The feature is the simplest and earliest—earliest typologically if not chronologically—member of a series of arches having soffit and/or face rolls, which may be regarded collectively as the 'soffit-roll system' of ornament. The historical development of the series is interesting and is discussed elsewhere.[24] Only the seven examples in Sussex need be considered here.

At Botolphs there is a soffit roll only. At Selham there are rolls down the jamb reveals but not round the arch soffit. At Sompting the soffit rolls pass below the imposts and down the jam reveals. At Clayton, a two-ordered chancel arch, the face rolls are on both faces with no capitals or bases. At Bosham and Stoughton, both of two orders, the face rolls are on both faces, the capitals showing development from Saxon type at Bosham to a mixture of Saxon and Norman at Stoughton. In the two-ordered arches the face rolls are really angle shafts.

Worth chancel arch is unusual in design; there are no soffit rolls and no attached jamb rolls; the north and south faces of the jamb reveals are half-round, the diameters of the half-rounds being only slightly less than the jamb thickness.

Botolph's arch head is of 16 voussoirs on the west face and 15 on the east; all are thin, but the north springer on the east face is very long and cut to curved shape. The soffit roll rests on corbels of unique design; each has four rows of elliptical depressions, not unlike some of those at Marton (Lincs) chancel arch (Fisher (b), fig 29). The bottom row has four depressions, and they decrease in number upwards to one in the top (fourth) row. The soffit roll is attached; it does not form an integral part of the head; it consists of 21 half-roll slabs of varying but short lengths, and the joints do not correspond with the joints between the voussoirs on either face. The voussoirs are through-stones only as far as the central roll. The head may therefore be regarded as of three rings (not orders)—an eastern, a western, and a central one which is the soffit roll. The square jambs are of small, brick shaped and sized blocks on the south (they may be brick replacements under the wash), and slabs, three or four per course, on the north. The tooling is mainly horizontal. The opening is 7ft 8in wide, and 7ft 3in high on the north to the base of the 9in impost (there is no impost on the south); that is, about 11ft 10in to the crown of the arch.

There may be early paintings hidden beneath the whitewash of the interior (André et al).

Further reading: G. Baldwin Brown; W. H. Godfrey (l); *P. M. Johnston; H. Poole; H. M. and J. Taylor; VCH, I, p* 444.

BUNCTON: *All Saints Chapel*

The village is some 1½ miles east of Washington and 2 miles north-west of Steyning.

This may be a very ancient place. A grant of land at an unidentified place, Gealtborgsteal, was made to Bishop Wihtun by one Ealdwulf, heretoga (ealdorman or sub-king) of the South Saxons, under and with the consent and licence of King Offa of Mercia in 791. It was dictated from the hill of Biohchandoune, probably Buncton.[25] The place is mentioned in Domesday Book as Bongetone. No church is mentioned.

It is a small church with a later western bell turret and very short later chancel. Its date is not known; it is only doubtfully Saxon. Bloxham called it Norman of c 1150–80; Johnston dated the nave and chancel arch to c 1070, the absence of buttresses suggests an early date. But the chancel arch certainly seems later. It has been suggested that this church may have been built by the monks of Beeding (or Sele) Priory c 1150–80, but this may apply only to the chancel which has pointed (perhaps Norman-Transitional) arcading on its north and south exterior walls. Or perhaps the arcading is of stones from Sele Priory built into the walls as ornamentation in the fourteenth century, a reputed date of the existing chancel. It is also stated that the chancel was merely shortened in the fourteenth century, as the east wall is of ashlar. This is not so; the bottom six or seven courses, the north half as far as the eaves and a narrow strip surrounding the east window are ashlar; above this is older work comparable with the rest of the church. The arcading projects only slightly from the wall face; it surrounds recesses which suggests it may be coeval with the walling, unless the recesses are later blockings. This seems unlikely. No indications of former annexes have been discovered. The ornamented faces are obviously exteriors, not just junctions with some outer annexe. It seems reasonable to regard the arcading as decoration and contemporary with the chancel walls. The chancel is 14ft 6in long (east-west) and 20ft wide on the exterior, an un-Saxon-like proportion. This unusual shortness, compared with the width, may have suggested the idea of a later shortening.

The Nave. The walls are of mixed knapped and unknapped flints, with Roman bricks here and there which may have come from a Roman villa about half a mile distant, the hypocaust of which was discovered in 1848. There is still much old plaster on the south wall.

The north-west and south-west quoins are of smallish slabs, side-alternate, with some diagonal tooling and some duplication; there is some brick repair work in the south-west quoin. There is no plinth. The nave is 34ft 9in long and 23ft 5in wide. The wall at the north door is 3ft ½in thick; at the chancel arch it is 2ft 8in thick.

There were two doorways, in north and south walls, placed a little east of central. The south one is blocked. It has a flat lintel of one roughly shaped and dressed stone above which was a plain, very flat segmental relieving arch, of which only a few stones remain. It seems too flat to be effective. The faces are flush with the wall face, and there is no projecting strip work. The jambs are of eight cubical slabs each, about half being duplicated; there is some diagonal tooling. The opening appears to be about 5ft high and 2ft 8in wide; on the interior it is 3ft 2in wide. The present entrance is on the north, exactly opposite the south doorway, and is of similar design but in much better condition. The flat relieving arch has ten voussoirs, all slightly tapering, the springers being of proper wedge-shape. The jambs are of ten small cubical stones, with some duplication. The imposts are thin, 3½in thick on the east, 5in on the west. The opening is 6ft 6in high to the imposts, and 3ft 1in wide. The interior head is carried up higher than, ie above, the exterior relieving arch. The inner opening is also wider by 4½in each side than the outer frame which is 9½in thick; the interior rebate for the door is therefore 2ft 3in deep. There is some diagonal tooling.

There are three small, apparently original, windows: two in the south wall and a narrower one in the north wall, all high up. Of the two in the south, one is east of the doorway and one to the west. The east one has an arched lintel, jambs of three slabs each, no sill, and a slight chamfer. The west one looks like a modern copy: it has arched lintel of two stones, jambs of two stones each, a turned up sill, and a wide chamfer all round. The window in the north wall is opposite the eastern one in the south wall. All are fairly widely splayed on the interior, the heads are of voussoirs, the jambs of side-alternate small slabs; there are no imposts.

The Chancel Arch. This is very fine and large. It is of one order on the east and two on the west, square-cut, flush with both wall faces. There are angle shafts on moulded bases standing on small square plinths. The capitals are of curious, possibly unique, design: the square abacus is brought to approximately circular shape by a chamfering of the faces; these flat chamfers are tucked in at the corners, or edges, the tucking in becoming deeper progressively towards the base to bring the capital to roughly circular shape to fit the column. The chamfered imposts are very curiously ornamented with three layers of carvings of Norman appearance: the top layer is of two rows of alternately raised and sunk squares, each raised or sunk being above (or below) a corresponding sunk or raised square; the second layer is a double row of very finely executed herring-boning with no spine; the chamfer has rather crude human faces and other ornament. It is in fact rather typical early Norman decoration. The imposts are returned to the nave wall face. The opening is 9ft 8in wide and about 9ft 3in high to the 9in imposts, ie about

14ft 10in to the crown of the arch. There was formerly early painting on the nave wall of which no traces remain (André et al).

Further reading: W. H. Blaauw; M. H. Bloxham; P. M. Johnston (l).

BURPHAM: *St Mary the Virgin's Church*

The place and its church are mentioned in Domesday Book as Bercheha(m). Burpham is probably an ancient place. Part of a Roman pavement was uncovered in the mid-1880's just beyond the east wall of the north transept. Nothelm granted land at Piperingas (now Peppering), near Burpham and in the parish, to Berhtfrith, Bishop of Selsey, c 700.[26] It was one of the 'strong points' in the chain of defensive fortresses extending from Plymouth to Surrey built by King Alfred. It is mentioned as such in the Burghal Hidage[27] a document dated to the reign of Edward the Elder (900–24). It was supplanted later as a strong point by Arundel, 2 miles south-west of Burpham.

The nave north and south walls are possibly pre-Conquest or, as Poole thought, of Overlap date with some Norman features. The walls are of knapped flints, with much old plaster remaining. The north and south transepts are early twelfth century, the chancel early thirteenth. The tower is fifteenth century. There is a gable-headed opening in the nave east gable, above the chancel arch and vaulting, and above a fine oak timber roof beam (in the nave). This opening may have led to, or lighted, an inter-roof space.

The nave is 38ft 6in long and 18ft wide. There is a small blocked window of primitive character in the north wall near the east end. It has a much worn single-arched lintel. Jambs are of one tall massive stone each, with small rectangular slabs above. The sill is of a very thin red Roman tile. It is very slightly chamfered all round, except the sill. A similar window near the west end was destroyed in 1892 when the more westerly of the modern two-light windows was inserted.

Page 71 : (*left*)
Selham, chancel arch
from west; (*right*)
Old Shoreham,
remains of Saxon
north doorway.

Page 72: (*left*) chancel arch
north capital; (*right*)
chancel arch south
capital.

The blocked doorway in the north wall is about centrally placed. On the interior it has a very flat (almost lintel-like) head of eight almost rectangular voussoirs. The upper half of the opening now has in it a modern coloured memorial window in modern surrounds. On the exterior the lintel is joggled, ie it is in three pieces; the centre stone is T-shaped, so cut that it rests on, and is supported by, the two outer ones. The jambs are of eight stones each, of side-alternate arrangement; it is not evident whether they are through-stones. The aperture is 3ft 2in wide on the exterior; on the interior it is 3ft 8in wide and 7ft 1in from the floor to the springing.

The modern main entrance, with a modern south porch, is a few feet to the west of the blocked north door. It is of similar dimensions; it may be a copy of an earlier south doorway or perhaps has some re-used early material in it. Remains of some thirteenth-century wall paintings were discovered in 1868 but were not preserved (André et al).

Further reading: A. Hussey; P. M. Johnston (l); M. A. Lower; R. H. Nibbs; H. Poole; F. W. Steer: he reproduces S. H. Grimm's drawing (1798) of the church from the north-east, and F. W. Saunders' drawing (1862) from the north-west.

CHICHESTER: St Olave's Chapel

St Olave or Olaf was King Olaf Haraldson of Norway, 1016–30. He came to England in 1013 and until 1016 he helped King Ethelred against the Danes—Sweyn and Canute. He became king of Norway in 1016, was driven out by Canute in 1028 and was killed at Stiklestad in 1030 when trying to regain his kingdom. Though not canonised, as a political saint, until 1154 he was regarded unofficially as a saint soon after his death and became the centre of a cult which spread rapidly throughout Scandinavia, and apparently England for besides Chichester the dedication occurs at ancient churches in London and at least eight other places in Great Britain. This dedication therefore does not preclude a date well prior to 1154, especially as there

E

was no reason for Olaf's popularity in England in Norman times. The church may indeed have been founded by Scandinavian merchants known to have been settled in Chichester (some say encouraged by Earl Godwin, the greatest Saxon landowner in Sussex). There are still Scandinavian family names in Chichester. A few Scandinavian names also occur as sub-tenants in the time of Edward the Confessor.

This church is puzzling, both as regards its date and many features of its fabric. P. M. Johnston wrote that 'evidence for pre-Conquest date though weighty [is] not convincing'. J. Cavis-Brown (op cit) stated, without giving any evidence, that the church contained work of the first, seventh, eleventh, twelfth and very early thirteenth centuries. P. Freeman considered the original church to be Saxon, not Roman, and perhaps late seventh century on account of certain close similarities to features at Brixworth; he suggested, merely as possibilities, that certain features might be of the first or fourth century. A writer in the *Gentleman's Magazine* for 1852 thought there were three building periods: c 680, due perhaps to Wilfrid, c 1040 and c 1310.

The church is not mentioned in Domesday Book. Chichester —the borough of Cicestre—is mentioned at some length, but the only church here is mentioned elsewhere under Pagham Hundred. This Hundred belonged to the archbishop of Canterbury who also owned land in the Pallant—a district of Chichester—and most writers consider that the church in Pagham Hundred was in fact All Saints in the Pallant.

In VCH the nave is dated to early twelfth century in the plan, but to the end of the eleventh century in the text. It is also stated that there was a small chancel which was rebuilt and enlarged in the late thirteenth century. According to L. Fleming the nave west wall is thirteenth century; it is shown in the VCH plan as early twelfth, the same age as the other nave walls. Much re-building was carried out in 1851. Tristram (op cit (b) pp 307 and 525) wrote that the church was demolished in the early years of the nineteenth century; later that it was 'rebuilt entirely in 1851; the chancel was originally Norman with later alterations'. This re-building does not appear to have been as complete as Tristram stated. The chancel arch was rebuilt. The perhaps thirteenth-century 3-light east window was replaced by a 2-light window (which was replaced by the existing 3-light window in 1956), and the thirteenth-century paintings around the old windows destroyed.[28] The earlier (thirteenth century) east window had replaced a still earlier single-light window the sill and lower parts of the widely splayed jambs of which were visible below the later window though they had been blocked with masonry when the later window was inserted. Freeman thought the earliest window to be Norman, perhaps on account of the wide splay.

The chancel floor, which had been raised at some time by several steps to 4ft above the nave floor, was lowered in 1851 to its present height of two steps, 12in, above the nave. The western doorway and the window above were replaced by the existing doorway and window in fourteenth-century style.

Since 1956 the church has been in use as an SPCK bookshop. The interior has been re-plastered and painted white and all architectural details are hidden, except those of the south doorway. The church is wedged between modern shops on north and south, and the east end is built round completely by modern private property and is quite inaccessible. Only the west front is visible on the exterior. This is of coursed flints with some scattered stones. The north-west and south-west quoins are of small stone work. The exterior east end is visible above the roofs of the modern cooling sheds of the neighbouring butcher's shop. The south-east quoin, upper part, is of smallish stone slabs; the north-east is rather similar but the stones are larger and look older; one is very large, almost massive.

Freeman reported that there were large Roman tiles in the south wall of the nave, herring-boning in the east wall of the chancel and square Roman tiles 'in vast numbers' all along the lower part of the nave south wall. He thought this evidence of an earlier date than medieval, but not Roman. This was a reasonable conclusion. The south coastal region of Sussex was in earlier days dotted with Roman villas from which the Saxon builders looted their bricks.

The nave is stated to be 25ft 6in long by 17ft 4in wide, and the chancel 13ft 8in by 13ft 10in. Freeman's measurements were, for the nave 25ft by 18ft, and for the chancel 16ft 6in by 12ft 6in. He wrote the 'east wall, seen in the lithograph [ie the interior east wall of the undercroft] is 12ft 6in wide'. The chancel north and south walls are not in alignment with the nave, but deviate to the north.

The south doorway is of Saxon type—tall and narrow. It is of one order, square-cut, round-headed, chamfered rather narrowly round the inner edge. The jambs are of small 'upright and flat' slabs of similar heights. The opening is 8ft 4in high and 2ft 7½in wide. A similar but smaller arched opening, nearly 7ft high by 2ft 1in wide, attached to the outer face was the original outer entrance; the inner may be regarded as a deep rebate for a door (there is an iron door hook of unknown date in the west jamb just to the north of the outer doorway). Like the inner arch, it has voussoirs and is of excellent masonry with fine joints. Freeman stated that the outer opening has an incised cross on a stone of the east jamb near the springing. The inner opening is 1ft 11in deep and the outer 5½in deep to the blocking. The thickness of the wall here is therefore 2ft 4½in plus the blocking. Actually it appears to be about 3ft thick.

The Undercroft. This was discovered in 1851 below the chancel floor: it had at one time been used as a cellar. It was very low; its floor was only 6ft below the then chancel floor and so only 3ft below the present floor. Fleming thought it may have been the work of the incumbent Trevet who in 1685 made 'a cellar under the chancell of the said church being very much hurtful to the said chancell'. This is unlikely. The structure described by Freeman has features very unlikely to be of the seventeenth century: he stated it to be of rough walling of stones and Roman bricks similar to other parts of the fabric.

What Trevet probably did was to convert a 2 or 3ft deep under-croft into a usable cellar of 6ft depth by raising the chancel floor to 4ft above the nave, and provide access to the cellar. (Now, there is no access either from the exterior or from the chancel.) To raise the chancel floor of so small a church 4ft above the nave would in itself be sufficiently 'hurtful to the said chancell' to call for contemporary comment. Trevet could hardly have built the undercroft walls which are in fact the foundation walls of the chancel.

In the east wall of the undercroft is a very much flattened head of an arch of Roman tiles, illustrated in Freeman, flat and radiating very irregularly from a centre. The arch is very flat even for a segmental head, and part of the crown is missing. It may have become depressed by a beam which at some time was inserted[29] in the hole just above the crown. The arch is rather similar to those at Brixworth of late seventh-century date except that at Brixworth the tiles are larger; here they are 16in by 11in by about 2in. Freeman reported that the mortar con-tained no pounded brick as Roman mortar usually had, and he rejected a Roman date on this account. The similarity with Brixworth suggested that Wilfrid may have been the builder: he was very active in Sussex in 680–85. Freeman also reported a similar window in the north wall of the chancel,[30] at about the same level, in which a layer of Roman tiles was laid flatly around the arch head—another resemblance to Brixworth. A writer in the *Gentleman's Magazine* (op cit (c)) wrote that this arch head was of stone voussoirs, but confirmed the flat layer of Roman tiles. The same writer regarded the eastern opening as an entrance to the undercroft. Freeman pointed out that the jambs did not extend to the original floor level but to about 3ft above it where there was a sill of projecting Roman tiles. He thought the window was the original east window of the chan-cel, the original chancel floor being that of the undercroft. This conclusion is difficult to accept. It would make the east window, less than 3ft above floor level, and it is less than 3ft high, of most unusual position and dimensions for a Saxon east window;

the Saxons liked their windows to be as high up as possible in very high walls. The problem is puzzling. Is the undercroft an intentional undercroft, vault or crypt? Or is it no more than a low hollow foundation to the chancel? If the latter, the windows are not easily explained. If the original nave and chancel floors (in small Saxon churches usually at one level) were at the same level as the present nave floor level, which is about the same level as the south doorway sill, the windows would be about half above and half below floor level—another curious position. The openings of the crypts at Wing (Bucks) and Repton (Derbys) are partly above and partly below ground level; but these are real crypts, probably used for burial purposes, with chancels raised well above them: the comparison with St Olave's seems hardly valid. The puzzle remains. It is unfortunate that the undercroft is not accessible for further examination. Freeman's writing is somewhat imaginative and in places obscure. But he does appear to be a reliable observer: one must accept his factual statements, and the puzzle resulting from them. The undercroft is not mentioned in VCH.

Urns. During the 1851 restoration two plain Roman urns were found in the chancel east wall, lying on their sides with mouths facing west. Freeman, giving full scope to his imagination, suggested—as possibilities only—that they may have formed part of a Roman columbaria (a sepulchral building having small apertures in its walls for the reception of burial urns) which may have been incorporated in the walls of the early church later built on the site; or alternatively that they may have been burial urns containing bones of martyrs of the early fourth century persecutions in Roman Britain during which St Alban was martyred.[31] It is more likely that the urns were placed there with the mistaken idea that they would improve the acoustics of the building. This idea was due to the Roman architectural writer Vitruvius (fl 40–28 BC). It was widely accepted after the discovery in 1414 of Vitruvius' book, by Poggio at the monastery of St Gall. Urns were apparently used for this purpose up to the sixteenth century.[32] Their presence is therefore no evidence of early date either at Chichester or elsewhere. Urns, not necessarily Roman, have been found in at least eight other places in England outside Sussex. There is a curious entry in the Churchwardens' Accounts quoted by Penny of Wimborne Minster (Dorset) under 1541: 'Payd for 2 pots of clay for wyndfylling of the chyrch, 8d'. They have also been recorded in Ireland, France, Italy, Germany, Sweden and Denmark. Sometimes the mouths would be sealed with membranes of plaster, and the acoustical ones would normally be on their sides. Most writers agree that though the reasons for this practice was often acoustical the idea itself is nonsense. It was however not the only reason, for such jars have been found in positions where the idea could not be applicable, eg in nave walls near the floor, and under the nave floor. In Sussex, urns have also been found at Arlington, Buxted (near Uckfield), East Blatchington (near Seaford), Ford, Slaugham, and Sutton (near Bignor and Petworth).[33] One urn found at Ford was in a specially constructed niche in the chancel north wall, and is said to have contained bones.

Further reading: L. Fleming; P. Freeman; Gentleman's Magazine, (b), (c) and (d); P. M. Johnston (l); E. W. Tristram (b); VCH, III, pp 162, 166, plan.

CHITHURST: *St Mary's Church*

The original dedication is not known. It is some 4 miles north-west of Midhurst. It occurs in Domesday Book as Titeherste; a chapel *(ecclesiola)* is mentioned. It is not certain whether this word in Domesday Book meant a chapel (as usually translated) or merely a small church—possibly of timber, such as a field church. Most of these *ecclesiolae* were in fact small. There are nine mentioned in the Sussex Domesday Book.

It was a small and poor 'parish', assessed at four hides with two ploughs, worth 40s in King Edward's time and 60s in 1086. It was relieved of taxation by Pope Nicholas in 1291 on account of poverty. In 1535 it was merely a chapelry of Iping, 2 miles to the east. Iping in Domesday Book was assessed at four hides with three ploughs and was worth £4; no church is mentioned.

Chithurst Church stands on a slight mound north of the small river Rother and of the road. It consists of nave and chancel only, both eleventh century, probably the ecclesiola of Domesday Book. Johnston suggested a date of c 1080. The walls are high for so small a church, about 15ft in the nave and 13ft in chancel, and thin, only 26in. They are of ragstone rubble of varying shapes and sizes with wide joints—and much mortar. There is some herring-boning. Much of the old plaster has peeled off. The nave north-west and north-east quoins, in good condition, are of hard yellowish sandstone of small slabs in side-alternate and end-on arrangement. The south-east quoin looks older, it is much worn, the slabs are larger and mainly side-alternate though some are so long, about 18in, that the side-alternate arrangement becomes 'on-end'. The south-west quoin, rebuilt c 1320 due perhaps to some early settlement, is of fairly large slabs, with some diagonal tooling, mainly face-alternate but with some side-alternate slabs and some duplications. The chancel north-east and south-east quoins are similar to the nave north-east and north-west ones.

There is no continuous plinth; it is visible only round the south-west corner of the nave and the south-east corner of the chancel; in between is modern flat brick footings. At the south-east the short plinth looks as though it was intended to support the quoin only—it is chamfered at its ends also.

There is a fine old open timber inner roof to nave and chancel with five heavy tie-beams: two immediately to east and west of the chancel arch, two across the nave and one near the chancel east end. The nave is 26ft 9in long by 14ft 9in wide and the chancel is 11ft 9in by 10ft 9in. There is a belcote over the west gable. The west porch is later. There may be wall paintings under the white wash (André et al).

The chancel arch is of one order, slightly horseshoed or stilted and set back behind the jambs; it has a slightly flattened round head of eleven square-cut voussoirs on the west face and twelve on the east, the interval is rubble filled. The jambs, of seven stones to each corner, are not of through-stones but of two or three stones per course; the imposts are 8in thick, plain chamfered below and at the ends, and are not returned. The jambs and imposts are of Saxon type but were re-tooled diagonally in 1830. The low chamfered plinths are 10in high on the south and 12in on the north. The opening is 5ft 4in wide and about 8ft 10in high to the springing, or about 11ft 6in to the crown of the arch. The jambs, ie the wall here, are 26in thick.

In the chancel north wall[34] is an eleventh-century window. It has a double-arched lintel and a narrow single splay, except the sill, jambs of two very large stones on the east and three on the west, and a massive sill turned up at the ends in Norman fashion; this is consistent with Johnston's suggested Overlap date of c 1080. The opening has no original provision for glazing or for shutters. The aperture is only 6in wide.

The font is interesting.[35] It is one of a group in Sussex of about twenty of Saxon or early Norman date. It is of circular tub shape, with sloping sides, and probably nineteenth-century vertical tooling. It stands on a later octagonal base which is on a still later square stone and brick base. The bowl is 15½in high, 2ft 3in across at the top, tapering downwards to about 18in; it is 3½in thick at the top.

Grave slabs. There are ten lying on the ground along the north wall of the church, including two small square ones which may have been head-stones. The larger ones are carved with crosses in half-round or flattish-segmental relief.[36] Three have latin crosses, one in plain and two in segmental relief. Four have double crosses in half-round relief. One has a peculiar kind of cross within a border: it is a double cross, the upper cross-bar being supported by two struts forming two triangles. There are seven similar grave slabs at nearby Stedham[37] and two at Steyning.[38] The three groups are so similar that they may be considered contemporary.

T. D. Kendrick[39] compares these three groups of Sussex grave slabs with the slab at Milton Bryan (Beds), an outlier of the well known group of grave slabs in the Cambridge–Norwich –Peterborough area, which he described as 'rude and rustic sculpture', and dated to 'probably . . . the first half of the eleventh century'. At Milton Bryan the panels between the cross arms are filled with single-strand interlacement; without this the stone would be almost indistinguishable from some of the Sussex group. Kendrick wrote: 'they are obviously such very late derivatives of the Cambridge type of grave slab that we must be prepared to find some of them are post-Conquest and may even be as late as the twelfth century.' The latter date is very likely when one recalls the conservatism of the Sussex masons.

Further reading: P. M. Johnston (l) and (n), plan, also pl 9 showing Sharpe's view of the church from NE as in 1804, and another view, as now, from SE; H. Poole; VCH, IV, pp 5–6, plan and (facing p 10) pl of church as in 1791.

CLAYTON: St John the Baptist Church

Clayton is 8 miles north of Brighton. It and its church were mentioned in Domesday Book as Claitune. In 1086 it was held by the wife of William de Watevile under W. de Warene (an unusual instance of a wife, not of royalty, with an estate held independently of her husband). It was given to Lewes Priory by de Warene in c 1093.

The nave, chancel arch and probably the western two-thirds of the chancel north and south walls are pre-Conquest. Baldwin Brown dated them to the Confessor's time; Poole thought them pre-Conquest, Rouse pre-Conquest and probably eleventh century. It has no long and short work and no original openings, except the chancel arch, which has definitely pre-Conquest, though late, features. There are no other specifically Saxon features except the relatively thin walls. Tristram considered the nave and chancel arch to be Saxon or early Norman and that the west wall was rebuilt later further to the west. There appear to be no clear indications in walling or quoins of later rebuild-

ing further west, and the nave length-breadth ratio of less than
2 : 1 does not support it. Tristram does not quote his sources so
the statement cannot be checked.

The walls are of uncoursed flint with wide 'joints' and much
mortar. There is no plinth. Much of the old exterior plaster has
peeled off.

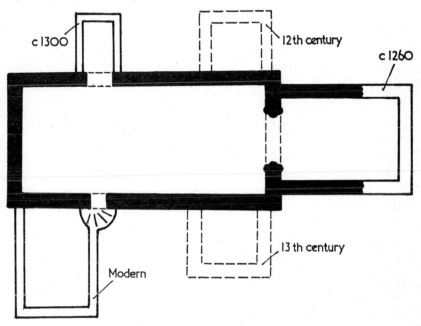

Fig 2. Clayton

The Nave. The north-west and south-west quoins are of slabs
mainly on their sides, some on end, of various heights but of
rather similar width; the lower ones are taller than those above,
up to about 3ft 1in by 14in by 15in, and dressed on the outer
faces only. The south-east quoin is of fourteen slabs on end
of which four are very long. The north-east quoin is plastered
or cemented over.

In the nave south wall near the east end on both exterior
and interior are remains of the south-western part of a curved

head of a blocked opening. On the north side are similar remains, above which on the exterior wall are marks of the gabled roof of a former chapel to which the blocked opening belonged. In spite of their Saxon appearance these remains are of porticus of post-Saxon date. The north porticus was of twelfth-century date; its foundations were excavated in 1918. The south porticus was of thirteenth-century date, the same as that of the chancel eastern part.

The walls are very high. The nave is about 43ft long and 22ft 6in wide on the exterior. The interior width is about 17ft 6in, making the walls about 2ft 6in thick. At the north door-way the thickness appears to be about 2ft 5in. The chancel is 19ft 6in by 13ft 3in on the interior; on the exterior the dimensions are 22ft by 17ft 6in, making the north and south walls about 2ft 1in, thinner than the nave walls. The chancel arch jambs are only 1ft 10in thick.

The only entrance to the church is the original north door-way, now within a fifteenth-century porch, near the west end. It has a head of five stones—four long curved ones and one short. The jambs have five stones each, one in each very long (19in and 24in respectively) and four short (8–10in). There are no imposts. The exterior opening 2ft 11½in wide and the jambs only 9in thick. On the interior the opening is taller and wider due to a deep rebate of 1ft 8in. The jamb on the east has two old square holes in one of which is a portion of an old iron door-latch of unknown date. The corresponding south door has been reconstructed; it is now a modern doorway leading to a modern vestry.

A short shingled bell-turret, probably of the fifteenth century, as the bells are, with a low four-sided pyramidal roof is *above* and *on* the nave roof at the west end. Nothing structural of this turret is inside the church, only bell ropes. The nave has a fine old open timbered interior roof. The exterior roof of nave and chancel are of red tiles, not original, except several of the lower courses of the nave roof which are of old Horsham slabs. The chancel roof is lower and at a lower slope than the original chancel roof, the marks of which are plainly visible on the nave east wall exterior.

The Chancel Arch. This is very fine (plate p 54). It is of two plain square-cut orders. There are half-round rolls down the east and west faces and reveals of the jambs, and round the east and west faces and soffit of the arch head. The soffit rolls project about 6½in and the face rolls about 8in. The square unchamfered plinths are 2ft 8in east-west and north-south and rise 15½in above the floor. They are not squarely under the jambs but rather too much to the west so the east face rolls do not stand entirely on the plinths and are so cut that their eastern

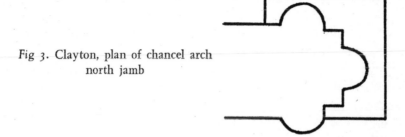

Fig 3. Clayton, plan of chancel arch
north jamb

parts extend to the ground. The thin, 6in, imposts have wide chamfers below but no quirks, and are returned only a few inches along each wall face. The arch between plinths is 6ft 3in wide and between the jamb reveals, ie behind the rolls, 8ft. The height is 8ft 9in between the plinths and the imposts, that is 10ft 6in above floor level to the tops of the imposts, and about 14ft 6in to the crown of the arch.

To each side of the chancel arch on the west face is a round-headed recess 1ft 4½in deep, about 3ft wide and sills 3ft 9in above floor level. Though now recesses, they may once have been openings, indications of which on the east face would be hidden by the later plaster. They are of thirteenth-century date.[40]

In the chancel east wall is a large circular window, high up above the east window and now filled with modern stained glass. It has very slight internal splay. It is probably thirteenth century, contemporary with the eastern part of the chancel. There was a font, probably Saxon, which has been lost since c 1830; its cushion stone base has been recovered.

The entire nave and chancel walls are plastered internally. There are remarkable early paintings all round the north, south and east walls of the nave. They are arranged in three horizontal zones, as at Hardham, and all are by a skilled painter. Tristram states that the sandy plaster, rather finer and more even than that at Hardham, is covered with a coating of lime putty to which the painting is applied. These are therefore not true frescoes. E. C. Rouse (quoted by A. Caiger-Smith, p 119) however is of the opinion that, like those at Whitley (Surrey) and Kempley (Glos), they are true frescoes. Most writers agree that the Hardham paintings date to c 1125. Tristram considered the Clayton frescoes to be rather later as they are better finished. Margaret Rickert agreed. Caiger-Smith thought the date controversial but probably late twelfth century. Dr Audrey Baker, in a later study than Tristram's, considered the Clayton paintings to be much earlier than the Hardham ones and suggested a date of c 1080. D. Talbot Rice (op cit, pp 110, 112, 172, 215) accepts this.

Further reading: G. Baldwin Brown; P. M. Johnston (l) and (q); R. H. Nibbs, *engraving of church from NE*; H. Poole; E. C. Rouse (b); E. W. Tristram (a), pp 28–9, (b) pp 113–15; VCH, VII, pp 142–3.

English Medieval Wall Paintings. Twelfth (and thirteenth) century wall paintings are not strictly relevant in a book on Saxon churches. There are however so many in churches which are considered to be Saxon, and in so many others in the county, that no book on Sussex churches should be without mention of them, if only to draw readers' attention to this little known branch of early English art.[41]

Twelfth-century paintings are or were (for many have been destroyed through the ravages of time or of too ardent restorers) wide-spread. Tristram (a) discusses paintings at 22 places in

Sussex, 12 each in Surrey and Gloucestershire, 11 each in Kent and Wiltshire, and in 63 other places in 24 other counties. Short references are given above and below to ancient frescoes at Aldingbourne, Chichester, Clayton, Coombes, Eastergate, Elsted, Ford, Hardham, Lyminster, Patcham, Slaugham, and Southease.

The Sussex and Surrey paintings form a group apart from the others. They appear to be all of Cluniac inspiration via the art school at Lewes priory, which was a daughter house of the great Burgundian abbey of Cluny. At least some of the painters of the Sussex frescoes were very probably monks from Lewes. The central school or scriptorium of Cluny influenced the art of western Europe, and especially that of central France, through the influence of its many daughter houses scattered throughout Europe, more than 1,200 by the end of the eleventh century.

Fresco painting was influenced by MS illumination, an ancient art which was practised at Cluny certainly as early as the second half of the tenth century (the abbey was founded in 910), and developed there to such a degree that Dr Joan Evans (op cit (b)) could write: 'in the most precise meaning of the words it may be termed Cluniac art'. Apart from its own intrinsic beauty it was a main source of motifs to the wall or fresco painter, the sculptor and the metal worker. The fresco painter in many cases was indeed the intermediary between the MS illuminator and the sculptor, although in fact all these arts influenced one another. Thus, the meander ribbon pattern, common in late Carolingian MSS, was taken over and developed in Cluniac illuminations and, via Lewes, it appears in a border at Clayton. Also, the Christ in Judgment over the chancel arch at Clayton is a derivative of the great fresco of Christ in Glory formerly in the refectory at Cluny and dating from the late eleventh century. This Clayton fresco in turn may be regarded as the forerunner of all the 'Dooms' which were to occupy the spaces above chancel arches in many English churches for the next three centuries. There is too some resemblance between many of the paintings of the Lewes school to the sculpture of Vézelay and

Moissac, 'the finest expression of Cluniac influence in France' (Tristram (*a*), p 34). There is also Byzantine influence in the Clayton frescoes, illustrated by the Phrygian caps and the Byzantinesque expression of some of the figures.

There is also much symbolism in these paintings, especially at Clayton. One example here is the angel at each of the four corners of the nave, symbolical of the angels at the last day who (in *Revelation*) 'shall gather together His elect from the Four Winds'. This symbolism is derivable ultimately from illuminated commentaries on *Revelation* which had great influence on Romanesque and Cluniac art, more especially those famous commentaries written and illuminated by Beatus, a Spanish monk of c 780, many copies of which were made in western Europe over the following three centuries (Joan Evans (*b*), pp 58 et seq).

Technically there were two types of wall frescoes. In true fresco painting the paint was applied to the fresh wet original plaster. The plaster and paint would dry out together and so become fully integrated with each other. This type apparently was not common in the Middle Ages. The usual technique throughout north-west Europe was to allow the plaster to dry; then it was newly wetted with lime water and given a coat of 'lime putty' to form a final smooth ground for the painting.

COCKING

The original dedication is not known; the church is now combined with the neighbouring parish of St Mary, Bepton. It is 3 miles south of Midhurst. Cocking and its church are mentioned in Domesday Book as Cochinges.

In VCH, in both plan and text, nave and chancel are dated to the twelfth century, but in the same text it is stated that there was a church here in 1086 and that the chancel arch is eleventh century. Johnston dated both nave and chancel to c 1080 and Poole called it an Overlap church with some Norman

Page 89: (above) Singleton, tower from west; (right) Southease, tower from south-west.

Page 90: Sompting:
(*above*) tower from north;
(*right*) tower arch north
jamb and capital.

features. The greater part of the chancel was rebuilt in ashlar in 1896.

The walls are of knapped flints. It is plastered on interior and exterior. The plaster is not necessarily, and certainly not entirely ancient. The church appears plastered in two plates: in Sharpe's collection, from the south-east as it was in 1804; in another, anonymous, plate of 1795 some herring-boning is shown in places in the chancel north wall.

The Nave. The nave south-east quoin was removed and used as building material in the early fourteenth-century south aisle. The north-west and north-east quoins were removed in 1865 when the north aisle was built and the nave and aisle walls integrated. The south-west quoin is presumably beneath the existing plaster.

The nave is 30ft 11in long by 18ft 5in wide at the east end and 18ft at the west.

High up in the centre of the south wall is an original window (Johnston (q), fig 4, and pl III, 2) blocked probably in the fourteenth century when the south aisle was built, and opened out in 1896. On the south, its former exterior (it is now between the nave and later aisle), it has an arched lintel, jambs of two very wide blocks each, and no apparent sill. The aperture is about 9in wide and about 2ft high. On the north face it is widely splayed and has a round head of five long voussoirs, cut to shape; there is plaster or rubble filling between interior and exterior heads. It is about 3ft 5in high to the springing. One roughly tooled impost is visible on the east; the remainder is plastered over like the walls. On the eastern splay are some remarkable thirteenth-century paintings.[42] A similar window in the centre of the nave north wall was destroyed when the north aisle was built in 1865. Three timbers, not rafters, in the nave ceiling, including a tie-beam, may be original; one is near the chancel arch. The corresponding chancel timbers were removed in 1896.

The Chancel. This is 15ft long and 14ft wide (Johnston's measurements); VCH gives the length as 16ft 6in. About one

F

half of an early gravestone was removed from the foundations of the chancel north wall during the re-building. It is now built into the interior of the north wall. It is 2ft ½in wide at the top and 2ft 5in long. It has on its face a roughly incised Y-shaped cross within a rectangular border.[43] It had presumably been re-used as building material in the original foundation as at Stedham. A gravestone at Chithurst has a similar design, but in relief. Incised ornament is earlier than relief so the Cocking stone may be older than the others which are reputed to be eleventh or twelfth century. There may have been other similar stones in the foundations which were not further investigated.

Parts of the arch heads and western jambs of two original windows, now blocked, are visible in the north and south walls (Poole, pl 10). They were exposed in 1896. They are about centrally placed. In the north window three short upright jamb stones and one springer stone and ten voussoirs are visible; in the south are three jamb stones and two voussoirs. All jamb stones are small—10–12in tall by about 5–6in wide; the voussoirs are slightly wider.

The chancel arch, (Johnston (q), fig 3, dr of W face; Poole, pl IX) is of one order. The head is of two rings, an eastern and a western, with plaster or rubble filling. It has fourteen small but variously sized voussoirs and is rather flattened; there has been some subsidence, the jambs are not strictly vertical. The jambs are square-cut, each of five 'upright and flat' slabs of similar heights, two only per course. The imposts are thin and plain chamfered at the ends also and are not returned. The arch is 6ft 6in high to the 7in imposts; it is 8ft 6in wide and hence some 11ft 4in to the crown. The jambs, ie the wall here, are 2ft 5in thick. Jambs and voussoirs have diagonal tooling, probably modern.

The western tower is thirteenth or fourteenth century. The western doorway may have been the original entrance to the church but has been re-constructed. The outer head is plain, pointed and of one order. The inner arch head is semi-elliptical and about 2ft above the outer pointed head. The jambs show random tooling; they are of fairly small slabs approximating to 'upright and flat' arrangement and with some of the uprights and flats duplicated. The opening is 4ft 4½in wide and 8ft 2in high to the springing of the interior arch head.

Further reading: P. M. Johnston (u), plan, fig 2; H. Poole; VCH, IV pp 45–7, plan.

COOMBES

The dedication is unknown. The manor and church are mentioned in Domesday Book as Cumbe. The village is situated mid-way between Steyning and Shoreham, about 2 miles from each. The church is of great interest and presents problems not all of which can be solved.

A plan in the church dates the nave north, south and east walls to the eleventh or twelfth century. A date of 1070–80 has also been suggested. This is a likely date, for the existing nave may well be the one mentioned in Domesday Book. Examination of the early wall paintings (discussed below) provides strong evidence for a pre-Domesday or, as Poole thought, a pre-Conquest date.

It is built of uncoursed knapped flints. There is no structural separation on the exterior between nave and chancel; on the interior they are separated by a heavy, early Norman-looking chancel arch, which however is Saxon. The nave is 36ft long by 15ft wide on the interior, ie the length-breadth ratio is $2\frac{1}{3}$: 1. If the nave before shortening had been only 5 (or 10) feet longer the original ratio would have been $2\frac{3}{4}$: 1 (or 3 : 1), a definitely Northumbrian Saxon ratio. The chancel is 18ft 6in by 17ft. The nave walls are about 2ft 8in thick. The chancel was rebuilt in the thirteenth or fourteenth century with north and south walls only 2ft thick; they might therefore be original, the rebuilding being only of the east wall, windows and roofing. Against this suggestion is a band of early twelfth-century painting in a key pattern on the chancel west wall. This does not extend to the north and south walls and so almost certainly indicates the width of the original chancel which apparently was only 9ft wide. The paintings on the north and south walls are late thirteenth- or early fourteenth-century date. It is the thin walls which make the chancel wider than the nave on the interior. The chancel east wall is 2ft 8in thick, like the nave walls.

On the exterior no plinth is visible, though the ground has risen so much, several feet in places, that it may be hidden. The roofing is later, perhaps eighteenth century when much was done to the church.

The west wall is problematical (plate p 35). The south-west quoin is of brick, obviously a replacement. There is no north-west quoin. Instead there is what appears to be a flint buttress jutting westwards from the west end of the north wall; closer examination shows this to be a short prolongation of the north wall, there being no indication of a quoin; the western edge of the prolongation is very ragged, just a tear-away. There is no similar prolongation at the south end of the west wall; it may have been removed and brick quoining substituted. In a measured plan in the church dotted lines are given indicating former prolongations westwards. Dalloway and Cartwright (II, pt I, p 112) in 1832 wrote that the church 'was formerly rather longer than it is at present, being reduced to its present size in 1724'. A short account of the building in the church also dates the west wall and window to 1724. This shortening was evidently due to the pressure of the rising ground outside which by now has risen at least 5 or 6ft. At some later date the bottom third of the interior of the west wall was thickened by about 13in.

About 2½ft from either end of the west wall are what appear to be old quoins left in the walls. The south one has a set of three stones—flat, upright, flat—with two smallish cubical stones above and one below. The north quoin is similar except that the top two stones are rather long and slope towards the north, the top one dying into the apparent buttress. Poole considered them to be the original quoins still in situ. He thought the nave was widened, perhaps in the early post-Conquest period. This conclusion is quite unacceptable. Such a widening would involve an almost complete reconstruction of the church, except the east and west walls. A far simpler method of widening is the universally accepted one of adding aisles. A widening would not be consistent with the evidence given above that the nave was shortened, not widened. The old quoins were presumably built into the wall as additional strengthening.

Owing to the risen ground outside, the western window, at a first glance, looks like a western doorway; its sill is almost at ground level. Its head is segmental and of five long stones cut to shape and chamfered. The jambs are of four stones each, 7–16in tall and on end. There are no imposts. The opening is 2ft 7in wide and 4ft 4in high to the springing. The frame of the window is thin; on the interior it forms the western face of a rectangular recess which has an old oak lintel. Apparently the original window was inserted in the rebuilt wall.

The Saxon south doorway, about centrally placed, is in a six-teenth-century porch. The doorway is 3ft 1in wide and 4ft 8in high to the springing (there are no imposts) above the porch floor and 6ft 9in above the nave floor. There are four steps down to the nave. A nave floor below exterior ground level is a common Saxon feature, but the considerable depth here, of 2ft 1in, may be due to a risen ground level outside, as at the west wall. The inner two inches, 7in thick, of this outer framework extend inwards, ie east and west, on each side and act as a door rebate. The wall here is 2ft 8in thick.

The remains of the blocked north doorway opposite are visible on the exterior wall (the interior is plastered throughout). There remain three western voussoirs, 9–11in long, of probably seven, all long and cut to curved shape; four roughly cubical slabs of the western jamb and the top one only of the east jamb remain; there are no imposts. There is what appears to be a sill of three or four slabs about a foot above the present ground level; about 15in above this is what looks like another sill of five slabs between the jambs. The opening was 4ft 4in wide and only 3ft

9in high to the springing, making a total height to the crown of about 5ft 11in.

Immediately to the east of the blocked central doorway, so close that the two jambs are in contact, is another blocked doorway of about the same height but narrower, only 1ft 10in wide. Of the east jamb three fairly large slabs below a missing fourth stone with a fifth slab above remain; no western jamb stone remains. Two slabs west of the top eastern jamb stone are presumably part of a flat lintel; one stone on the east, and marks on the wall, suggest strongly a former round head above a flat lintel. The position of this former opening is puzzling: two doorways so close together would not be required and if one was built subsequently to the blocking of the other it would have been easier to cut the new doorway through the blocking of the old. The eastern doorway appears to be the original north doorway contemporary with the walls.

The blocked doorway to the west has white, ie unpainted, plaster behind it on the interior wall; the early paintings here were presumably destroyed when the doorway was made. F. W. Steer dates this doorway to late fourteenth century, or early fifteenth. If this is so, it is a crude piece of work for that date (cf the long 'voussoirs' cut to curved shape in the Saxon manner).

There are two other blocked openings, and one not blocked in the north wall; five altogether, three doorways and two windows.

In the chancel north wall, 9ft 6in from the east end is a blocked doorway. It has a slightly segmental lintel of two stones only, a west jamb of eleven and an east jamb of nine stones, all on end; the top stones where the imposts should be are very thin, the others vary in size from 7in by 6in to 20in by 11in. The opening was 1ft 9in wide by 7ft high from the lowest jamb stone which is 18in above ground level. This doorway, though it looks old, was the entrance to a fifteenth- or sixteenth-century vestry or chapel off the chancel, long since destroyed.

Near the west end of the north wall, about 4ft 3in from the

west corner and about 6ft 6in above the ground, is an original window, not blocked. It has an arched lintel, jambs of two stones each—a big flat one with one of similar size on end above it. There is no sill. The aperture is 6in wide and 20in high. On the interior it is single-splayed rather more widely than is characteristic of Saxon windows but rather less than is usual in Norman windows. The interior head is of five voussoirs; the jambs have four slabs each on end, all roughly finished, but there are some indications of diagonal tooling.

Towards the east end of the nave north wall are five stones of the western jamb of a blocked window. It is at about the same height above the ground as the western one; there is no indication of size or date.

In the south wall are the remains of two blocked windows. One is near the west end about opposite to the corresponding window (referred to above) in the north wall. It has an arched lintel; only three eastern and two western jamb stones are left; it is very narrow; the stones show some diagonal tooling. On the interior the wall plaster has been cut away to expose three western jamb stones.

The other blocked window is immediately to the east of the south porch, the porch east wall being in line with the window west jamb. It has a double-arched lintel with no tooling. Only two stones, with diagonal tooling, of the west jamb remain. Nothing is left of the east jamb as this was cut into by a six-teenth-century three-light window.

These two windows and the one near the west end of the north wall appear to be original. Perhaps there were three in each wall.

The chancel arch has a round head of two rings of voussoirs, an eastern and a western one, all plastered so details are not visible. It has chamfered imposts, not returned; on each inner corner of the east face is carved a human face of later date than the arch. The jambs are of three stones per course, with diagonal tooling: they are (ie the wall here) 2ft 6in thick. There is a consecration cross on the second jamb stone below the south impost on the west face. The opening is 6ft 1in wide and 5ft 2½in high to the 5½in imposts, ie 5ft 8in to the springing and about 8ft 9in to the crown.

In the chancel south wall are two, much later, low-side windows, one of which very unusually is circular.[44] The interior of nave and chancel is plastered. On the nave north, south and east walls and chancel arch (both faces and soffit) are early wall paintings[45] uncovered by E. C. Rouse in 1949, and treated by him in 1951–2 (op cit, and Pilgrim's Trust op cit). He considered the earliest to be of eleventh to twelfth, or eleventh- or twelfth-century date. N. Pevsner and Ian Nairn dated them to perhaps not later than c 1100. A. Caiger-Smith dated them to c 1170–80, a few years later than the completion of the Canterbury paintings which he placed at c 1170. This late date for the Coombes frescoes is not widely accepted. According to Rouse they are, like those at Clayton, 'true' frescoes whereas the great majority of the Lewes school of wall paintings are not true frescoes. The Clayton frescoes were dated by Tristram to later than c 1125. Dr Audrey Baker in a later study than Tristram's suggested a date of c 1080. Accepting this earlier date, the unusual 'true' fresco character of the Clayton and Coombes paintings would seem to give additional support for a Saxon date for Coombes.

The paintings on the chancel walls are of the fourteenth century; and those on the west wall (above the later thickening) are very much post-1724.

Further reading: H. Poole; E. C. Rouse.

EASEBOURNE: *St Mary's Church*

Easebourne is near Cowdray Park, about 2 miles east of Midhurst. Eseborne or Esborne Hundred is mentioned in Domesday Book, but no specific manor of that name, and no church. However, Tadeham, modern Todham which was (at least as early as 1326) and still is in the parish of Easebourne, is mentioned, but no church. The earliest mention of Easebourne village or manor appears to be in a deed of 1105 by which Savaric fitz Cane and Muriel his wife, gave the church of 'Isenburne' to the Norman abbey of Séez; if this is so the church must have been recovered later for in c 1248 or earlier a priory of Augustinian nuns was founded here and the church was given to the nunnery as part of its endowment. It became the conventual church. The nuns used the chancel as a presbytery and the eastern half of the nave as a choir. The chancel was rebuilt square. The nave south door was blocked and a new doorway opened immediately to the west of it. A wall, with a central doorway, was built across the nave immediately to the west of the new doorway. The narrow early twelfth-century north aisle was widened to 21ft and this, with the western half of the nave and perhaps the ground floor of the late twelfth-century tower, became the parish church. Few traces of these alterations are now visible except the blocked south doorway. It was drastically restored by R. Blomfield in 1876. The partition wall in the nave was removed, a new chancel built at the east end of the north aisle, which thus became the nave; the earlier Saxon nave is now the south aisle. Further restoration work was carried out in 1912–14 and in 1925.

Originally the church may have been a 'hundred' church, or 'ordinary minster', supporting a number of secular priests who would be responsible for looking after the spiritual needs of neighbouring villages, too small or too poor to have churches of their own. In this connection it may be significant that chapels (that is, field churches, little churches, perhaps the *ecclesiolae* of Domesday Book) at Todham, Midhurst, Fernhurst and Lodsworth were attached to it at least as early as 1291.

The church consisted of a nave and chancel, the latter possibly apsidal (St J. Hope, but there is no evidence for this), with perhaps a small wooden belfry over the west gable.

The nave was 55ft long by 18ft wide internally, a ratio of length to breadth of 3:1, a Saxon proportion. The walls were of yellowish sandstone rubble of irregular sizes and with wide joints. The south wall (except the immediate surroundings of the mainly modern windows and some modern external re-facing to the east of the thirteenth-century doorway) is original, as is also the west wall to the north and south of the tower arch. It is stated that the late twelfth-century tower arch was cut through the old nave west wall. The existing nave east wall and arch leading to the south chapel (formerly the nuns' presbytery which was on the site of the Saxon chancel) are of modern ashlar but apparently made to the original Saxon thickness of 1ft 9½in. The Saxon wall at the south doorway is 2ft 5in thick. The Saxon south-west quoin is of large slab work, becoming smaller towards the top and in no particular arrangement; a few stones have diagonal tooling, others have none. The west face of the quoin is hidden by the north wall of the late thirteenth-century cloister. The south-east quoin is hidden by the south wall of the early thirteenth-century nuns' presbytery, and the north-west quoin by the remaining bit of the west wall of the early-twelfth-century narrow north aisle now incorporated with the modern nave. The interior of the church is plastered. There is no herring-boning visible, as stated by some writers, in the south wall exterior. If there was any it is either behind the modern refacing on the exterior, or hidden by the plaster on the interior.

The blocked south doorway was 8ft 1in high above the modern tiled floor and about 2ft 8in wide, a height-breadth ratio of 3 : 1, typically Saxon proportions. All that remains are the six eastern voussoirs of the round head visible on the interior, and three massive bottom stones of the eastern jamb visible only on the exterior, hidden on the interior by the plaster. The voussoirs are about 12in wide and numbered originally nine. The massive size of the remaining jamb stones suggest a date not later than c mid-eleventh century; VCH gives the date at c 1080 and Hope 'perhaps' c 1100.

Further reading: H. E. Hinkley, plan; W. St J. Hope, pp 100–6; P. M. Johnston (l); VCH, IV, pp 52–3, plan on p 45.

EASTDEAN: *Church of St Simon and St Jude*

Eastdean (East Sussex) should not be confused with East Dean (West Sussex). It is situated about midway between Eastbourne and Seaford, about 4 miles from each, and only ½ mile from Friston. The manor but no church is mentioned in Domesday Book as Esdene.

Baldwin Brown rejected it as Saxon as it has no specifically Saxon features but thought it was built within fifty years after the Conquest. Poole does not mention it. Probably it is very late eleventh century. The tower now abuts on the north of the extreme east end of the later, very late twelfth century, nave which was built up against the south wall of the earlier tower. There is no common wall between tower and nave, but two walls in contact: the tower south wall and the nave north wall. The tower is really a separate, independent building.

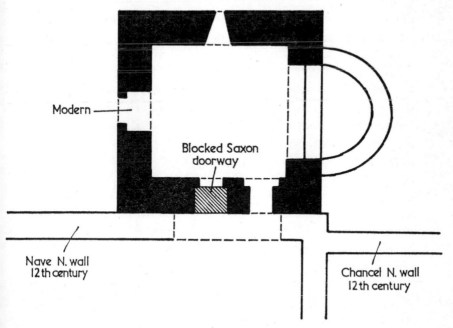

Fig 4. Eastdean

Originally the church consisted of the square tower and an eastern semi-circular apsidal chancel. It was a turriform church; that is the ground floor of the tower was the nave, (as at Barton-on-Humber and probably Broughton-by-Brigg (Lincs) Earls Barton (Northants), and Fingest (Bucks)). This accounts for its rather squat Norman-like appearance, turriform church towers being necessarily wider than normal Saxon towers. Originally too it may have been built as a semi-defensive tower as a refuge against the frequent raiders from the sea. On the exterior it is 18ft wide (north-south) and 17ft 10in east-west. On the interior the south wall is 11ft 11in long and the west wall 11ft 8½in. The west wall is 3ft thick, the north and south about 3ft 2in.

The tower is of three low slightly recessed stages separated by two string courses, chamfered on the upper edges. The ground stage occupies about two-fifths of the total height; the two upper stages are of about equal heights. The walls are of knapped flints. The quoins are of rather small grey stones (green sandstone), roughly dressed, with no tooling, and are almost cubical, varying in size from about 8 to 12in.

In the ground stage the western doorway is modern. Another modern doorway in the south wall, east of centre, allows the tower to be used as a vestry. There is a blocked doorway, a little west of centre, in the south wall, now hidden on the former exterior by the nave of the later church; this was presumably the original entrance. It has a single-arched, flatly segmental lintel. The west jamb is of two tall stones, about 2ft 6in high; the east jamb has one long stone about 4ft high with one short, 11in, stone above. These are definitely Saxon features; the Normans did not use such long stones. The opening was about 2ft 4in wide and about 5ft 4in high. There is a window in the north wall similar to the other windows above but wider; it has a wider splay and no sill.

In the second stage are two windows one in the west and one in the east wall (but not one in the north wall). The west window is comparatively tall and narrow, with arched lintel and single slab sill resting on the string. The jambs are of three

large irregularly shaped slabs each. It is chamfered all round.
It has a single narrow splay. It is about 30in high but the
aperture is only 4½in wide at the base tapering upwards (an
early feature) to about 3½in at the head. The window in the
east wall is similar but has no sill; it rests on the string.

In the third stage are three similar windows—in west, north
and east walls. The west one is similar to the one in the stage
below, but is wider and has jambs of two slabs each, on end.
All have arched lintels, and sills, are chamfered all round and
all are well above the strings.

The apse no longer exists but its plan is evident on the
ground to the east of the tower and there are marks of it on
the exterior wall. The arch, now blocked, leading to the apse
is of one order of 17 rather small voussoirs, not through-stones.
The jambs have eight stones in each, of roughly comparable
sizes; some have diagonal tooling. The imposts are 4in thick
and plain chamfered below. The width between jambs is 8ft 4in
and the jambs are 5ft 6in high to the imposts, the height to the
crown of the arch being about 10ft 2in.

Further reading: A. A. Evans (b); P. M. Johnston (l).

EASTERGATE: St George's Church

The village is 4 miles west-south-west of Arundel. It and its
church are mentioned in Domesday Book as Gate. It was held
by Earl (later King) Harold.

Baldwin Brown thought it was built within fifty years after
the Conquest but not really Saxon as it has no distinctive
Anglo-Saxon features (but cf the window, below). Johnston
considered it possibly pre-Conquest, and Poole that it is the
Domesday Book church; Tristram considered the chancel to be
Saxon.

The nave exterior is covered with rough-cast. The chancel
north wall has old plaster much of which has peeled off; the
south wall is not plastered and is of broken flints with much
mortar. There is much herring-boning in Roman bricks, of about

8in square by 1–2in thick. Below the herring-boning is one horizontal course of long Roman bricks, seven or eight, 18in long by 1–2in thick, laid flat. Johnston stated that there is herring-boning too in the lower part of the nave south wall, beneath the rough-cast.

The nave south-east quoin is of small stones above, mainly face-alternate; if there is duplication (as stated by some writers) it is hidden by the rough-cast. The lower stones are larger: the lowest three are 2ft 4in, 18in and 12in long. The chancel quoins are of large stones, though smaller than the larger nave ones, and side-alternate; one stone only in the north-east quoin is duplicated.

The nave is 42ft 6in long by 18ft wide; the chancel, almost square on the exterior, is 15ft 3in long and 13ft 6in wide on the interior.

A narrow original window is in the chancel north wall (Poole, pl x). On the exterior it has a double-arched lintel, and massive jamb stones, three per jamb, in flat—upright—flat arrangement. It has a sloping large sill which is the central portion of the long bottom jamb stone. That is, the two bottom jamb stones and the sill are of one long slab, the central portion being scooped upwards to form a sloping sill. The opening is slightly chamfered all round, except the sill. On the interior it is single splayed, including the sill. The round head is plastered over but the lower halves of the two springers are visible; these are more worn than the jambs, which may be renewals. The jambs are of three slabs each, tall, side-alternate. The window is rather wider than is usual with Saxon openings of this type; this with the chamfer may suggest a late or post-Conquest date.

Tristram refers to remains of twelfth-century paintings round the window and thought there might be others under the lime wash. André et al also referred to these paintings.

Further reading: G. Baldwin Brown; P. M. Johnston (l); H. Poole.

ELSTED: *St Paul's Church*

The dedication is modern; its earlier dedication was to
St Michael. Elsted is midway between Petersfield and Mid-
hurst, about 4½ miles from each, and 2 miles south of
Chithurst. It and its church are mentioned in Domesday Book
as Halstede. It was held by Bishop Osbern of Exeter under King
Edward.

The church was originally a single chamber, about 30ft long
and 18ft 6in wide on interior. The east end was used as a
chancel. It was built of thin shaly rubble and hard chalk rag
laid entirely in herring-boning (Poole, pl VIII). Poole considered
it to be of Overlap date with some Norman features; the
Norman features however were due to Norman alterations and
additions and were not part of the original church. A separate
chancel was added in the twelfth century when a Norman
arcade and north aisle were built. It was rebuilt in the thirteenth
century (see Sharpe's dr no 124 of 1805). The chancel arch was,
and is, very similar to the contemporary nave arches but larger
(see Sharpe's dr no 125 of 1805). It is lofty and slightly stilted,
has a square-cut round head of one order of two stones per
course. The jambs are plain, of two or three stones per course,
and have imposts, 8in thick, chamfered below. The opening is
7ft 8in wide and 9ft high to the springing, ie 12ft 10in to the
crown. The jambs (the wall here) are 2ft 2in thick, a Saxon
not a Norman dimension.

The north aisle was removed later and the arches blocked
but the two arch heads are still in the wall, visible on both
interior and exterior. The church was in a bad state in 1873
and was restored. In 1893 a tree was blown down on the nave
and serious damage done to the roof which was neglected. Later
the whole roof fell in and was left. By 1951 most of the north
and parts of the west wall were still standing; only a few feet
in height of the east end of the south wall remained, the rest
of the south wall to the west was only about two feet or so high.
The chancel was intact. The nave was restored in ashlar, the

seventeenth-century south porch rebuilt and a vestry built in 1952. The north wall has much ashlar around the Norman blocked arches. The original herring-bone work is visible inside and out along the lower part of the south wall as far as the south door; west of this all is new. In the west wall the bottom 10–12ft on the north and 4–5ft on the south are original herring-boning. The nave east wall is still mainly of its original herring-bone rubble, but has rectangular ashlar-like repair work above the eaves and around the central rubble.

The later corner-diagonal buttresses at the west end hide most of the quoining. The top three stones of the north-west quoin and the top six of the south-west are visible, all small stone work renewals, except one stone. The north-east and south-east quoins are in side-alternate arrangement.

The seventeenth-century porch was built round the original eleventh-century south doorway. This doorway was removed in the 1873 restoration and placed against the nave interior north wall. In 1952 it was re-erected in the new porch. It is only 6in thick. Its round head has seven voussoirs, the top one very thin. The jambs have eight stones each, roughly side-alternate. It has no imposts and is chamfered all round. It is about 3ft 2in wide, 5ft 4in high to the springing and 7ft to the crown.

An old gravestone was discovered during the last restoration. It is plain with chamfered edges and diagonal tooling. It is now used as a seat in the south porch.

A stone with an incised cross on it has been built into the north wall, interior, of the chancel. It is a plain latin cross with rectangular ends to the arms and head, and stands on a two-stepped base. The stone is 1ft 10in high by 10½in. It is of soft very white stone, chalk of some variety, smooth (presumably re-dressed) and does not look Saxon as it is stated to be in an account of the church hanging in the church. It is too neatly incised; it looks almost machine made, due perhaps to its whiteness and redressing.

The two neighbouring, small and poor parishes of Didling and Treyford were amalgamated and have now been absorbed

Page 107: (left) Stopham, south doorway; (right) Stoughton, chancel arch from west.

Page 108: *(left)* West Dean (West Sussex), north doorway exterior; *(below)* Westhampnett, chancel south wall exterior.

by Elsted which is formally known as Elsted and Treyford-cum-Didling.

Tristram refers to some thirteenth-century wall paintings in the chancel and suggested there may be more under the lime wash. Johnston gave a drawing of some in the nave and also thought there may be more under the wash of the north and east walls. André et al also mentioned them.

Further reading: P. M. Johnston (f) and (l); H. Poole; E. W. Tristram (a), p 122; VCH, IV, pp 9–10, plan.

EXCEAT

The name has been written Exceat (pronounced locally Ex-sét) since the seventeenth century. Its thirteenth-century spelling was Excete. In Domesday Book it was written Essete; no church was mentioned. As a separate parish it came to an end in 1528 when it was united with Westdean.

The old church (W. Budgen) was almost due south of the village of Westdean, about 300yd from and south of the present main road leading over Cuckmere river bridge to Friston and Eastbourne. It overlooked the mouth of the river and was only about a mile from the sea and about 500yd from the river.

Vestiges of the ruined church were perceptible in the mid-nineteenth century when the ground was ploughed over. It was excavated in 1913. Originally it consisted of a nave, a semicircular apsidal chancel, slightly stilted, and probably a south porch. The interior dimensions were: nave 31ft long by 16ft 3in; chancel, from the east face of the base of the chancel arch, 12ft 3in wide and about 7ft deep (east–west); the chancel arch opening was 6ft 6in wide. It was one of the smallest churches in West Sussex. The walls were mainly of flint and stone rubble. The walls, including the apse walls but excluding the nave east wall were about 2ft 9in thick. The nave east wall was more than 5ft thick to the north of the chancel arch and about 4ft to the south of it. Why this unusual thickness? Was this wall a foundation footing only which supported a thinner wall

above? Against this suggestion, some original plaster remained
on the west face. The remains were about 9in below the surface
of the wheat field. Budgen, and P. M. Johnston agreed, dated
the remains to c 1050–80.

The south porch appeared contemporary with the nave—ie
eleventh century—but the foundations were not bonded in. It
had a very narrow external south doorway (perhaps as some

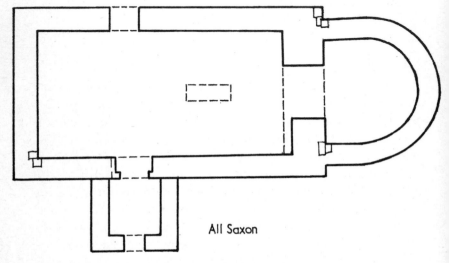

All Saxon

Fig 5. Exceat, plan of former church

protection against the south winds), much narrower than the
inner south doorway to the nave which was almost as wide as
the porch interior.

A north doorway (Budgen, two plates facing p 164) exactly
opposite the south one was narrower than the south one. The
remaining four stones of the sill had a 3in plain chamfer along
the outer edge, perhaps to reduce wear. Johnston thought this
sill was part of a thirteenth-century casing of greensand within
a wider eleventh-century opening: the stones were continued
across the jambs to east and west; it certainly appeared to be a
lining. The foundations of the south wall stopped short at the

door jambs; those of the north wall ran along beneath the sill. Some graves were excavated below the chancel floor and one in the nave floor. The latter had a plain gravestone above, about 5ft 6in long by 2ft 6in, tapering slightly, rather irregular and broken at one end. It had no chamfer, ornament or inscription. A skeleton and parts of another were found within but no other object of interest. The stone appeared to have been disturbed at some time, perhaps to admit the other part-skeleton, perhaps from the apse grave.

The ruins were reburied and the site reserved. An inscribed 10-ton block of Portland stone was erected in the centre.

FORD: *The Church of St Andrew-at-the-Ford*

Ford is about 3 miles south-south-west of Arundel and about 2 miles from the sea. It is on the opposite bank, the western, of the River Arun and about 1½ miles from Lyminster, and 1½ miles east of Yapton to which it is now joined ecclesiastically. Climping is less than a mile to the south. The church is among trees in the middle of a field some distance from the road. The derivation of the name is obvious. That there was a ford here, and perhaps a very ancient one, is undoubted (Allcroft (c)).

In 1927 A. S. Peckham (quoted by Allcroft (c)) located the remains of a definite bar across the river some 200yd above the church. The bar juts out from both banks, about 12–15ft in the west and 20–25ft in the east, with no trace of it in the centre. Allcroft also refers to 'Ford Dock' marked on an old map of 1788 and inferred that Ford (not Lyminster as thought by P. M. Johnston) was the port of Arundel. Ford, a smaller place than Lyminster, may (as discussed below, pp 142–5) have been part of Climping manor and may have been given by Earl Roger to Lyminster. In this case Ford may have become a kind of port-suburb of Lyminster. A port would have been a source of wealth; no port is mentioned in Domesday Book under Ford (which is not mentioned at all) or Lyminster, but a reference under Arundel does indicate that Arundel owned a port, though it was not at Arundel; it was apparently lower down the river, perhaps at Ford.

The place is certainly ancient. Peat and Halstead wrote that 'on the north side of the church . . . was found in 1899 a singular interment. Six skeletons placed in a circle, the heads innermost, and radiating from a centre, were found at about 5 feet below' the then existing ground level. No pottery or grave goods were found. The authors inferred that the burials were not Christian, but pagan Saxon or pre-Saxon. Allcroft ((*a*, *i*) pp 282–3; (*c*) p 68) pointed out that some undoubtedly Christian radial burials are known at a few other places in Britain. The absence of grave goods at Ford suggests Christian rather than pagan burial. He also referred to an early example at Ephesus where the bodies were arranged radially with heads inwards round a central spot which was traditionally supposed to be the tomb of St John the Evangelist. It would appear that Ford, at least as a Christian burial ground, may date back to the very earliest Christian times in Sussex, ie to Wilfrid's day.

Ford is not mentioned in Domesday Book, but Climping (Clepinges) is, where two churches are mentioned. Earl Roger, after the death of his countess in 1082, divided his manor of Climping into two equal halves, each with a church, and gave one half to the abbey of St Martin at Séez, in Normandy. The other half he gave to the abbey of Almanesches, also in Normandy, of which his daughter was abbess and from whence he had settled a colony of nuns on his estate at Lyminster, or Nunneminstre.[46] One of these churches at Climping may have been Ford (Johnston (*b*); Allcroft (*c*)). L. F. Salzman (in VCH, I, p 430) however, states definitely that it was at Atherington one mile south of Climping and on the coast. The point is of interest as it affects the dating of Ford church; it is discussed in more detail below (pp 142–5).

Baldwin Brown denied the church to be Saxon as (so he wrote) it has no distinctive Saxon features (but cf the two early windows in the nave north wall); he dated it to within fifty years after the Conquest. Poole thought it doubtfully Saxon. Johnston

dated the earlier parts of the nave to c 1040, the western part
of the south wall to c 1420, and the eastern part to c 1180.
Tristram called it Norman with some early Saxon fabric in the
nave.

The nave west and north walls and the north-east corner as
far as the chancel arch, two windows in the north wall and a

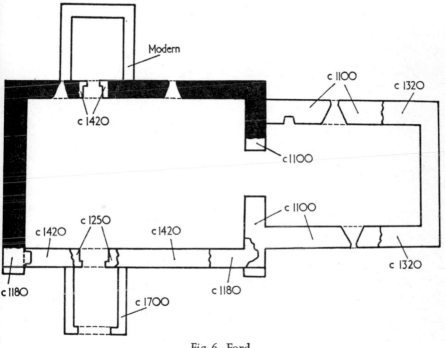

Fig 6. Ford

stone with interlacement ornament in the north doorway jamb
appear to the writer to be Saxon and may be pre-Conquest. The
nave walls are of uncoursed flints, with many small blocks of
Caen stone here and there[47] and some bits of red, perhaps
Roman, bricks. The exterior has old plaster but much of it has
peeled off. The later chancel, of two dates, is also of flints but
very regularly coursed and has modern pointing. The nave walls
are high and the north one has noticeable batter on the interior.

The quoins are of small stone work, some side-alternate, with many duplications in the later south-east and some in the early north-east quoin. This small stone quoining has been used as an argument against a Saxon date. But there is similar work at Eastergate, Friston and Lyminster, and typical Saxon 'long and short' or 'upright and flat' work is rare in Sussex.

The south porch is of brick and may be of the seventeenth century. The north vestry opposite is modern. A south aisle, long since destroyed, was built c 1180 when the south wall was rebuilt. A respond of the western pillar of the arcade was left (Johnston (b), fig 4 and plan) embedded in the south wall when the western half was rebuilt in 1420.

The nave is 31ft long by 21ft 6in (interior measurements); the west wall is about 3ft thick, the north and south walls 2ft 6in. In the nave north wall are two narrow windows with narrow single splays (cf the much wider splays of the two later lancets in the same wall). The apertures are only 6in wide and 2ft 4½in high. The rebate is curious, cut only for a shutter and not for glazing; it appears to be the only one of its type in the county. The western window of the two has an arched lintel, jambs of three massive stones each, and a sill of one very thin slab, possibly later. The outer jambs are of Caen stone, the inner one dressed in chalk and plaster. The eastern window was discovered under the later plaster by Johnston. The stone dressings had gone and it was blocked with flints. It was reconstructed by Johnston to correspond with the western one.

There is a plinth of only 1½in projection, with a shallow chamfer, along the west and north nave walls. There is a later plinth along the chancel north wall which joins the older one of the same height, but it has a greater projection—of 3in—and is laid differently.

There is no western doorway, nor are there any indications of a former doorway in the west wall exterior. The north and south doorways, near the west end of the nave, are in the usual Saxon position, but are not Saxon. The north doorway is of the fifteenth century and is built of Norman stones as indicated by the diagonal tooling. It now leads into a modern vestry. Built into the exterior arch head, and visible now only from the ill-lighted vestry, is a stone with supposed interlacement ornament. (It is shown in situ in drawing of the doorway in P. M. Johnston (b), p 116, fig 4; the ornament is shown in his fig 5, p 119.) The stone itself, deep brown in colour, differs from any other in the church. Interlacement is a northern or celtic ornament and is rare in southern England. This stone may be part of a Celtic cross imported into Sussex, conceivably by Wilfrid in the late seventh century. There is a much larger fragment—about 4 feet high—of a reddish sandstone cross in Brixworth church (North-ants). This has some resemblance to the famous fishing stone in Cumberland and is of a similar stone. (The native stone of Northants is white oolite.) Wilfrid spent several years in Northants and may have built Brixworth church. He also built churches during his five years residence in Sussex. Why he should import (if he did) large, heavy, carved crosses from Nor-thumbria to Northants and to Sussex is by no means clear. P. M. Johnston and J. Romilly Aller suggested any date for this carving between 700 and 1040, surely a reasonably safe guess!

The Ford stone appears to be the end fragment of a square-ended cross arm. The ornament consists of four narrow half-round bands, round-ended and staple shaped. They do not interlace but are parallel and the ends concentric with one another. Above is a similar set of staple ornament, at right angles to the first, with the staple ends cutting across those of the first. Below there is just sufficient indication of a similar set. The ornament may properly be described as tri-lobed, each lobe consisting of a four-stranded staple, the upper and lower may have been a double-ended staple (like long chain links) cutting across and through the horizontal ornament. This cannot properly be regarded as interlacement and is quite unlike any interlacement known to the writer.

There are fragments of early painting on the nave walls, of various dates[48] from the twelfth to the fifteenth century. At one point there is a consecration cross, just to the west of the north

door. Both Johnston and Tristram agree it may be Saxon. It is
not in ordinary distemper colour 'but is painted on a hard sort
of mastic, incorporated with the original pebbly plaster'. Here
there are two layers of paint; the upper layer is supposed to be
twelfth-century patterning (Tristram); the cross is below this.
It is enclosed in a quatrefoil. Such quatrefoils occur in the Missal
of Robert of Jumièges, an illuminated MS of the Winchester
school dated by T. D. Kendrick (op cit, p 14) to 1013–17, and
by D. Talbot Rice (op cit, pp 190–1) to 1000–15.

The Chancel. The western two-thirds, the chancel arch and
the southern half of the nave east wall are early Norman, dated
to c 1100. The eastern third of the chancel is later and was
dated by Johnston to c 1320. A straight joint is plainly visible
between the two parts. The north and south walls are 3ft 6in
thick, ie about a foot thicker than the nave walls; the east wall
however is 2ft 6in thick.

The chancel arch (Johnston (b), figs 7 and 8) is round-headed,
of two rings, an eastern and a western one, plaster filled. The
head is of 19 small voussoirs, is slightly stilted and about 7ft
wide. The jambs are of two to four stones per course. The
imposts have star or saltire ornament with narrow hollow
chamfer below. They are not returned but the ends also have
saltire ornament. The imposts are of oolite, probably from
Wight, which occurs nowhere else in the church. The rest of
the arch is of Caen stone, with axe diagonal tooling.

Excavations carried out in the 1899 restoration showed that
the original chancel floor was about 7in below the nave floor.
A lower chancel floor was unusual in Saxon churches though a
similar arrangement occurs at Warlingham church in Surrey
(thirteenth century) and originally at St Mary's, Eastbourne.
The Ford nave floor may be original; it is not known when the
chancel floor was raised. It was also discovered that the chancel
arch jambs rested on shallow, chamfered plinths of small projection.

In the south wall of the chancel, just to the west of the
straight joint (ie in the early—1100—part) is an early window

(Johnston (b), fig 10). It has an arched lintel, jambs of four stones each and a chamfered sill of one stone turned up at the ends in Norman fashion. It is comparable in size with the later lancet in the eastern, later, part of the north wall.

In the chancel north wall, in the western early part, is a niche (Johnston (b), fig 9). It is 3ft 9in high to the springing, 1ft 4in wide, very slightly splayed rather more on the west than on the east, and 1ft 1in deep. It has a round head of seven voussoirs, with narrower keystone (keystones were unusual in Saxon work), and with two extra voussoirs on the west. The jambs are of thin upright slabs. There are two interior grooves in the jamb walls, about 1in by 1in, near the front, and to about 8in above the niche floor. This may have held a board originally built in to protect some object inside, perhaps relics. It is reported that in 1879, when the chancel was restored, an urn of black or dark earthenware containing supposed charred bones was found in the niche.

Another urn was found in the nave north wall just to the west of the north door and only a few feet above the floor.[49] It was broken, but the neck was seen to be about 10in wide. One, or perhaps two more were found just below the wall plate in the north-west corner of the chancel.

There is an early font perhaps pre-twelfth century. It is cubical, very roughly dressed, probably by axe. It has no fillet or ornament round the lip which however has been repaired in cement. It is 2ft square and 18in deep on the exterior. It stands on a modern base.

Further reading: A. H. Allcroft (a) and (c); G. Baldwin Brown; P. M. Johnston (b), plan; (c); and (l); H. Poole; A. H. Peat and L. C. Halsted; E. W. Tristram (a), p 124.

FRISTON: *The church of St Mary the Virgin*

Friston is situated about mid-way between Eastbourne and Seaford, about 4 miles from each and only half a mile from Eastdean. It may be an ancient place; its name is Saxon, perhaps

derived from Fritha's tun or enclosure. It is not mentioned in
Domesday Book. Baldwin Brown thought it had no distinctive
Saxon features but was probably built within about fifty years
of the Conquest. The greater parts of the nave north and south
walls and a blocked window and doorway in the south wall
are probably Saxon. A corresponding north doorway, now leading to a vestry, appears to be of the same age. There is a late
eleventh-, or perhaps early twelfth-century south doorway, now
the only entrance, near the earlier blocked one, and less than
two feet to the west of it. This was cut when the nave was
extended westwards by 8ft and a new west wall built in the
early Norman period.

The nave is of uncoursed knapped flints, with some blocks of
stone (Eastbourne rock) here and there especially along the base
of the south wall. On the exterior it is about 46ft long and
about 22½ft wide. The walls are 2ft 3in thick, a Saxon dimension. The nave north-east quoin is of modest sized slabs, side-
alternate. There are heavy later buttresses at the extreme east
and west ends of the south wall and integrated with it; at the
east end only the top two quoin stones, side-alternate, are visible
above the buttresses; no south-west quoin stones are visible.
Similar buttresses are against the west wall but not at the
extreme ends; the north-west quoin is of Norman small stone
work.

The blocked south window has an arched lintel on the
exterior, no sill, no imposts, jambs of two slabs each below with
one thin flat above. On the interior it has a round head of five
voussoirs, no imposts, no sill—only splayed walling—and jambs
of three slabs each. The exterior aperture was 7in wide; it is
single-splayed on the interior (open as far as the thin blocking)
rather widely to 2ft 3in. The jambs have diagonal tooling.

The blocked doorway: on the exterior only the eastern half
of the round head, six rough voussoirs, hardly real ones, remains.
On the interior four western voussoirs and two eastern ones are
visible; the central upper part of the head is missing. There are
no imposts. The jambs remain except the top stone of each—

six stones in each dressed only on the exposed faces. They have diagonal tooling. The opening was 3ft 3in wide and 7ft 9in high to the crown of the arch. It is not known whether the diagonal tooling of this doorway and of the blocked window is original; it may have been retooled when the Norman doorway, further west, was built.

The nave has a beautiful old open timber roof of c 1450.

The chancel is dated to c 1300. There may have been an earlier chancel, perhaps apsidal similar to the neighbouring churches at Exceat, Eastdean and Norman Newhaven. The chancel arch is low, with flat segmental head and has no imposts or capitals.

Further reading: G. Baldwin Brown; W. H. Legge.

GUESTLING: St Lawrence's Church

The village is 4 miles north-east of Hastings and 2 miles from the sea. Guestling, as Gestelinges manor in Gestelinges Hundred, is mentioned in Domesday Book, but no church. It was held by Ulbald of King Edward, and later by Geoffrey de Floc of Robert Count of Eu. In the same hundred was the unidentified manor of Rameslie, a large estate which at one time included Rye, Winchelsea and a part of Hastings and belonged to the Abbey of Fécamp in Normandy. Rameslie had five churches one of which may well have been Guestling (others may have been those formerly at Pett, Fairlight, Icklesham and Udimore). Later, Geoffrey de Floc(is) gave the church at Guestling to a prebend (held probably by his brother Hugh) of the collegiate church of St Mary at Hastings, founded by the Count of Eu c 1090 but which may have been a refounding of an earlier foundation of the Confessor (VCH, II, p 112).

Poole considered the church to be of doubtful date; the present writer agrees. Johnston dated it to c 1120. VCH gives the eleventh century for the nave; the tower and narrow north aisle (rebuilt and widened and with a new north arcade in modern times) were dated to the early twelfth century, perhaps as early as c 1100. Possibly the nave north wall above the arcading is original as are the two western quoins of the nave which indicate that the early nave was of the same width, if not the same nave, as the existing one. The nave eastern quoins also appear, in the VCH plan, to be original.

Initially the church consisted of an aisleless nave and chancel, with perhaps a timber western tower. The chancel was rebuilt in the thirteenth century. The present tower may have been built partly for defence, that is as a refuge from the frequent raids from overseas, as it had no external opening in the ground floor; the existing western doorway and eastern arch are modern neo-Norman.

The walls are of local sandstone and ironstone. They are very high, an early feature. The nave gable is sharply pointed, the roof ridge reaching almost to the tower eaves. All roofs are of red tiles, apparently not original. The walls are 2ft 7in thick except the west wall which is reported to be about 3ft. The tower walls are 4ft thick.

The nave north-west quoin is of rather small slab work of irregular arrangement; one or two shorts are on end. The slabs do not project from the wall face. There is a straight joint between nave and north aisle and the quoin is clearly visible. The south-west quoin has been removed as the wall here is integrated with the originally fourteenth-century south aisle, rebuilt in the modern restoration. No north-east or south-east quoin is visible, both being hidden by the late thirteenth-century north and south chapels. The chancel quoins are modern. The nave is stated to be 31ft 6in long and 18ft 6in wide.

The attractive tower is of slender Saxon proportions (cf Bishopstone tower, p 17). It is of three stages with no separating string course between the two lower stages; the only string is below the belfry, which is recessed. It is not bonded into the nave west wall, which indicates that it is of later date. It has a very tall pyramidal roof with rather deeply projecting eaves which make the roof look like a cap. A large square stair turret, with an internal newel staircase, is at the north-west corner.

It is contemporary with the tower and has three windows, vertically disposed. The tower south-west, south-east and north-east quoins (the latter two visible above the aisle roof) and the turret quoins are all similar: the stones are of irregular shapes and sizes in side-alternate arrangement; a few have diagonal tooling, most have none.

The tower has two windows in west, north and south walls of the two lower stages, that is one window in each of the three walls of each stage, six windows in all. All are closely similar except the lower ones which are taller than those above. They have arched lintels, no imposts, sills of single slabs, and are chamfered all round. The upper windows have two stones per jamb, a small upper stone and a massive lower one. Some stones are renewals. These windows are disposed rather curiously. Of the lower range those on the north and south are slightly east and more markedly east, respectively, of central; the west one is slightly south of central. Of the upper range, the north and south windows are west of central, the west one south of central. They have rather wide internal single splays, but hardly wide enough to be considered typically Norman. The turret windows are similar to the corresponding tower windows but shorter: they have arched lintels, jambs of two slabs each, rather long single stone sills, and are slightly chamfered all round. There is a similar window, though much taller, with six small stones per jamb, in the north aisle west wall. It is widely splayed on the interior. The exterior may be original fitted into the rebuilt aisle.

The belfry windows in the north, west, and south walls are high up, well above the string course and rather close to the eaves. They are the usual Saxon double openings, but of the later, Saxo-Norman Overlap type. They have arched lintels, one to each half-head, jambs of five small stones each, sills but no imposts, and are slightly chamfered all round. They have tall slender columns, not baluster shafts, with capitals and bases which are flush with the wall outer faces; that is, they are not mid-wall. The capitals have chamfered faces and edges to bring them to roughly circular form below. The bases are square and shallow with rounded tops. No east belfry opening is visible on exterior or interior; if there is one it is below the nave roof ridge and above the nave ceiling.

In the upper stages are parts of old timber framing which, some think, may possibly be parts of the supposed early timber tower.

Further reading: Anon (c); P. M. Johnston (l); H. Poole; VCH, IX, pp 182–3, *plan*.

HANGLETON: St Helen's Church

The village is now part of Hove, embedded in suburbia and about 2 miles from the sea. The population is now about 15,000; in 1831 it was 68. The manor, but not a church, is mentioned in Domesday Book as Hangetone. It was close to the western border of the Rape of Lewes; it was part of Chingestone (Kingston Buci), a manor of W. de Braose, just across the border in the Rape of Bramber.

Lower thought the church was Norman, Clayton as Early English and later: but a church here is mentioned, with others, in a grant to Lewes Priory made by Bishop Sigrid II of Chichester (1180–1204) (Hussey, p 252). Baldwin Brown rejected the church as Saxon as he thought it had no specific Saxon features but that it was built probably within about fifty years of the Conquest. Johnston thought the nave might be pre-Conquest, but dated the chancel to the late thirteenth century. VCH dated the nave to the twelfth century, the tower to the early thirteenth and the chancel to c 1300. Poole does not mention the church. The nave is certainly the oldest part of the fabric. It has few specifically Saxon or Norman features; but the high-up, narrow-splayed ancient windows and some of the quoining suggest Saxon workmanship though it may well be post-Conquest, as Baldwin Brown thought, or even post-1100.

The nave north and south walls (plate p 125) are of mixed broken and unbroken flints, mainly in herring-boning. The north-east and south-east quoins are of rectangular slabs, mainly in the not uncommon alternate arrangement though a few stones are 'upright and flat'. The south-west quoin is a modern brick replacement. The north-west quoin is partially obscured by the modern vestry. The nave is stated to be about 37ft long by c 17ft wide. The later chancel is very slightly narrower than the nave. The wall at the south doorway is 3ft 1in thick. Traces of early wall paintings are supposed to be under the wash (André et al).

The north and south doorways are opposite each other, about one-third of the nave length from the west end. The north doorway, formerly blocked, has been opened out and a modern porch built round it. The interior details are hidden by plaster. On the exterior the head has six voussoirs, not wedge-shaped but of various lengths, some rather long and cut to appropriate curved shape. The jambs have seven stones each, in alternate arrangement. There are no imposts. The opening is 34in wide and 5ft 11in high to the springing. On the interior it is 39in wide and 6ft 9in high.

The south doorway has a round head of ten stones, narrower than those in the north doorway and wedge shaped. Some writers say it has been altered, so it may not be original; Hussey described the church in 1852 as being 'in a melancholy condition'. The opening is 33½in wide and 5ft 1in high on the exterior, and 41in wide and 6ft 1in high on the interior; ie both doorways have interior rebates for doors.

East of the north doorway is a contemporary narrow window, of narrow single-splay and high up. The head is an arched lintel and the jambs are of one stone each, on end. There is a corresponding and similar head only in the south wall, an arched lintel. Both openings are about one-third nave length from the east end; there may have been two in each wall.

Further reading: G. Baldwin Brown; C. E. Clayton; A. Hussey; T. W. Horsfield (b), I; P. M. Johnston (a 2), pp 130–2; M. A. Lower (a), I, p 209; VCH, VII, p 281, plan, Sharpe's plate of church from SW in 1804 facing p 276. The literature is scanty and not entirely reliable. Much of the information given above has been supplied by the vicar, Rev E. F. Taylor, BSc, to whom the author is glad to record his indebtedness and thanks.

HARDHAM: St Botolph's Church

Hardham is a mile south of Pulborough. It, but not its church, is mentioned in Domesday Book as Heriedha(m). The nave and chancel may be of the eleventh century though most writers attribute it to the early twelfth. Johnston considered it to be eleventh or early twelfth century, and Tristram as 'a small Norman church of the early part of the twelfth century'. Baldwin Brown does not mention it. Miss Audrey Baker, D. Talbot Rice and Miss Margaret Rickert dated it to c 1125, the accepted date of the frescoes which they considered to be contemporary with the fabric, though there is no actual evidence for this. The building looks extremely primitive, and yet it was considered sufficiently important to have its entire interior walls covered with fine frescoes.

It is built of local sandstone and firestone rubble with considerable inter-mixture of Roman materials, especially in the chancel. Here, in the north and south walls are patches of Roman tiles, some flat and about half an inch thick, some corrugated and only about one-quarter inch thick. There is also a group of 15 or 16 thin flat Roman tiles, with original mortar, forming the third 'stone' from the base in the chancel southeast quoin. The nave and chancel quoins look ancient and are all similar—rather large slabs up to 20in by 15in by 7in, very roughly dressed, side-alternate; some stones are duplicated. There is no plinth.

The nave is 31ft 6in long by 19ft, and the almost square chancel is 17ft by 15ft 6in (interior measurements). The walls are 2ft 9in thick. The chancel east wall and the nave west wall converge towards the south. The modern belcote above the nave east gable is of timber and slates; it replaced an earlier one in the same position. The earlier one is stated to have been

Page 125 : *(above)* Woolbeding, south wall exterior; *(below)* Hangleton, north wall exterior.

Page 126: Worth: (above) exterior from south-east; (left) nave south wall, west end exterior.

built largely of Roman bricks, flue tiles and stone work from a nearby Roman station. Perhaps much of the walling material of the chancel came from the same source.

The nave and chancel roofs are of old red tiles. The inner roofing is of ancient oak, possibly coeval with the fabric in the nave; in the chancel it may be later, perhaps renewed in the fifteenth century, as one tie beam above the altar has one four-rayed star or flower carved on, and projecting from, the centre of the soffit.

A blocked south doorway, two loop windows in the nave north and south walls (one in each) and one in the chancel north wall, and the chancel arch are original features.

The south doorway, blocked with bricks probably in the seventeenth century, is very archaic looking (dr in Johnston (d), p 76). It was about 7ft high and about 3ft 8in wide. It is not visible on the interior, being under the plaster. It has a thin flat slab lintel tapering towards its ends, that is cambered above, and is cracked vertically. It has square-edged jambs of six or seven large blocks each; those on the west are on end, the eastern ones on their sides. One or two stones show signs of rough diagonal tooling. There are no definite imposts. Above the lintel is a very rough relieving arch, too flat and crudely built to be of any use (cf the cracked lintel below), of very roughly shaped stones.

The nave loop windows are about 4ft east of centre, but not quite opposite to each other: the south one is a little further west than the north. The apertures are only 6in wide, they taper upwards (an early feature) and the single splays are narrow. On the exterior the north window (dr in Johnston (d), p 73, of interior p 93) has an arched lintel, the upper part roughly triangular, the jambs are of one long stone on end with one shorter one above, and the sill is short. There is no apparent provision for glazing or for a light shutter. The south window is similar but has a roughly made double arched lintel.

The chancel loop window in the north wall has a rather wider splay than the nave ones and its sill is more widely splayed

H

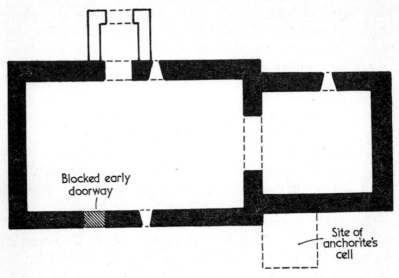

Blocked early
doorway

Site of
anchorite's
cell

Fig 7. Hardham

than the jambs. On the exterior it has a shallow rebate for a
board or light shutter. It narrows upwards and has exterior
jambs of two uprights each, of equal heights. The narrow thin
sill has bits of red brick showing through the plaster. There
is a narrow chamfer all round. All the stones are roughly tooled.
In fact in the whole church there is only an occasional instance
of diagonal tooling: here and there in the quoins and in the
chancel arch.

The chancel arch (Johnston (*d*), pl 2) is of one square-cut
order; it has no mouldings except on the imposts, or ornamentation. It is stated to be very slightly horseshoed—actually it is
merely stilted by one voussoir. The head has thirteen voussoirs,
rather long and irregular, with alternate ones, including the
keystone, projecting laterally (ie above the extrados) beyond the
others. The keystone and every alternate stone are through-
stones, that is, each springer and then nos 3, 5, 7, 9, 11; the
others are two stones per course. The imposts are small and
hollow chamfered below a narrow half-round beading. Jambs

are of seven stones each, all of similar heights, two per course, with no through-stones. There is a little rough diagonal tooling on a few stones. The opening is 9ft wide. It is 6ft 4in high above the chancel floor to the underside of the 8in imposts; the chancel floor is 7in above the nave floor, so the crown of the arch is over 12ft above the nave floor.

The chancel east window, the nave west window and a lancet near the east end of the nave north wall are thirteenth century; the two-light window in the chancel south wall is c 1330.

The west window is pointed and very wide; it is within a round-headed recess of rather wide single splay. It replaced an earlier one. Its exceptional width, 2ft 8in, is due to its developing out of a large circular window, of a kind not uncommon in eleventh- and twelfth-century gables. The circular head was prolonged downwards and the upper half of the head converted clumsily to a pointed shape.

A crude, wide, ugly and badly formed or mis-shaped recess in the nave exterior south wall near the east end may be of the late fourteenth or early fifteenth century. Its purpose is unknown.

In the chancel south wall is an anchorite's squint, of perhaps c 1250, discovered and opened out in 1900. Remains of the anchorite's cell were also discovered. The anchorite is reputed to have been a woman, with the curious name of Myliana.

There was a famous yew tree here, possibly older than the church. It is shown in Horsfield's view of the church as it was at the end of the eighteenth century. According to Lower, twenty-seven people could stand together within its hollow trunk. Dalloway and Cartwright ((b), p 295) gave its dimensions as: height to the first branch 17ft; girth at 1ft above ground 21ft, at 4ft above ground it was 23ft and at 10ft it was 19ft. The top was blown off in 1824 and it was cut down sometime after 1832.

There are ancient wall paintings covering the whole of the nave and chancel walls and even the window splays[50]. Originally they extended also round the chancel arch but the plaster here was removed in 1862 and the arch pointed in cement. Some are in good condition, some indistinct, some perished or obliterated. All are of the twelfth century. Tristram dated them to c 1140, earlier than the Clayton frescoes which he thought were better finished and which he dated to c 1160. Caiger-Smith dated them to the late twelfth century as he thought them less skilled than those at Clayton and Coombes. Dr Audrey Baker, Miss M. Rickert, and D. Talbot Rice all accept c 1125 as the date of the paintings and of the fabric.

The frescoes are in three horizontal rows as at Clayton. Among them are some interesting, characteristically Saxon, revivals, mainly at the west end of the chancel. These appear to be of the same date as the rest and 'even to be by the same craftsman'. Tristram regarded them as a Saxon revival, rather than a survival, and probably copied by the artist from an illuminated MS of an earlier date than his other sources, in fact of Saxon date. He suggested this source may have been a copy of the seventh-century Caedmon's poems, illuminated in the early eleventh century, and now in the Bodleian Library at Oxford (MS Junius II). T. D. Kendrick[51] dated the MS to 1030–50.

Further reading: T. W. Horsfield (b), II, p 183; P. M. Johnston (d), plan on p 74, (e) and (l); M. A. Lower (a), I; P. D. Mundy.

HORSTED KEYNES: St Giles' Church

Horsted Keynes is 5 miles south of East Grinstead. It, but not a church, is mentioned in Domesday Book as Horstede. It was held by Ulreve of King Edward, and later by W. de Cahaignes, hence the name.

It is built of local sandstone with wide joints and is now a deep brown in colour, especially the older parts of the building. It is mainly of the Early English and Decorated Periods, but possibly parts of the nave fabric may be ancient—Norman or Saxon.

There is a probably Saxon doorway re-erected in the later

(post-Norman) north aisle near the west end. It is not very similar to that at Bolney as it is shorter and has no ornamentation. It has a round head of nine thin (about 5in) voussoirs on the interior and seven on the exterior. The tooling is mainly diagonal. The jambs on the interior are of five slabs each, mainly side-alternate: three massive slabs separated by two smaller ones, all roughly dressed and finished, the large ones having roughly pointed ends on their bonded faces. The exterior jambs have six smaller slabs each, better finished, side-alternate, and have chamfered imposts. The opening is 3ft 1in wide on the exterior; on the interior it is 3ft 5½in wide and 5ft 10in high, that is with an interior rebate of about 3in all round.

The church appears to have been originally of nave, four-arched crossing, chancel and a large south transept, too large to be called a porticus. It is dated by some writers to c 1220, but has some features which might suggest an earlier date. The north crossing arch now has a later window; there is no evidence of a former north transept; perhaps, as at Wootton Wawen (Warwickshire), there was no north transept. The north arch head is a renewal in modern style. The western arch head is not original, it is pointed. The eastern (or chancel) and south arch heads, and all four square piers, appear to be original. A later tower was erected over the crossing. All four piers are 4ft thick. The chancel arch imposts are of two stones each; the eastern seven inches of the north impost and the eastern four inches of the south one are later renewals in a different kind of stone. This might perhaps be taken to suggest (no more than suggest) that the jambs may have been thickened to support the extra load when the tower was built. All are plastered so few details of structure are visible.

The chancel arch is 7ft 10in high to the rather thin (5in) imposts, and 7ft 2in wide; the total height to the crown is therefore about 11ft 10in. The imposts have hollow chamfers below quirks, an Overlap or Norman feature. The plinths, of the same width or depth (east-west) as the jambs, project only 3in beyond the jamb north and south faces. The jambs are of three or four rather large slabs per course, the corners are mainly side-alternate; the top two slabs on the south are tall, 19in and 21in, on end. The arch head, of one square-cut single order, has ten long curved voussoirs on each—east and west—face; two are very long. The north and south openings are similar to the chancel arch but smaller. The south arch head has eight voussoirs, long and curved; four are very long. The jambs and imposts are like those of the chancel arch. Each opening is 6ft 4in wide and 6ft 4in high to the imposts, say, nearly 10ft high to the crown.

The exterior of the south transept (which is now a vestry) looks old. It is covered with old, not necessarily original, plaster much of which has peeled off. The quoins are of rather small slabs, side-alternate in the west and face-alternate in the eastern quoin.

Further reading: P. M. Johnston (l).

JEVINGTON: *St Andrew's Church*

This church is in a fine position in the South Downs, 2 miles south-south-west of Polegate and 4 miles north-west of Eastbourne. The nave and western tower are at least in part Saxon but were so drastically over-restored in 1873 that many original features have been destroyed or obscured. Baldwin Brown dated it to the Overlap. The whole church is built of uncoursed flint except the nave south wall which is of roughly dressed square stones below with some flints above. In the tower south wall are many large and small stones among the flint rubble, and there are some courses of large stones just above the Saxon blocked window in the north wall. There is also some flint herring-boning high up in the tower especially below the north belfry opening. Herring-boning is supposed to have been used for strengthening purposes and is usually found in the lower parts of buildings, sometimes as at Breamore in Norman repair work. Here, at Jevington, it is high up where no extra strengthening is needed. The north-east quoin is of rather large slabs in

irregular upright and flat arrangement. The north-west and
south-west quoins do not appear to be original; the south-east
quoin is largely hidden by a buttress; the upper part appears to
be modern. There is no plinth, only a modern dressing of cement
round the north wall of the tower and north aisle. The tower is
capped with a low pyramidal roof.

The tower looks massive and low, though it has thin walls. It
is 18ft square on the interior and about 23ft on the exterior;
the walls are about 2ft 6in thick. It is of two stages, the upper
one recessed above a string course. In the north and south walls
are two round-headed modern windows, one in each wall, about
10ft from the ground. Above these are the remains of the heads
of two earlier windows turned in Roman bricks; they are not
strictly gable-headed but, as W. H. Legge put it, are 'not round-
headed, but inclined to be obtusely angular'. In Grimm's drawing of the south face of the tower as it was in 1784 (reproduced
by Legge) the window now blocked is shown as open and no
belfry opening is shown. The present belfry openings in the
north and south walls are of the 1873 restoration and are in
neo-Norman style. They are double round-headed openings with
plain jambs and each is enclosed under a wide pointed arch with
its own jambs outside those of the double opening. The mid-
wall shafts are original and re-used; they are banded and lathe-
turned like those at St Albans Abbey and some formerly in St
Mary-in-Castro, Dover. Above each double opening and within
the enclosing arch head is a circular sound hole; there are two
others above each pointed enclosing arch. They are modern or
modern renewals.

The western doorway is in modern neo-Norman style. The
tower arch was much altered in 1873. The jambs appear to be
original; they are of upright and flat slabs some of which are
through-stones. The imposts are plain with slight hollow chamfer and are returned along the walls as string courses; they are
undoubtedly renewals. The arch head is recessed on both faces,
though not deeply, but is not really of two orders. There is no
separate outer order built on an inner order; each voussoir is com-

mon to both rings, being cut to appropriate shape. The head has two rings of voussoirs, an eastern and a western, with ashlar soffit. It is a renewal. The two smaller arched openings, one to the north and one to the south of the main arch, are also of the 1873 restoration. There is strip-work round the head and down the sides of the jambs. The opening is 5ft 8in wide and the jambs 2ft 1in thick.

The fine carving of Christ now attached to the nave interior north wall near the west end was discovered in the tower in 1785. It is no part of the architecture of the church and cannot be discussed here. It has been dealt with by T. D. Kendrick and by D. Talbot Rice who consider it to be one of the very few remaining pieces of Saxon sculpture in the country showing the Scandinavian Urnes type of ornament. The two grotesque animals at the feet of Christ consist almost entirely of complicated Urnes interlacements. Talbot Rice thinks it probably very late pre-Conquest c 1050; Kendrick that it must be post-Conquest, probably c 1100.

Further reading: W. H. Legge.

KINGSTON BUCI: *Church of St Julian le Mans*

Kingston Buci is near the sea, some 2 miles east of Shoreham. It is mentioned in Domesday Book as Chingestone or Chingestune. It was a manor of W. de Braose, the tenant-in-chief of the Rape; his sub-tenant was Ralph de Buci from whom the manor took its second name (sometimes written Kingston Bucy or Bowsey, and now corrupted to Kingston-by-the-Sea). It included the 'estate' of Hangleton (Hangestone), about 2 miles to the north-east. No church at Hangleton was mentioned; but there were two at Kingston Buci. The second church was probably at Southwick, about a mile to the east, no trace of which remains.

Godfrey and Poole consider the nave walls to be of the eleventh century, though there are no specifically Saxon or Norman features. The chancel, south porch and doorway, and central axial tower are of the thirteenth century. The tower is one of eleven post-Saxon axial towers in an eastern or central position in Sussex; it is of the same width as the nave.

The nave walls are of roughly knapped flints with wide 'joints'. There is much original plaster on the north wall, but none on the others. The walls are only 2ft 3in thick and are high. They were at one time higher; there are stones in the tower west and east faces which indicate the position of the former nave and chancel roofs. Both had steeper gables than the existing ones. The present roofs are of red tiles, except several courses in the lower part of the nave south roof which are of Horsham slabs. The western wall was lined on the interior in the fifteenth century, when the western window was inserted. Around this window on the exterior the flint work is clearly later than the rest; and above are some roughly cubical stones among the flints which may be original. These changes may have been made when the nave and chancel walls were lowered.

The nave is 51ft long by 21ft on the exterior. The north-west and south-west quoins are of rather large sandstone slabs; one stone is 2ft 3in long by 12in by 13in. They are mostly side-alternate, roughly dressed and with no definite tooling. In the south wall, about 13ft from the west end and west of the south porch, are ten stones vertically disposed which Grayling thought were remains of the original south-west quoin (the nave, he considered, having been lengthened at some time). These are not quoin stones : only three are of sandstone, seven being of a harder greyer stone; also the western edges are chamfered as no quoin stones would be. It seems likely that they are the remains of the eastern jamb of a former window. Further east, east of the porch and close to the eaves, are the remains of similar grey stones, of what at first sight looks like a two-membered string course. The upper course of five stones is flush with the wall face, the lower of four stones project. They may however well be part of a former window, their closeness to the eaves being due to the former lowering of the wall.

In the south wall, west of the porch and very near to the

supposed old quoin, is a tall narrow window. On the exterior it has a double arched lintel of two stones, and jambs of 'upright and flat' stones, nine to each, of different lengths; the sill is of two slabs side by side and head and jambs are chamfered. It is definitely of Saxon type. On the interior it is widely splayed, including the sill; the head, slightly pointed, is of voussoirs; the jambs are of side-alternate stones approximating to 'upright and flat', with some renewals. The interior, north of the glass line, which is near the exterior, is clearly later than the exterior and may be part of the thirteenth-century rebuilding.

Further reading: W. H. Godfrey (*a*), pp 112–13, *plan;* F. Grayling; H. Poole.

LEWES: *Church of St John-sub-Castro*

Lewes is mentioned in Domesday Book as Laquis, Lawes and Lewes. Archbishop Lanfranc held land there. It was a thriving borough in King Edward's time, but no church is mentioned. This is perhaps surprising for it is known from charters and land grants that there were at least nine churches in the borough in Saxon times.

The old church no longer exists. Its site is a few yards to the east (the present church is orientated north-south, so its true east wall is its ceremonial south) of the existing modern (1839) building. The site of its high altar is railed off and marked with a stone cross. It was built very high up in an encampment.[52] There was, and is still, a steep bank on north and west, with a ditch also on the west where the road now runs. On east and south there was another steep embankment with a broad and deep fosse. Elliott (quoted by Horsfield (*a*)) in 1775 suggested that a causeway was, or may have been, built across the brooks to the east from Lewes to the Ouse and the encampment erected to guard this passage from the Danes who were beginning to infest the county. This may have been the work of Ceolnoth, Archbishop of Canterbury, as he seems to have been given nearby Malling by King Egbert and his son Aethelwulf in 838.[53]

Perhaps King Alfred later rebuilt the fort in stone and possibly a church here, though an earlier one than that pulled down in 1839. This later church consisted of un-aisled nave, chancel and western tower. William Camden ((b), pp 314–15) in 1586 described it as 'all desolate and beset with briars and brambles', and John Speed (op cit) in 1611 as 'a little desolate church at Lewes in Sussex'. When Camden wrote the chancel was standing, but was pulled down soon afterwards, probably in 1587 when the rest of the church was restored. According to Rowe (quoted by Horsfield (a)) it was repaired again in 1635.

Good plates of the church are given in the Burrell Collection (reproduced in VCH, VII, p 38) of c 1780; in the Sharpe Collection (No 208) of c 1804; and in Horsfield (pl XXII) c 1824.

Burrell's plate shows no chancel but the head and jambs of the blocked chancel arch in the east wall, and also 'tear-away' on each side of and close to the jambs indicating that the chancel arch was almost as wide as the chancel. There was an arch head only in about the centre of the south wall (possibly the Mangnus monument), and just east of it and just below the eaves a blocked small rectangular window. At the extreme west end were marks of a gabled roof below which was a blocked opening, perhaps the old south doorway in situ (now built into the east end (exterior) of the aisle of the new church). Marks of an earlier nave roof, above the then existing one, were visible on the tower east wall. The tower was of slender proportions, with a pyramidal roof and a single window in the belfry south wall. Sharpe's plate is very similar to Burrell's. Horsfield's is similar too but shows only the head and no jambs of the south doorway. It plainly shows herring-boning in the south wall, a feature reported also by J. D. Parry (op cit). Horsfield reported that there were steps leading down to the nave at the west end, a not uncommon Saxon feature.

Baldwin Brown dated the church to his period C, ie between late tenth century and c 1100. Poole thought it pre-Conquest. The only remains now above ground are the original south doorway rebuilt into the ceremonial east end, exterior, of the north aisle of the new church, and the inscribed arch head only of the Mangnus monument now in the south wall exterior.

The old south doorway[54] has a round head and jambs of large stones. The voussoirs are long and cut to curved shape and do not radiate from a centre, but look almost corbelled out as though, perhaps, to avoid the use of centring in its construction. Three roll mouldings separated by two wide flats run round the head and down the jambs. The arch rolls are rather flatter, more segmental, than those down the jambs. There is rather similar ornament round the undoubtedly Saxon arch at Strethall (Essex) (Baldwin Brown, p 481). The jamb stones and voussoirs are about 5–7in long and wide enough to include all three rolls. Small irregular bits of voussoir and jamb stones project from the outer edges, suggesting that a flat band of stones, and not a hood mould, ran round immediately outside the rolls. The imposts are long, almost long enough to be called strings, 3ft by about 4½–5in thick. They are square-cut with two quirks on the faces, between which is a wide flat segmental band; these bands are returned along the inner ends of the imposts, but the outer ends are cut off plain. The arch head is about 3ft 7in wide and the archivolt about 1ft 5in. The imposts are about 4ft 3in above the present ground level.

The Mangnus Monument was broken up in the destruction of the chancel and rebuilding of the nave in c 1587. The remains were collected later, perhaps in the 1635 repairing, and built into the south wall of the old nave.[55] Godfrey ((g), p 6) called it the old chancel arch head. This is unlikely. An earlier writer stated it to be 'in the circumference of the chancel door'. This is consistent with Camden's drawing which shows a narrow round head and two tall jambs,[56] the inscription being written in two rows up the left jamb, round the head and down the right jamb. This presumably was the arrangement in the original church, but, again presumably, converted to a wider round head only in the later re-assembling. The question arises: was it really part of a narrow doorway, or of a monument, perhaps tomb, of Mangnus?

The head is of fifteen stones, all short but cut to appropriate curved shapes, about 7in wide and 7 or 8in long. The interior width of the head (there are now no jambs) is about 2ft 10in. Speed (op cit) wrote of it as inscribed 'in the gaping chinks of an arch in the Wall, in a rude and ouerworne Character'. The inscription reads:

[CLAVDITUR : HIC : MILES : DANO] RUM : REGIA : PROLES : MANGNUS : N̂OME : EI : MAN [GNE] : NOTA : fGENIEI : [DEPONENS : MANGNUM : SE : MORI] BUS : INDUIT : AGNUM : fRETE : fVITA : FIT : PAR[VVLV]S : ARNACORITA.

The letters in square brackets are seventeenth century replacements. (Horsfield (a), pl XXIII). In Camden the wording is very slightly different in a few places; the only significant difference however is that he wrote MAGNUS instead of the very unusual form MANGNUS. The inscription has been translated: 'Here is immured a knight, Mangnus by name, offspring of the royal race of the Danes, well known as of a good race; laying aside his greatness he assumed a lamb-like nature, and in place of an active life, became a lowly anchorite.'

Nothing really factual is known about Mangnus, but tradition made him the third son of King Harold II. The three sons of Harold—Godwin, Edmund and Magnus—raided the West Country from Ireland in 1067 and again more seriously in 1068. They were driven off by Beorn, Earl of Cornwall,[57] and returned to Ireland from where they went to Denmark for good. Nothing is known of the third son Magnus except that he did not join in the second raid and did not go to Denmark.

Further reading: G. Baldwin Brown; William Camden; W. H. Godfrey (g); T. W. Horsfield (a) and (b); P. M. Johnston (l) and (r); H. Poole; VCH, VII, p 37.

LURGASHALL: St Lawrence's Church

Lurgashall is about 4½ miles north-east of Midhurst and about the same distance north-north-west of Petworth. Neither place nor church is mentioned in Domesday Book. The church is built of thin shaly rubble with wide joints. There is some herring-boning exposed to view, by a cutting away of plaster, in the nave north wall. Also in the north wall, above the centrally placed modern window, is a row of thin rubble slabs arranged on end looking like part of a segmental arch head; they might be the remains of the head of a former window replaced by the modern one below.

The south wall is 3ft thick, a Norman thickness; Tristram considered it Norman. The north wall and its blocked doorway may be Saxon. The nave quoins look very Saxon. The northwest quoin has one long flat at the base, then two uprights and five which are on their sides, but not alternate, the remainder are face-alternate. The south-west quoin has two massive uprights at the base, then one small upright and smaller work above mainly side-alternate. Both quoins stand on small corner plinths, as at Rumboldswyke. The two other quoins are hidden by the later transept and vestry.

The blocked early north doorway is exactly opposite the later south doorway which may or may not have replaced an earlier one. The round head is of five long thin slabs cut to appropriate curved shape. There are no imposts. The jambs are of nine short uprights each, only about 5in wide though they may go further east and west beneath the plaster. The opening is 8ft 1in high to the springing above the modern tiled floor, and 4ft 1in wide between the jambs, and about 10ft high to the crown of the arch. It is 6in deep to the blocking. There is no indication of a doorway in the wall exterior.

The chancel is thirteenth century and there are traces of thirteenth-century paintings on the nave south wall.[58]

Further reading: P. M. Johnstone (l).

LYMINSTER: St Mary Magdalen's Church

Lyminster is about a mile east of the River Arun, about 1½ miles almost due south from Arundel and about the same distance due north of Littlehampton. It is an ancient place and was important in Saxon times. Johnston thought it was the 'Portus de Arundel' until some time after the Norman period when it was displaced by Littlehampton, lower down the river. It seems more likely however that the port was at Ford, near the west bank of the river (see p 111). The church is on a spit of rising ground.

It was formerly a property of Alfred the Great who left the 'twune of Lullyngaminster' to 'my cosyn Osferthe'.[59] King Athelstan and his Great Council met here in 930. This king may have founded the nunnery stated to have been established here about mid-tenth century. There are no remains though it has been supposed that it (or the later one) was south of the church where the present farmyard is. One tradition has it that it was the abbess here who was abducted by Sweyn, eldest son of Earl Godwin, c 1046, for which deed he was exiled from England for some years. Lyminster has sometimes been confused with Leominster (in Herefordshire), due to their similarly sounding names. The balance of historical evidence however shows that Sweyn abducted the abbess of Leominster, not of Lyminster, during his return from his war against King Gwynedd of South Wales.[60] Tradition is strong that this Saxon nunnery at Lyminster existed. The name Nonneminstre suggests that there may have been nuns resident here from an early date. But there appears to be no documentary evidence concerning it.[61] The name Nonneminstre has no necessary connection with a nunnery; though it was used occasionally for a nunnery it was not in general use with that meaning.

As Lolinminstre and Nonneminstre the place occurs in Domesday Book under two separate entries, each with a church. Undoubtedly the separate entries represent separate manors. Lolinminstre was held by King Edward in demesne. It contained 20 hides of land and was worth 'in the time of King Edward and afterwards as now' £50. Nonneminstre was held by Esmund the priest of King Edward. It contained 13 hides and was worth £20 in King Edward's time, and £25 in 1086. Later, both places were held by Earl Roger. He granted an estate at Nonneminstre to the abbey of Almanesches (in Normandy) of which his daughter was abbess, and settled a colony of nuns there from Almanesches.[62] Later, in 1082, after the death of his countess, he divided his manor of Climping (about 2 miles south-west of Lyminster), which had two churches, into two equal moieties one of which he gave to the Abbey of Almanesches, and the other to the Abbey of St Martin at Séez. These two estates—at Nonneminstre and Climping—were the only properties in Sussex at this time owned by Almanesches; the church at Poling was added probably some time after 1086. In 1178 Pope Alexander III confirmed to the nuns of Almanesches all their rights in the manors and churches of Climping (Climpinges), Ford (Fordres), Poling (Palingnes), Rustington (Rosintone), and significantly the *manor* of Preston (Presintone) and the *church* of Nunneminstre. Why this difference in phraseology? Why should the abbey have rights in the *manor* of Preston (no church mentioned) and the church of Nunneminstre (no manor mentioned)? Allcroft was of the opinion that the church at Nunneminstre was the same as the Nonneminstre of Domesday Book, which was Nunna's minster (Just as Lyminster, the Lolinminstre of Domesday and the Lullyngminstre of Alfred's will was Lulla's minster). Nunna was a kinsman of King Ine of Wessex (686–726), and his name appears as a witness in several Anglo-Saxon charters of that time. Allcroft considered Presintone (= Priest's tun) to be West Preston, a manor which certainly existed but is not mentioned, under that name, in Domesday Book though the neighbouring manor of East Preston is, as Prestitone. Allcroft's view is (his argument appears convincing) that the Nonneminstre of Domesday was the manor of West Preston and that the church was the minster built by Nunna in West Preston manor. It would therefore be south-east of its neighbour Lyminster.

Earl Roger had also given land at Arundel to St Martin of Séez to found a priory there, subordinate to the abbey, though this priory (of St Nicholas) was not actually founded till 1102. Later, he gave it (as stated above) half of Climping; and it also

Page 143: Worth: *(right)* south doorway interior; *(below)* nave north wall exterior.

Page 144: Worth, chancel arch and arch to south porticus, from north-west.

held the villages of Eastergate and Fishbourne. A ballivate was established at Atherington,[63] on the coast, about a mile south of Climping, to look after the abbey's estates in Sussex. The question arises: which church (at Climping) was given to which abbey? If Climping, the predecessor of the existing fine later church, was given to Nonneminstre it seems reasonable to suppose that the other church was at Atherington[64] in view of the ballivate of Séez stationed there. If, on the other hand, Climping was the church given to Séez then the other church (given to Nonneminstre) may have been Ford (as suggested by P. M. Johnston and A. H. Allcroft), which is less than a mile north of Climping and about equally close to Lyminster and Nonneminstre. Neither Ford nor Atherington is mentioned in Domesday Book. But it does not follow from the two churches referred to in Domesday Book under Climping that there were no more than two churches in that considerable manor (not one of the nine churches known to have existed in Lewes at this time is mentioned). Both Ford and Atherington may have been included in Climping. The point is of importance as it has some bearing on the dating of Ford church (see p 112), which some writers deny to be of Saxon date.

The long, very lofty, narrow nave, the chancel arch and perhaps parts of the chancel are of Saxon date. Poole thought the church pre-Conquest; Johnston dated it to c 1040. Baldwin Brown considered it to have no distinctive Saxon features but may be reckoned to date about half a century after the Conquest. It is built largely of flints with wide 'joints' and much mortar.

The Nave. This is 63ft long by 21ft 6in and the walls barely 2ft 6in thick. The length-breadth ratio of 3 : 1 is a typical Saxon proportion of northern type, almost specifically Saxon: the Normans did not use such great length-breadth ratios, or such thin walls. The walls are about 20ft high; they were raised by about 5ft in 1170 when the north aisle and very tall north arcade were built. The existing fine interior timber roof may be of this date. The outer roof was formerly of Horsham slabs, replaced in modern times by red tiles.

I

The quoins are of sandstone. The south-east one is mainly side-alternate with many duplications. The north-east is hidden by the modern vestry and north aisle except the top four stones which are of slabs, side-alternate on the east faces; the north face is hidden by the aisle.

The western doorway (Johnston (g), pl 30) to the nave is now the only entrance to the tower which has no western doorway. The doorway is a fine specimen of very early Norman work of perhaps c 1100–20; it is of later date than the nave fabric and earlier than the ground stage of the tower (c 1200). The

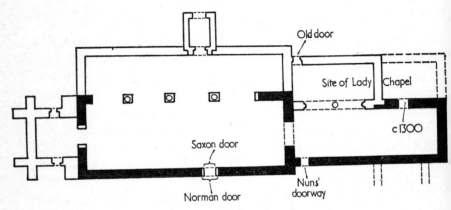

Fig 8. Lyminster. Tower arch, c 1120; north aisle, c 1170; tower, c 1200; north porch, c 1425; vestry modern, on site of old Lady Chapel; nave and much of chancel, c 1040

head is of finely axed Caen stone. On the interior, east, face it is of one plain square-cut order. The segmental head is of thirteen almost rectangular voussoirs, the springers of which are properly shaped. The opening is chamfered round head and jambs. The jambs are of red sandstone, three or four stones per course with many renewals and repairs. There are no imposts. It is 5ft 5in wide and 9ft 4in high to the springing, ie nearly 12ft to the crown. The outer, western face is of two orders and is rather lower than the inner frame.

The north aisle is dated to c 1170. It is 18in narrower at the

east end than at the west. The aisle windows are modern (1864).
The remains of a blocked one high up in the west wall appear
to be original, ie Norman. It has been stated that the stonework
of this window may have come from Saxon windows blocked or
destroyed when the aisle was built.

An original south doorway, (plate p 53), now blocked, in the
centre of the south wall may have been the original, Saxon,
entrance to this church, ie before the more monumental western
portal of c 1100–20 was built. Only the head remains visible on
both interior and exterior wall faces. A lower doorway, of
Norman date, was built in the blocking of the earlier doorway.
It too is now blocked. The Saxon doorway was cut straight
through the wall, ie with no rebate. It is 8ft 6in high and was
3ft 4in wide. It had no imposts. The head is of nine voussoirs of
equal widths, with a narrower keystone. The Norman doorway
was 2–3ft lower than the Saxon one, and rather wider. On the
exterior it was about 3ft 11in wide and about 3ft 6in high
between sill and springers, ie about 5ft 6in to the crown of the
arch. The head is of fourteen small, about 8in wide, and squarish
voussoirs. The jambs are of six stones each; the top one on the
west is of grey stone, different from the others and longer laterally as though to act as an impost. The two springers are
duplicated laterally. Jambs and head are chamfered. The sill, of
four irregular slabs, is badly worn.

Apart from their different dimensions these two doorways
are very similar, roughly and even crudely built. So similar are
they that if their dates, separated by perhaps a century and a
half, were not known they might well be considered to be the
work of the same mason. It is not unlikely that the later doorway may have been built by a local mason, using the traditional
methods of his Saxon forbears, who was assisting Norman
masons in the rebuilding. Yet one doorway is called, and is,
Saxon; the other is described in the literature as Norman. There
seems little justification for such discrimination. The present
writer prefers to regard the tall doorway as tenth- or eleventh-
century Saxon and the other as twelfth-century Saxon.[85]

There is an early window (Johnston (g), fig 4) in the nave north wall, partly cut away by the late twelfth-century arcading. On the exterior (aisle side) it has an arched lintel of one irregularly shaped block, and jambs of large slabs. On the interior (nave side) it has a round head of eleven voussoirs, with rubble filling in the single wide Norman-type splay. It was perhaps one of four, two in each north and south wall. Johnston dated it to the eleventh century, but it is about 17ft above the floor, ie above the original height of the wall, 15ft, and so may be a Norman insertion when the wall was raised in height and the arcading cut. But the arcade cuts into the window which must therefore be older. Its dating remains a problem.

The Chancel. The chancel is quite exceptionally long, 46ft long by 14ft 6in wide, with a length–breadth ratio of 3 : 1. It has been so much altered by later rebuilding that it is not possible to say how much, if anything, in the fabric is original. It narrows slightly towards the east end, and the walls are 2ft 6in thick. There are no original openings. The small doorway (which may have opened to a Lady Chapel long since destroyed) in the north wall near the east end, and the small window above are later, c 1200. Possibly the chancel became the nuns' church and the nave the parish church. It is stated that the remains of an early doorway, possibly the nuns', were found in the extreme south-west corner of the south wall; it is indicated in Johnston's plan. There are indications, near the south-east end, of a blocked archway which may have opened to a chapel, no remains of which have been found. The roof, of fifteenth-century date, was reconstructed to a different pitch in 1884.

The chancel arch (plate p 54) is fine, 19ft 3in high to the crown and 8ft 4in wide. The jambs are in two stages; that is, there are two sets of imposts, one set half-way up the jambs. Possibly the arch was raised when the nave walls were raised for the erection of the rather high arcaded north aisle in 1170. The lower imposts have hollow chamfers below, the upper ones have plain chamfers below a quirk. The jambs are of two or three stones per course and are, ie the wall here, 2ft 6in thick.

The head is plain, square-cut, of one order, but of two rings, an eastern and a western one. There is an almost straight joint round the soffit about one-third the distance from the west face. Each ring is of through-stones as far as the joint. There are eleven voussoirs on the east and eighteen on the west, thin and rather long and cut to appropriate curved shape. The lowest (springer) stone on each side is a through stone to both rings.

There is a small plain red consecration cross low down on the north jamb, perhaps of the twelfth century (André et all; E. W. Tristram (*a*), p 137).

Further reading: A. H. Allcroft (*c*); G. Baldwin Brown; A. Barr-Hamilton; A. Hussey; P. M. Johnston (*g*), *plan in pl 31, facing p 202, and (j)*; H. Poole; Rosemary Sisson.

NORTH STOKE

The dedication is not known. The church is about 2 miles north-north-east of Arundel and 1½ miles south-south-west of Amberley. The manor and church are mentioned in Domesday Book as Stoches. The word 'Stoches' seems to imply the presence of a ford. There is evidence of very early, perhaps pre-Roman, fords at North Stoke and South Stoke (see A. H. Allcroft (*b*)). The manor had 8 hides of land and was worth £20, a considerable sum.

The church consists of nave, chancel, north and south transepts, and a small timber bell turret raised over the west end of the north side of the nave; the turret rises not far through the nave roof. It has been stated that the nave is not much later than 1200, the chancel c 1240, and the transepts c 1275–80. It has also been supposed that the unusual width of the nave, 21ft 6in on the interior, is due to its being built round an earlier, perhaps the Domesday Book church, so that the early church could be used during the re-building; this however is conjecture. The nave undoubtedly is the oldest part and it has some details which are consistent with an earlier date than 1200, in particular its very high walls. In the west wall the height to the eaves is nearly that of the width, 27ft 3in. Although not easy to determine, the wall thickness at the south door seems to be about 2ft 10½in to 3ft including the plaster. Poole's measurement was 2ft 9in; this was before the heavy plastering in the 1962 restoration. The jamb of the elaborately moulded chancel arch is 3ft thick. Poole thought the church to be of Overlap date, with some Norman features, eg the wall thickness, but examination of the fabric suggests that it can hardly be considered more than doubtfully Saxon.

The walls are of large knapped flints with wide 'joints' and much mortar; the nave has old exterior plaster much of which has peeled off. The north-west and south-west quoins are of large, worn, rather thin slabs, side-alternate with some duplications. The lower slabs are up to 20in by 18in by 8in; the upper ones are smaller; a few show diagonal tooling, most of them none. The roof, not highly pitched, is of red tiles. There is no plinth to nave or transepts. There is a corner plinth at the north-east of the chancel, but not at the south-east, and a tall flint thickening along the east wall. The nave is 36ft 3in long by 21ft 6in on the interior.

The two, north and south, doorways opposite each other and near the west end have been re-modelled to a pointed style and lowered. The south doorway, the present entrance, is in a later porch. The jambs are thickly plastered hiding all details. It is 3ft 2½in wide (the writer's measurement). The north door is blocked, but not being plastered on the exterior the stone work is plain. The outer jambs are of seven fairly large slabs each, side-alternate and of at least three stones per course; a few have diagonal tooling, most have none.

There are two small original tall and narrow windows high up in the nave north and south walls, one in each wall. The north one is blocked and plastered on the exterior. Both are partly hidden by the west walls of the later transepts; the transept walls are canted at these points to avoid blocking the windows. The south window on the exterior has an arched lintel, the west jamb is of two massive stones, there is no sill or chamfer. On the interior both windows have rather wide splays but not as wide as is usual with late Norman windows. The interior round head of the south window is of voussoirs, slightly wedge-shaped, of which three on the west and one on the east remain. Five jamb stones on the west and two on the east remain. The round head of the north window is more complete; it has six roughly shaped voussoirs, the two springers being tall and cut to shape. Four western jamb stones only remain. Rather, unusually the church is orientated 34° north of east.

The font is interesting and possibly ancient, even Saxon. It is tub-shaped with vertical tooling, as on some other old fonts in Sussex. It has a double moulded fillet round the lip. The bowl is about 17in high, 2ft 3in in diameter and the lip is 3¼in thick. It stands on a cylindrical stem which looks as old and has vertical tooling. The flat square base is thin and has a thin double moulding; it may not be so old as the rest. The stem and base are about 2ft high.

Further reading: H. Poole; J. H. Round.

OLD SHOREHAM: *The church of St Nicholas of Myra*

St Nicholas, Bishop of Myra in Lycia (Asia Minor), died c 352. He was the patron saint of mariners, merchants and bakers, and especially of children. It was a popular dedication of ancient churches near the sea in Sussex; others are or were at Bramber, Brighton, Portslade, Arundel, Poling, Worth.

Shoreham is about 6 miles west-north-west of Brighton and 5 miles east-north-east of Worthing. It and its church are mentioned in Domesday Book as Soresham. After the Conquest it was a manor of W. de Braose, the tenant-in-chief of the Rape of Bramber under the Conqueror. De Braose gave 'the tithes of the church of Sorham' to St Nicholas of Bramber in 1073. In c 1075 he founded the priory of Sele (Beeding) and gave to the Abbey of St Florent at Saumur, in Anjou, St Nicholas of Old Shoreham together with other properties in the neighbourhood as far south as the mouth of the River Adur.[66]

Baldwin Brown dated the church to post-c 950, Poole simply as pre-Conquest which it undoubtedly is, or was. It consisted of a nave with a western tower (or porticus) and square chancel slightly narrower than the nave. The nave was 45ft long (including the tower which was about 15ft square) and about 17ft wide; the chancel was of the same dimensions as the tower, 15ft square (interior measurements). The nave north wall is only 2ft 2in thick; the tower north wall (plate p 71) is a little over 3ft, thinning a little towards the east. The curious off-set in the north wall indicates the north-east end of the tower; it measures 12in north-south on the exterior and 1ft 11½in on the interior, the difference representing the difference in wall thickness on the east and west of the off-set. It is about 20ft on the exterior from the tower west wall. There is no off-set on the south; the tower and nave walls are here flush as they were refaced in the earliest Norman rebuilding of c 1070–1100. This work is usually called Norman, but in view of its date and the crudeness of the few positive remains it may as justifiably be regarded as Saxon as Norman. At this time the nave was lengthened westward by removal of the tower east wall (and presumably the upper stage or stages) thereby incorporating the ground floor with the nave. The Saxon north doorway to the tower was blocked and a new doorway cut in the south wall just to the east of the former tower east wall. A window was inserted in the south wall near the west end and opposite the blocked north doorway.

The next rebuilding was c 1130–50 when the Normans built the existing beautiful tower on the site of the Saxon chancel; the corners of the old chancel are apparently embedded in the four Norman tower piers. At this period too were built the north and south transepts, each with an eastern apsidal chapel, and further east a new and longer chancel, with apsidal east end, of the same width as the earlier chancel. The square stair turret between the north transept and the tower is also of this date, as is also the richly ornamented nave north doorway.

In the late thirteenth century the transeptal apses and the chancel were removed and a larger chancel, the existing one,

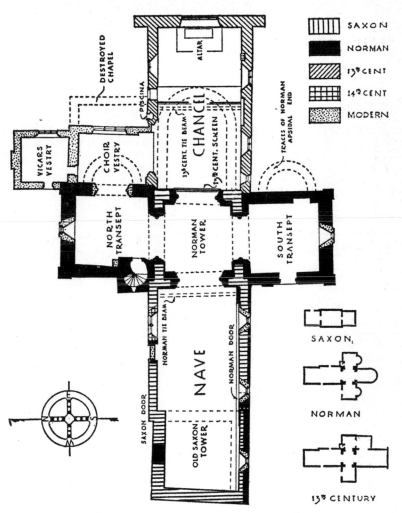

Scale [_____|_____|_____] feet
Measured & Drawn by J.H.Warner

Fig 9. Old Shoreham

erected. It is square-ended, only 9ft shorter than, and of the same width as, the nave, ie slightly wider than the earlier chancel.

The two-light window near the east end of the nave north wall is of fourteenth-century date. Other changes to the east of the tower, and the north and south windows of the transepts and the range of three windows in the nave south wall are modern.

The interior has modern plaster throughout which hides all interior early details except the north doorway. The church was in a ruinous condition in 1840. The north transept was almost a ruin; the yard soil so highly piled up that it hid the walls for several feet above the level of the interior; the jambs of the Norman doorway in the west wall of the south transept (now the main entrance to the church) were hidden, only the arch head being visible. It was completely restored in 1840–2.

The Saxon church was built of roughly knapped flints, with wide 'joints' and much mortar; no plinth is visible above ground. The quoins of the former west tower are mainly renewals, of side-alternate slabs. The north-east quoin is visible in the nave north wall 17ft 8in from the west corner. It is of irregular, not very big slabs, with one long one on end and four renewals at the top. The west wall is not at right angles to the nave side walls: the south-west angle is more acute than the north-west.

The blocked Saxon north doorway (plate p 71) is 8ft 4in from the west quoin, ie at about the centre of the former tower north wall. From the appearance of the wall-work and strip-work the opening was round-headed. The fragmentary jambs are of long massive blocks. There was strip-work round the head and down the jambs. The strip-work round head is of rough rubble stones; the verticals are fragmentary, more so on east than west, and of short 'longs' on end. Small flat slabs act as imposts to the strip-work; no imposts to the inner head are visible. The strip-work is about 6ft 4in high to the rough springing, ie to the imposts, and 3ft 11in wide. The inner opening, ie the doorway itself, was about 2ft 10in wide.

The only opening in the west wall is one high up in the gable, perhaps originally Saxon. It is large, gable-headed and now glazed. The dressings are of stones, five stones in each jamb and three to each face of the gable head. It is apparently double-splayed, but has a flat sill. The outer faces of the head and jambs were grooved and moulded at some later date.

In the nave south wall the three single-light round-headed windows are modern. The western one is cut through the blocking of the early Norman (or Saxon) window (the one opposite the blocked north doorway). Of this some west and east jamb stones, one rather big, and a few stones of the round head remain. The opening was about 4ft wide. Further along the south wall, between the middle and eastern modern windows, are some square jamb blocks, extending to close to the eaves, of what may have been a Saxon window; it is higher in the wall than the blocked western window, and so may be earlier, perhaps one of the original Saxon windows.

The middle modern window cuts into the eastern part of the head of the blocked early Norman south doorway. This had six small voussoirs in the western half of its round head which enclosed a tympanum with a flat lintel below. This may not have been a real lintel; it consists of a row of small slabs wedged in between the jambs. Many small slabs similar to the jamb stones appear as a kind of lining to the jambs, with a straight joint between. Possibly all these odd stones are parts of an earlier blocking than the present one. The tympanum is filled with flat irregularly shaped slabs; the jambs of small blocks in no particular arrangement; the width was about 3ft 4in and the height to the springing about 6ft 10in.

The north doorway, about centrally placed, has modern blocking and is of one order. On the exterior it is 2ft 10in wide and 4ft 4in high to the springing. It has a plain round head of fourteen small, very regular voussoirs, no imposts and jambs of six slabs each, side-alternate. On the interior the jambs and head appear to be renewals, voussoirs are thin, jambs of side-alternate slabs, and the round head is decorated with Norman chevron ornament, resembling in this respect the beautiful tower arches. It is rebated, perhaps later, for a door on the interior where the width is 3ft 8in. Its height from the nave floor is about 6ft 5in, about 2ft higher than on the exterior due probably to differing ground levels.

Further reading: G. Baldwin Brown; H. Cheal, pp 165–81; Gentleman's Magazine, (a); W. E. Godfrey, plan; P. M. Johnston (s); J. M. Neale; H. Poole; F. S. W. Simpson, plan.

OVINGDEAN: St Wulfran's Church

This is an unusual dedication, rare in England and the only one in Sussex. St Wulfran was a late seventh-century archbishop of Sens (France).

The village is 3 miles east of Brighton pier and about a mile from the coast. It is mentioned in Domesday Book as Hovingesdene, Hovingedene and Ovingedene. A chapel (ecclesiola) is mentioned. Although usually translated chapel, the word literally means a little church, ie a field church, which is what this church probably was. According to VCH no traces remain of this early church, the existing building being of the very beginning of the twelfth century. Johnston wrote 'evidence in favour of a pre-Conquest date, though weighty, is not conclusive'. Baldwin Brown thought it not Saxon as it has no distinctive Anglo-Saxon features, but was probably built within about fifty years of the Conquest. Poole considered it to be the Domesday Book church and dated it to 1066–86. It has many Saxon-looking features: nave and chancel walls, blocked north doorway, chancel arch, some windows. In view of the primitive character of Sussex Saxon work which persisted long after the Conquest, Ovingdean may well be considered a Saxon church in spite of its post-Conquest, perhaps early twelfth-century date.

The walls are of small, roughly coursed, knapped flints, with considerable restoration work here and there. A flint plinth (Saxon plinths are rare in Sussex) is along the chancel south

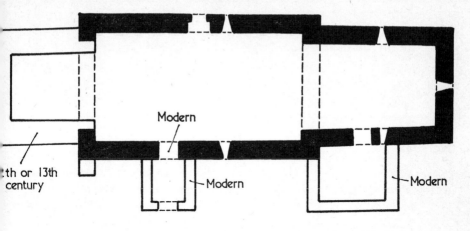

Fig 10. Ovingdean

wall, a mere thickening of the wall, with no chamfer, very
different from the higher plinth round the thirteenth-century
tower. The nave walls are high, nearly 20ft; the roof ridge
reaches nearly to the tower roof eaves. The chancel walls are
also high, only 5 or 6ft lower than the nave. Both roofs are
highly pitched.

The nave north-west and north-east quoins are of small face
—and side—alternate slabs; many in the north-east are duplicated and these fill the entire wall space between the nave quoin
and chancel north wall, about 1ft 10in. Here the chancel also
has a quoin, ie at its north-west corner, side-alternate and similar
to those of the nave. The chancel south-east quoin is just flint
walling except four stones near the top, which look later insertions, and three slabs above which look older and may be
original. The chancel north-east quoin is mainly side-alternate
and is similar to the nave quoins. The nave south-east and
south-west quoins are hidden by the later vestry (on the south)
and buttress (on the south-west).

The nave is 34ft long by 17ft 6in, and the chancel 19ft long
by 14ft on the interior. On the exterior the chancel is 22ft 2in

long by 19ft 1in. Hence the chancel north and south walls average 2ft 6in thick and the east wall 3ft 2in. The nave wall at the south door is 2ft 9½in thick and the east wall, at the chancel arch, is 2ft 11½in thick. The chancel is rather long, ie it does not approximate to the more usual nearly square shape. There is a vertical crack in the north wall about 7ft from the east end exterior; if there is one in the south it is hidden by the later chapel. This crack, together with the greater thickness of the east wall, may indicate, though it does not prove, a later lengthening of the chancel. This would make the original chancel of more normal proportions, ie 12ft long by 14ft wide. Such a lengthening seems however on other grounds unlikely: it would invalidate a Saxon date for the chancel south-east flint quoin, the east window appears to be original, and the original windows in the chancel north and south walls are centrally placed.

There are two wide pointed arch heads in the exterior of the nave south wall, eg two blocked arches, covering almost the whole length of the wall. There is a similar arch head in the chancel south wall. These are the remains of a late twelfth- or early thirteenth-century south aisle. This aisle was destroyed, probably in 1377 by French raiders who are known to have raided the south coast in that year. There are some stones in the flint walling of reddish colour indicative of fire damage.

The only entrance to the church now is a south doorway, through a porch, both of mid-nineteenth-century date. Almost opposite in the north wall, almost centrally placed (its western jamb is on a level with the eastern jamb of the south doorway) is a blocked doorway. This is stated to have been the original entrance. It is not known whether the modern south doorway replaced an earlier one; but a single entrance in the north only was unusual as this was the side of the church where the Devil was supposed to lurk. On the exterior the head is of two plain orders only slightly recessed by about two inches. The outer order is of thirteen voussoirs of even lengths and the inner of ten. There are no imposts; the jambs are continuous with the inner order. The outer order has no jambs; it is really a kind of hood mould 10in wide; the inner head is 11–12in wide. There are six approximately square stones to the western jamb with two thin ones of perhaps Roman tiles. The interior has a head of one order, and has no imposts or through-stones. The head has twelve voussoirs and there are eight jamb stones on the east and ten on the west. Here it is 6ft 5in high to the springing and 3ft 10in wide. On the exterior it is about 6ft high though only 4ft 10in is above the ground, the lower parts of the jambs being now below the risen ground surface. The exterior width is 3ft 3in which indicates an interior rebate of 3 or 4in. This rebate is not apparent; it is presumably hidden by the blocking which is about 2ft from the interior wall face. Such deep rebates are not uncommon: others are at Bolney and Chichester. This type of doorway, with only slightly recessed two orders on one face and a single order on the other, is not uncommon in Saxo-Norman Overlap churches. Some others are at Bolney, Wivelsfield and at Pattishall (Northants). It is a late Saxon, post-Conquest, feature rather than early Norman.

Just east of the north doorway and high up is a narrow loop window now glazed. On the exterior it has an arched lintel, jambs of four slabs each, of similar sizes though the bottom eastern one is larger, and a sill which looks later; the opening is chamfered all round. On the interior the head is of voussoirs; the single splay is not very wide, ie not of Norman width. There is stated to be a similar head only exactly opposite in the south wall, not visible on the interior. On the exterior there is one only fairly large stone, in the flint walling, just above and about half-way along the western half-head of the thirteenth-century blocked arch. This stone might be a remnant of the window, which was cut into by the later arch; it is about opposite to the north opening.

A circular, slightly splayed opening is high up in the nave east gable and above the chancel arch. It is badly worn on the exterior but appears to be hollow-chamfered all round. It is of voussoirs on the interior. Openings in this position are a Saxon feature.

The chancel east window and the two centrally placed in the chancel north and south walls are closely similar, and similar also to the nave north window; all are original. They are single lights with apertures of about 5in wide, with not very wide internal splays (the splay of the east window is rather wider). On the interior the heads are of voussoirs, about six to each, with the eastern springers long, on end, and cut to curved shape. The jambs are of three to five stones each, side-alternate; there are no imposts. The chancel windows show diagonal tooling. On the exterior they have arched lintels, jambs of four massive stones each, with a fifth thin slab acting as impost, single stone short sills, and are chamfered all round. The south window was cut into by the thirteenth-century aisle arch. When the modern south-east chapel was built this window was opened out and restored; its renewed south-west corner now cuts into the later arch (Johnston (a), sketch p 180).

To the east of the chancel south window is a lancet and to the west a low-side window, both of thirteenth-century date, though the lancet has modern internal dressings. There is no other window in the north wall.

The chancel arch is rather similar to that at Rumboldswyke; it is triple, though not originally so. The central arch is stated to be original; the lateral ones are modern replacements, or conversions of niches.[67] The central arch is of one order, of two rings—an eastern and western—with rubble or plaster filling between. The imposts are plain-chamfered renewals; the jambs are of three or four stones per course. The head has fifteen voussoirs. The face has diagonal tooling. The opening is 9ft 6in high and 5ft 8in wide.

The low tower is very late twelfth or early thirteenth century. Three openings high up in the north, south and west walls are of crude almost Saxon-type workmanship.

The roofs are modern reconstructions of red tiles, except for a few lower courses of the original Horsham slabs in the nave south roof. Some of the old Horsham slab roofing tiles are now set in the floor on the north side of the chancel; some have holes for the iron nails originally used in the roofing.

Further reading: G. Baldwin Brown; G. M. Hills (a), *plan in fig 3;* P. M. Johnston (a 1) *pp 179–81, and* (l); H. Poole; VCH, VII, *pp 231–2, plan.*

PAGHAM: *The Church of St Thomas the Martyr*

The village is 5 miles south-south-east of Chichester. It is an ancient place. The estate of 'Pecganham' was given to Bishop Wilfrid by King Caedwalla of Wessex[68] c 683 'during the short time that he had power over the South Saxon kingdom'. This grant was 'with the consent and pious agreement' of the under-king Ecgweald. This name appears again in Barker's Charter No II, and nowhere else, with the variant spelling Aethwald and this is probably another variant of Aethelwahl, King of the South Saxons who had been conquered temporarily by Caedwalla and was acting as under-king to him (see also under Aldingbourne, p 27). Wilfrid transferred the estate to the See of Canterbury after his reconciliation with archbishop Theodore and his return to Northumbria in 686. It remained the property of the see for centuries for it was still held, in demesne, by Archbishop Lanfranc in the Conqueror's time. The manor and a church are mentioned in Domesday Book as Pageham.

About half the chancel south wall at the west end is possibly eleventh century. Poole thought it Saxon but was doubtful as to whether it was pre- or post-Conquest.

West of the middle window in the chancel south wall is a line of old quoining; west of this is stated to be remains of herring-boning: all this may be part of the original church indicating a chancel length of about 15ft. This old walling is of irregularly sized and shaped rubble with wide joints. The old quoining is of ten smallish blocks in rough approximation to upright and flat arrangement; not very clearly so as the blocks are of similar sizes, about 7in by 8in; two are duplicated. The supposed herring-boning is not real herring-boning: there are some courses of long thin rubble slabs, eg up to 18in by 3in, a few single courses of which are laid in herring-bone fashion, ie sloping.

The walling east of the old quoining and the rest of the chancel are thirteenth century, largely refaced in the restoration of 1837.

The church was converted to cruciform, transeptal type with no central tower but probably with the existing western tower, in the thirteenth century, when the nave was rebuilt. There has been so much refacing, restoring, rebuilding and enlargements (eg addition of north and south aisles), all in well coursed even-sized rubble, that it is now substantially a beautifully finished modern church.

Further reading: H. Poole; VCH, IV, pp 231–2, plan.

PATCHAM: *All Saints' Church*

The village is about 2 miles inland from Brighton pier. It is the most northerly suburb of Brighton but still retains something of its village character, eg the green with the church beside it. The manor and church are mentioned in Domesday book as Piceham. The manor was held in demesne by W. de Warene.

The only remains of an earlier church are of a north door-way, blocked, and now built into the north wall of the modern north aisle (Poole pl VII). Poole considered the doorway to be pre-Conquest. The nave and chancel arch are stated to be twelfth century; whether late Saxon or early Norman it is diffi-cult to determine in the absence of specific details, other than the doorway; the doorway may be of this date. On the exterior it has a large monolithic flat lintel, 10in thick, with a slightly stilted round head above of eleven voussoirs of about equal lengths and about 8in wide. The tympanum is built up with slabs of ashlar. The blocking, like the walls, is of flints. The opening below the lintel is low, about twice the width: it is stated to be 7ft 6in high (but only 6ft 10in are above ground) and 2ft 9in wide. The jambs are of five slabs each of comparable sizes except the top ones which are wider to serve as imposts. On the interior there is no lintel, only round head and jambs. The dimensions are 8ft 9in high and 3ft 4in wide, indicating an interior rebate of 3–4in.

There are, or were,[69] early thirteenth-century paintings on the interior walls. The well-known 'Doom' round the chancel arch was dated by Tristram to c 1225–50.

Further reading: H. Poole.

POLING: *St Nicholas' Church*

The village is less than 3 miles south-east of Arundel and a little more than a mile east of Lyminster. It is an ancient place. There may have been a Roman settlement here, for a gold coin of Cunobeline and the foundations of a villa were found here. At some time after, perhaps not long after, 1086 the church and manor were given to the Norman abbey (nunnery) of Alma-nesches; in 1178 the abbey's rights in these properties were confirmed by Pope Alexander III.[70] Only Poling Hundred is mentioned in Domesday Book, and no church. Poole thought the church to be pre-Conquest; Baldwin Brown dated it vaguely to 1040–1100. The Knights Hospitallers were established here in the late twelfth century; the south aisle was built by them c 1190–1220.

The nave north, west and south walls are original and Saxon, as indicated by the double-splayed window. They are of knapped flints; the exterior is covered with plaster of 1875 date, much of which is peeling off. The nave is 24ft 6in long by 13ft 2in wide, and the north wall is 17ft 6in high to the wall plate. The north wall is 2ft 4in thick and the south 2ft 5in.

The chancel was originally c 10ft square. It was rebuilt entirely, widened and lengthened and made as high as the nave in c 1380; the north and south walls were carried outwards to be in line with the nave walls. The nave east quoins were partly removed for use in the new chancel (as stone was scarce) as

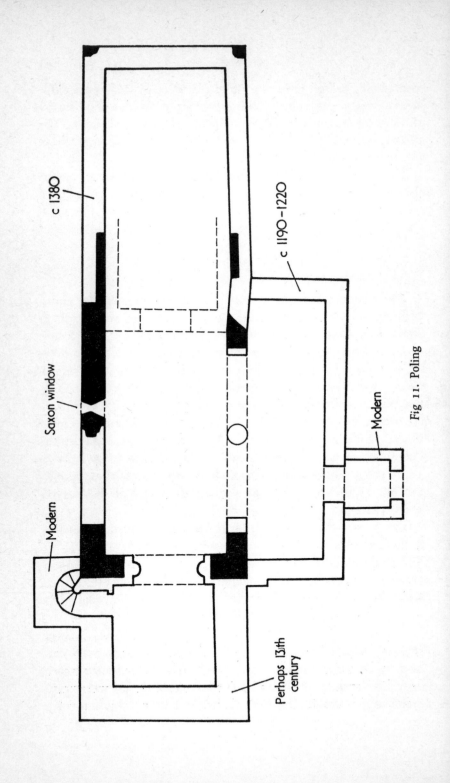

c 1380

c 1190–1220

Saxon window

Modern

Modern

Perhaps 13th century

Fig 11. Poling

inner facing to the west ends of the north and south walls. The Saxon chancel east quoins were rebuilt into their new positions at the east end of the new chancel (Johnston, dr in fig 3). These are arranged in irregular mixed upright and flat and side-alternate manner. Six stones only of the old nave north-east quoin remain, to a height of about 3½ft, in the north wall. The other nave quoins are hidden by the later western tower and buttresses. Some of the quoin stones are of Caen stone but most are of Quarr Abbey stone from the Isle of Wight or similar beds on the Sussex coast.[71]

A slight difference in colour of the plaster led P. M. Johnston to uncover a Saxon window in the nave north wall in 1917. This window had been carefully blocked, perhaps in the fourteenth-century rebuilding. The walls were replastered in 1875. The window is double-splayed (Johnston (t), drs and plan in figs 1 and 2). The aperture is 3ft high and 10in wide; it is splayed out to 1ft 10½in on the exterior and to 2ft 6in on the interior; the outer splay is 12in deep and the inner is 18in. The head is of rubble and flints. The exterior and interior jambs, not entire, are of three thin stones each: two shorts on end below and one long above. The jambs, but not the head, were recessed for a light shutter. Two pieces of oak rebated together, 8½in and 9½in wide respectively, about 8 to 9in high and ⅛in thick, part of the shutter, hang in a frame on the wall below the window. Head and jambs are plastered, presumably original for traces of painting are on the eastern splay: an angel in red outline, now very faint and almost unrecognisable.

The low massive western tower, of grey flints and Pulborough sandstone, is dated by some writers to early fifteenth century; but E. W. Tristram ((b), p 590) dates a consecration cross in it to the thirteenth century. Other consecration crosses in the church have been reported in earlier literature (André et al). The south porch is modern, c 1830; the south doorway is perhaps thirteenth century; there is a scratch dial on its eastern jamb. The church is orientated 17° north of east.

The font may be Saxon. It is small, circular, tub-shaped and of hard gritstone. It has a flat fillet round the lip, 1½in wide and of about ½in projection. The lower half of the bowl is widely chamfered downwards to meet the octagonal fifteenth-century stem. The bowl is about 18in high and 2ft 2in in diameter.

Further reading: Anon (a); G. Baldwin Brown; P. M. Johnston (t); H. Poole.

ROTTINGDEAN: St Margaret's Church

The village is on the coast about 3 miles east of Brighton pier. The place but not a church is mentioned in Domesday Book as Rotingedene; Haminc held it of Earl Godwin.

Baldwin Brown thought the church had no distinctive Saxon features but was built probably within fifty years of the Conquest. Johnston considered the south-west quoin and north doorway to be Saxon, as does the present writer. H. Braun, writing in VCH, considered the nave north wall to be early twelfth century, the tower and chancel thirteenth century, and the nave west wall a fourteenth-century reconstruction. Wynne et al considered the nave north wall to be pre-Conquest, that a tower was built c 1080–1100 on the foundations of the old chancel and a new chancel erected east of the tower; also that a south, and perhaps a north transept (or porticus) of similar dimensions to the chancel was built at the same time. Parts of the foundations of the south transept were discovered, and reburied, in 1909; no actual remains of a north transept have been found.

The transept and part of the chancel were demolished when the tower fell within a century of its erection. The chancel was rebuilt and the present tower built c 1200. The tower walls are over 4ft thick and are flanked on north and south by contemporary buttresses.

Originally the church, of rubble and flints, was probably of nave and chancel only. The nave, long and narrow, is 64ft 6in long and 20ft 6in wide, the length-breadth ratio being 3 : 1, a

Saxon proportion. The chancel was 16ft square and slightly skew to the nave, being inclined towards the south. The later and present towers, being built on the earlier chancel foundations, were similarly skew to the nave, and the later chancel and transept, in line with the tower, were similarly skew.

About 1200, when the present tower was built, it is believed that the nave may have been widened slightly on the south and a south aisle built. The church is reported to have been burnt, with its neighbour Ovingdean, in 1377 by French raiders when the south aisle and nave west wall and roofs were destroyed. The west wall, but not the aisle, was rebuilt and the nave arcade built up with masonry. The church was restored in 1856 by Sir Gilbert Scott who widened the nave by 2ft on the south and built the existing south aisle.

The nave north wall is original. The north-west quoin is of large yellowish sandstone slabs, some up to 15in by 13in by 8in, in mixed face- and side-alternate arrangement; some stones are duplicated; there is no tooling.

The remains of the lower part of the north doorway are about centrally placed. Four eastern and three western jamb stones remain; they are of similar stone and of similar sizes to the quoin stones, one jamb stone is 18in by 12in by 10in; there is no apparent tooling, the stones are badly dressed. The sill is short, between the jambs, and is of a different (grey) stone; it has a chamfered outer edge and may be later. The opening was 3ft 8in wide; the height of the existing portion is 2ft 8in and 11in deep to the blocking.

A stone with colour on it was discovered in the 1856 restoration. There may have been early paintings on the church walls (André et al).

Further reading: G. Baldwin Brown; VCH, VII, pp 236–7, plan; A. E. Wynne, L. Verey and D. Corrie, plan.

RUMBOLDSWYKE: *St Mary's Church*

According to Lower, the original dedication was said to be to

St Rumbold. There are two saints of this name in the Roman calendar; one was a seventh-century Northumbrian. This might suggest that an early church here might have been built by Wilfrid; this however would be pure conjecture. It is more likely that the Rumbold of the manorial name may have been a Saxon thegn who held the manor. The manor is mentioned in Domesday Book as Wiche and as existing in King Edward's time. No church is mentioned. It is situated less than a mile south of Chichester but is now a suburb of the city, known locally as Wyke.

Baldwin Brown thought the church had no distinctive Saxon features but was built probably within fifty years of the Conquest. Both nave and chancel however are probably Saxon in part. VCH attributed it to the eleventh century with only minor alterations till the nineteenth. Johnston also considered it to be of eleventh-century date.

There was some rebuilding in 1866 when the north aisle was built, and again c 1890 when the organ chamber, now a vestry, was erected north of the chancel. The north-west and north-east corners of the north aisle have some original quoin stones, seven in each, taken from the nave north-west quoin when that was integrated with the aisle west wall. The nave north-east quoin is hidden by the aisle. In the south-east quoin the two lowest stones are very long—one is 2ft 3in—on end, and are separated by a single Roman tile about ¼in thick. The rest of the quoin and the chancel quoins are of regular sized roughly dressed slabs in side-alternate arrangement. The lowest six stones in the chancel south-east quoin have vertical grooving about 3in from the edge, suggesting re-used stones from elsewhere.

The walls are of knapped flints with large roughly dressed stones here and there, and with wide joints. There is some herring-boning in Roman bricks in the chancel south wall and a little here and there in the nave west, south and east walls. Johnston wrote that the nave and chancel walls were 'disturbed' in the 1866 rebuilding and that originally the walls were largely of Roman bricks with 'massive' quoins. This disturbance however must have amounted to substantial rebuilding for the present quoin stones are evidently not original, and there is little Roman brickwork now in the walls. The little herring-boning left is of single courses of sloping stones, not real herring-boning.

The nave is about 44ft long by 23 or 24ft wide on the exterior; the walls are about 2ft 2–3in thick except the nave east wall, at the chancel arch, which is 2ft 1in thick. The chancel is about 6ft narrower than the nave. The nave had a north door-way, probably contemporary with the church, which was removed when the aisle was built. The south doorway, the present entrance, is thirteenth century.

The chancel arch, of sandstone, is fine and very large. It has a round head of thirteen voussoirs, with the top one narrow; they are not through-stones. The imposts, 9in thick, are plain chamfered below on east and west and are not returned. The jambs of two or three stones per course have some renewals on the west; on the east they are of three uprights, one long flat, one upright and one short flat. The eastern face has no renewals. The opening is 7ft 6in wide and 8ft 7in high to the imposts, ie about 12ft 7in to the crown. This arch is not original. VCH wrote that it is modern (1890) with imitation random tooling. According to J. Tavernor-Perry (in P. D. Mundy, pp 54–71) the original Saxon arch was entirely of Roman bricks (like that at nearby Westhampnett) and was destroyed in the 1890 rebuild-ing. Dalloway and Cartwright (II, pt I), writing in 1832, do not mention a Roman brick chancel arch here though they refer to the church. Hills wrote in 1868 that the north doorway and the then existing chancel arch were early work, original and contemporary with the church. He stated further that when the plaster was stripped from the interior walls in 1866 the lancet windows and one door (he did not say which, but presumably it was the south door) of the same date (thirteenth century) were 'palpably seen to be insertions in a much older wall'. There are now no original windows; the oldest are the lancets men-tioned by Hills.

The interior of the church is plastered white and is beautifully maintained.

Further reading: G. *Baldwin Brown;* G. M. *Hills* (*a*), *p* 40*n and plan;* P. M. *Johnston* (*a* 2), *p* 151; M. A. *Lower* (*a*); P. D. *Mundy;* VCH, IV, *pp* 172–3, *plan.*

SELHAM: *The Church of St James the Apostle*

The dedication is modern; up till the early sixteenth century it was known as St Mary. The village is mid-way between Midhurst and Petworth, about ½ mile south of the main road. It occurs in Domesday Book as Seleham, but no church is mentioned.

The nave, with its north doorway, the chancel and chancel arch are of the eleventh century. Poole thought the church to be post-Conquest as there are mouldings and, so he wrote, no through-stones. It is built of shaly rubble, like Bosham, and plastered. Much of the plaster, of more than one date on the chancel, is peeling off. There is herring-boning, without spines, in the chancel east and north walls and in the nave north wall, and some very rough work about half-way up in the nave south wall; there is none in the west wall which looks as though it might be of later date. The walls are high for so small a church, and at the north doorway only 1ft 11in thick. The nave is 25ft long by 14ft wide, and the chancel 13ft by 11ft.

The nave, north-west, north-east and south-west quoins are similar; the lower stones are long and thin, some being on end, the others side-alternate; the stones are shorter higher up but still side-alternate. The south-east quoin is probably similar but is partly hidden by the later south chapel and some later plaster.

The nave north doorway (Poole, pl V) is of roughly dressed stones. It has a plain round head of two rings with six voussoirs on the exterior and seven on the interior. The jambs are square-cut and have five stones on the west and six on the east; there is some plaster repair work which hides some of the joints, but the top stone in each jamb appears to be a through-stone (Poole wrote that there were no through-stones). The opening is slightly splayed, being 2ft 8½in wide on the nave side and 2ft 9½in on the exterior; there is no rebate for a door, a late feature. The imposts are badly worn but appear to be hollow chamfered below a quirk. The opening is 6ft high to the 7in imposts; the overall height to the crown is therefore about 8ft.

There is a round-headed narrow light of single splay very high up in the west gable, a common Saxon feature. It appears to have been renewed and glazed on the exterior. It has an arched lintel, jambs of five flat stones each—three larger and two shorter into the walls—and a turned up sill.

The chancel arch (plate p 71) is large and fine and elaborately ornamented. It is round-headed, of two rings of voussoirs—an eastern and a western—of eight voussoirs on the east and ten on the west. The voussoirs are rather long and cut to appropriate curved shape. The east face is square-cut, plain and flush with the wall face. The western face of the arch head has three half-round mouldings, the inner one of greater projection and about equal in width to both the two outer ones. There is no soffit roll but there are ¾-round attached columns down the jamb reveals. These columns have three-membered impost-capitals and Ionic bases, and stand on square-cut plinths which are two-stepped on their reveal faces only. The height of the opening from floor to crown of arch is 11ft 3in; the width is 6ft 3in between the jamb faces, and 4ft 4in between the plinths which project inwards from the jambs 11½in on each side. The detailed heights of the various parts are: plinths 6in; column bases 5in; columns 5ft; plain half-round neckings 1in on the south, 2in on the north; lower members of the capitals 11in on the south, 10in on the north; upper members 8in; imposts 7in.

The ornamentation of the impost-capitals needs describing in detail as the photographs are not sufficiently revealing. The lower capital on the south (plate p 72) has on it an intertwined

monster and serpent; the monster is biting its own tail and its
head forms the western volute. A second snake, not intertwined, has a head which forms the eastern volute; its body
passes round the capital reveal and its tail, formed like an
acanthus, is below the western volute. Projecting from the
snake's mouth on the east face of the capital are two stems, each
ending in three acanthus leaves. The upper capital has a two-
strand interlaced acanthus scroll on the west and reveal, but not
on the east face. The top member, or impost or abacus, is square
and has two-strand, half-round interlacement on the west and
reveal; the eastern face has been cut roughly back to the wall
face.

The lower capital on the north (plate p 72) is voluted and
roughly composite; each volute—west and east—ends below in
a triple acanthus. The upper member has two-strand, half-round
interlacement. The top member or abacus, has acanthus ornament on its western face and a hollow chamfer between two
half-round mouldings on its reveal face; the east face is cut
back to the wall face. These abaci project from the arch head
3½in on the north and 1½in on the south. All the acanthus
leaves are of Saxon type; ie three leaves per stem, bending back-
wards and of increasing size from front to back.

At first sight it might be thought that the ornamentation is
of two periods; the roll mouldings of the archivolt west face, the
Ionic bases to the columns, and the quirked chamfers on the
north abacus seem later—Norman—than the undoubtedly
Saxon animal and interlacement ornament. Probably however
the work is merely that of different masons, one Saxon and one
Norman or Norman-trained.

The fine timber roof supporting the outer tiled roof is
fifteenth century. All the windows, the north porch and the
south chapel are modern.

There is an early font, one of many Saxon and/or early
Norman fonts in Sussex. It has vertical tooling. It is circular
with gently sloping sides and stands on a hexagonal base, probably later, also with vertical tooling. The bowl is 2ft high and

2ft 7in across the top. The lip is 4in thick; it has a ¾-round fillet around the outer edge, and two quirks forming an inverted V are round the top.

Further reading: H. Poole; VCH, IV, p 81, plan; P. D. Mundy.

SINGLETON: St John the Evangelist's Church

Singleton is situated about 5 miles south-west of Midhurst and 6 miles north-east of Chichester. The village and church are mentioned in Domesday Book as Silletone. The place was of some importance for the church is stated to have owned three hides and one rod of land, a considerable possession. The tower is dated to c 950 or 1000; the aisled nave and chancel are mid-thirteenth century.

The tower (plate p 89) is built of flint with some later ashlar above as repair work. The quoins are of well-dressed big stone work arranged side-alternately. The tower is of three stages with later plain battlemented parapet. The lower stage is plastered; the upper stages, which are not recessed, are rough-cast. There is a small chamfered plinth.

The tower is about 14ft wide (north-south) on the interior and 21ft 11in on the exterior, which makes the walls about 4ft thick, rather thick for a tower of this date; Baldwin Brown gave a thickness of 2ft 8in. The interior length (east-west) is 17ft. Though longer east-west than north-south it is not a porch tower and there is no indication of a western doorway.

In the ground stage there is a round-headed double-splayed window in the north, south and west wall. The heads are of voussoirs, jambs of three slabs each and they have no imposts. The south window is hidden by a later buttress; the west one is at a higher level than the others. In the second stage on the north are two single-splayed round-headed windows close together; the heads are of voussoirs, jambs of slabs and no imposts. There are no openings in this stage on the west or south. In the east wall, above the tower arch, is a larger tall opening, unsplayed and therefore probably a doorway. It has a gabled head, unusual in so large an opening, and the jambs slope inwards at their lower corners making the sill appear three-sided.

In the third or belfry stage in the north wall is a single round-headed window with head of voussoirs, slab jambs and chamfered all round. There is no opening in the south or west. In the east, on a level with the north opening, is a large later opening with perhaps original jambs. The head is a flat lintel narrower than the opening, so the jambs are curved inwards to meet it.

The tower arch is pointed though the jambs have some through-stones; it was probably reconstructed in the thirteenth century. It is about 9ft 10in wide and 7ft 6in to the imposts. The jambs are 2ft 8in thick.

SLAUGHAM: St Mary's Church

The village, pronounced locally Slaffham, is about midway between Horsham and Cuckfield and about 5 miles from each. Neither the place nor the church is mentioned in Domesday Book. Dengate called it Norman; E. W. Tristram thought it had some Norman remains. VCH dates the nave and perhaps the chancel north wall to the twelfth century. They are of yellow Bargate stone of various shapes and sizes.

Originally both nave and chancel were of the same width with no separation between them. The nave is 41ft long by 19ft wide.

In the nave north wall is an early doorway, apparently contemporary with the nave and so, perhaps only doubtfully, Saxon. It is rather similar to the doorway at Horsted Keynes 8 miles east-north-east of Slaugham. On the interior the sill is 3ft 1in above the floor; on the exterior it is level with the ground. On the exterior it is 3ft 7in wide, 6ft 9in high to the crown; the jambs are 5ft high; there are no imposts. The interior round head has nine voussoirs. On the exterior the head has eight voussoirs, which are therefore not through-stones; the jambs have six slabs each of mixed face- and side-alternate arrangement and are apparently through-stones. There are imposts, 15in long by 6in thick, chamfered below a quirk.

There were early paintings[72] on the nave interior walls. They were discovered in 1874 but subsequently destroyed.

Further reading: W. A. Dengate, plan; VCH, VII, pp 184–6, plan.

SOMPTING: St Mary's Church

Sompting is 2 miles east-north-east of Worthing. The church is of complex plan developed through various additions in the twelfth to the fourteenth century. The tower and part of the nave are Saxon. The village and the church are mentioned in Domesday Book under the name of Sultinges. The original dedication is not known; the earliest mention of it is in a grant of land made in 1442 to 'the church of St Mary of Sultinge'. Baldwin Brown dated the tower to the Overlap, Clapham to the early eleventh century; it is almost certainly pre-Conquest.

The tower (plate p 90) is built of uncoursed flints with some Roman bricks here and there in the north and west tower walls. It was formerly plastered, but much of the plaster has peeled off. It is of two stages on the exterior separated by a curiously decorated string course. The string is square-cut with a series of curved hollowed-out depressions, half-ellipses, cut round the lower edges. It has been described as a kind of billet ornament but is really quite different. The ground stage occupies little more than a quarter of the total height. On the west there are no openings above the ground stage and below the belfry, which is not separated on the exterior from the stages below. On the south there is one small window above the string course suggestive of a second internal stage; and on the north there are two ranges of window openings between string and belfry indicating four internal stages including ground stage and belfry.

The south-east quoin is of genuine long and short work, though rather irregular above the string course. The south-west quoin below the string is of big stone work arranged mainly on end in rough long and short arrangement; above the string this quoin is, like the south-east one, of rather irregular long and short work. The north-west quoin and north-east quoin above the string course are similar; they are of small square or short slabs on end throughout the entire height. On both sides of the south-west quoin, ie in the south and west walls, and extending to the string course are real long and short thin buttresses. There is evidence that there may have been similar small buttresses at the north-west quoin, replaced by the later larger buttresses. Fletcher and Jackson maintain that the apparent south-east quoin below the string is not a real quoin for the nave and tower are of the same width and the nave north and south walls are continuous with the tower north and south walls. The apparent south-east quoin below the string is a projecting long and short pilaster-buttress at the junction of nave and tower walls. Similarly there is no north-east tower quoin below the string course but faint indications remain of a projecting pilaster-buttress, as on the south-east.

There are centrally placed pilasters on the north, south and west walls. Below the strings they are now fragmentary on north and west. Below the strings they are square-cut, of 'long and short' arrangement, and stand on projecting bases. Above the strings they are complete on all three walls, are of half-round section, and not of 'long and short' arrangement (as stated by H. M. and J. Taylor), but of a series of long shorts (fig 12). The pilasters extend upwards into the apices of the helm-shaped roof where they end below projecting square corbels; according to Rickman's drawing the corbels were hollow chamfered round the lower half. Below the belfry openings these pilaster strips are interrupted by capitals, which are presumably decorative for they could serve no useful purpose where they are. Two of them are floriated, closely similar to those on the soffit roll capitals of the tower arch. The capital on the west is too badly worn to be recognised but according to Rickman's drawing it was decorated with a human face. Fletcher and Jackson consider that the pilaster strips below the string course are all genuine structural

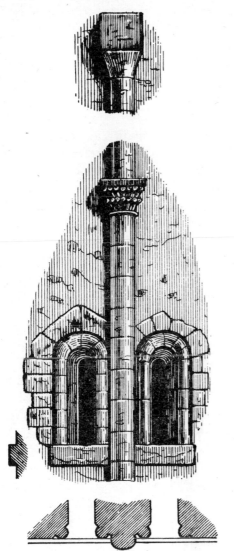

Fig 12. Sompting, pilaster on
north face of tower

buttresses, but that the strip-work above is decorative; this arrangement is similar to that at Barnack. It should be noted that the north-west and south-west quoins below the string are, rather abnormally, flush with the wall face and were originally plastered like the walls; the quoins above the string project in the usual manner and were not plastered. The south-east apparent quoin below the string projects like the pilaster buttresses; which is further evidence that this is really a buttress and not a quoin.

There is neither a window nor a doorway in the south wall of the ground stage. In the west there is a tall narrow blocked round-headed opening to the north of the central pilaster. It has slab jambs, no imposts, thin sill and a half-round head cut from a single stone. It is rebated all round, including the sill, possibly for the fixing of lighting slabs; it is too far above ground level to be a doorway. The other two openings on the west, one a window the other a doorway, with their north jambs cutting into the central pilaster are later. In the north wall to the east of the central pilaster is a tall single round-headed window, splayed all round.

Above the string course, in the south wall of the second stage is a small gable-headed window to the east of the central pilaster. The gable is of two thin slabs, each jamb has a tall massive centre slab with a smaller slab above and below; the sill is one slab between the jambs.

In the north wall are two ranges of windows above the string and below the belfry. The lower pair is of small gable-headed openings, one of the pair being on each side of the central pilaster. The central common jamb is a single massive circular pillar stone. The outer jambs are of single stones with half-round outer faces. The sill is too badly worn to be recognisable as a sill. According to Rickman's drawing it was massive with some queer incised carvings on the face; it may possibly have been a cross fragment re-used. Higher up are two separate single windows, close together, one on each side of the central pilaster. They are larger than those below. They are round-headed and both heads and jambs have half-round outer faces (plate p 90 and fig 12). Both heads are below and enclosed by a larger round head in the wall turned in Roman bricks not shown in Rickman's drawing. Both have massive sills apparently formerly decorated, like the gable-headed pair below. These windows above the string course and below the belfry (ie two pairs in the north wall and a single one in the south; there are none in the west and east walls) are peculiar in that those gable-headed on the exterior are round headed inside, and vice-versa. The east and west single belfry openings are gabled on both faces.

The north and south belfry openings are alike; those on the west and east are alike but differ from those on north and south. The east and west windows are pairs of single gable-headed openings; the gable sides have half-round edges. The eastern pair have stone jambs; the western openings have jambs of Roman bricks. The north and south openings are interesting and unusual. They are tall double openings of the usual Saxon belfry type, two pairs in each wall one on each side of the central pilaster. The round heads are not cut from single stones and heads and jambs are half-round on their outer edges. The sills are square-cut and sloping. The central mid-wall shafts are plain and straight, not bulging balusters, and do not support mid-wall projecting imposts. Instead their upper ends are corbelled out to north and south to support the double heads above. Such corbelled-out capitals occur also at Jarrow and Bolam; all three are of late eleventh-century date. Baldwin Brown thought this form originated in Italy; that it passed from there to the Rhineland, where it became popular, and then to England in the late eleventh century. There is a very similar capital at Trier Cathedral in the Rhineland of the same date. These Sompting capitals are carved with foliage stems with lobed terminations similar to the Viking Ringerike ornament (Baldwin Brown, fig 98). This, according to W. G. Godfrey, might suggest a date early in the century, ie earlier than that suggested by Baldwin Brown. On the other hand, T. D. Kendrick states that the Ringerike style did not reach England until 'the closing years of Cnut's reign', (say c 1030) and continued up to the Conquest though it had only slight influence on southern English art.

The tower roof is of the Rhenish type, a form developed in the Rhineland where it became popular. There are fine, though later, examples at the Abbey Church at Laach, at Andernach and Coblentz Cathedrals and at the Apostles' Church at Cologne. It consists of a four-sided gabled roof with the apices of the gables placed centrally in the tower walls and the lower corners of the gables above the tower quoins; the roof faces are trapezoidal. It is the only Saxon tower which is known to have retained its original roof form. There was a similar one at Flixton, Suffolk, until it was pulled down and rebuilt last century. There may have been one at St Benet's, Cambridge (Fisher (b), p 160).

The tower arch is fine and of unusual interest (plate p 90). Its round head is of voussoirs. The jambs are of slabs, face-alternate and approximating to upright and flat in that some of the stones are thinner than others and run further into the walls. They stand on very thin square-cut plinths. There are soffit rolls, a late Saxon feature, round the head and down the jambs and which stand on chamfered half-round bases. There are thin, square-cut abaci below the arch head cut to appropriate shapes, and below the abaci are capitals with unusual decoration. The capitals of the soffit rolls are foliated and similar to those on the exterior half-round pilaster strips. Clapham describes the ornament as 'imitated more or less remotely from classical examples'. Each has three layers of rather crudely stylised leaves, with turned back tips, similar to those at Scartho (Lincs). Clapham thought them derived from the palmette which was easier to reproduce than the acanthus and which is found occasionally in Saxon work down to the end of the Saxon period. This may be so; but it could be equally well explained as an attempt to reproduce a type of Norman foliated capital not yet very familiar in Saxon England. Moreover, the acanthus is found elsewhere in the church. The capitals above the jambs on either side of the soffit roll capitals are quite different. They are voluted capitals of original design. The corner volutes are boldly carved, reminiscent of those at Glentworth (Lincs) but simpler. They might be described as trumpet spirals with clusters of grapes at their centres.

The arch, and the fifteenth-century western doorway (which may have replaced an earlier one) are placed well south of central to allow, presumably, for an altar to the north against the tower east wall; altars in this position in porches were common in Saxon churches. The arch is 6ft 11in high from the nave floor to the base of the capitals, which are 12in high with 3in abaci above; the total height to the springing is therefore about 8ft 2in. The opening is about 7ft 1in wide so the overall height to the crown of the arch is about 11ft 8in. The thickness of the jamb, ie the wall here, is about 2ft 5in.

The late twelfth-century nave is of the same exterior width as the tower, about 19½ft, and with walls only about 6in thinner; the tower walls are about 3ft thick. These are Saxon dimensions and suggest that the rebuilt nave and chancel were erected on the original Saxon foundations. The chancel was extended eastwards and there is no structural division between nave and chancel; the two form an uninterrupted rectangle 78ft long by 15ft wide on the interior, a length-breadth ratio of over 5 : 1. If the original Saxon chancel was square (a common Saxon dimension) and was extended later to twice its length, the Saxon nave would have been about 48ft long, with a length-breadth ratio of rather more than 3 : 1.

In the chancel, south of the altar, is a gable-headed piscina with rather primitive but highly finished interlacing acanthus ornament. Identical carving occurs on the flat lintel of a rectangular recess to the north of the altar, and on three strips of frieze behind the altar incorporated in a later reredos. All are probably re-used portions from an earlier larger design.

In the south chapel is a carving of a bishop or apostle, for he is nimbed. It is very primitively Anglo-Saxon in execution : the body is in a frontal attitude, the head in profile; one enormous eye is in the top side of the forehead; the hands are very large;

the pastoral staff stands apparently unaided on its point. It is interesting as it has simple palmette ornament rather similar to that on the tower arch soffit roll capitals, and a stiff leaf ornament on the capitals which might almost be the originals of the Jews' harp ornament at Stow (Lincs) and elsewhere.

Further reading: M. B. Adam; J. L. André; G. Baldwin Brown; A. W. Clapham (a) and (c); E. G. M. Fletcher and E. D. C. Jackson; C. R. Peers; T. Rickman.

SOUTHEASE

The dedication is unknown. The village is mid-way between Newhaven and Lewes and about 3 miles from each. Southease is an ancient place. A church here, with 28 hides of land, was given by King Edgar in 966 to Newminster Abbey, later called Hyde Abbey, Winchester. This abbey had been founded not as a monastery but as a house of clerks by Edward the Elder (899–924). The lives of these clerical houses (there were others at the Old Minster (Winchester), Chertsey (Surrey), Milton Abbas (Dorset) and elsewhere) deteriorated later and Edgar in 966 drove out the clerks and replaced them by monks. His foundation charter (BM, Cotton, Vespasian, A VIII) is thought by T. D. Kendrick (op cit, pp 5–6) and by Margaret Rickert (op cit, p 42) to be the earliest of the beautiful MSS of the famous Saxon Winchester school of MS illumination. It is written in letters of gold[73] with three full-page illustrations, one of which in gold and other rich colours on purple vellum shows King Edgar, between the Virgin and St Peter, holding the charter aloft to heaven where Christ sits in a mandorla surrounded by four angels.[74] The book is open at this page under a glass case in the British Museum and may be seen by visitors.

The grant of '*Sueisse cum viginte octo hides et ecclesia*' is written in an addendum (folio 34)[75] to the charter. This too was written in letters of gold but according to Birch, the editor of *Cartularium Saxonicum*, is probably of early twelfth-century

date. It is written in a later and different hand; the scribe
attempted to imitate the script of Edgar's time, ie the original
hand of the charter.[76] It is followed by other folios, some of
which are also in imitated archaic script, containing grants of
King Henry I's time (1100–35). It is not known whether folio
34 is a copy of the original grant of King Edgar. There is some
probability that it is because the grant, whenever made, was
prior to the date of the folio: the manor and its church are
mentioned in Domesday Book as Suesse and as belonging to
Hyde Abbey in King Edward's time and as still belonging to it.
It remained in the possession of Hyde Abbey until the dissolu-
tion of 1538.

Nothing is known of the early church of King Edgar's time.
According to VCH the existing nave 'is apparently of the pre-
Conquest period', ie part of the Domesday Book church, the
western round tower being twelfth century. Poole considered it
to be post-Conquest, of the Overlap period, with some Norman
features. Godfrey wrote 'The tower and nave can be dated with
certainty to the twelfth century, and, judging from the blocked
window high up in the north wall of the nave, early in that
century'. E. C. Rouse agreed. Without disputing the twelfth-
century date the present writer, for reasons discussed above,
(p 9) considers the church to be essentially a Saxon church.

Originally it consisted of a long nave and square chancel
slightly narrower than the nave. The nave was 46ft long and
16ft 6in wide; the length-breadth ratio of nearly 3 : 1 is a Saxon
feature. Only the foundations of the chancel remain, under-
ground, excavated and re-buried. The present chancel is the
eastern third of the nave, formerly separated from the rest by a
fifteenth-century oak screen and rood loft. The chancel is now
slightly lower, by a foot or so, than the nave so the roof was
presumably lowered at some time. The nave and chancel roofs
are now of red tiles, except the three lowest courses of the nave
south roof which are of Horsham slabs. The tower roof is of
shingles.

Short north and south aisles, or perhaps porticus, were added in the late twelfth century; of these only foundations remain. Fragmentary remains of the round head and jambs of an arch (blocked in the fourteenth century when the aisle had presumably fallen into decay) to the north aisle are visible on both exterior and interior of the nave wall. Fragments of a piscina of the north aisle also remain in the nave wall exterior near the east end.

More than half—the western half—of the nave walls and the north-east and south-east corners are original. Stretches of walling towards the east, and most of the east wall, including the three-light east window, are fourteenth century. The walls are of mainly unknapped flints with some, not much, stone rubble here and there. The walls are high, 15 or 16ft, and at the south doorway the wall is 2ft 5in thick. There seems to be a rough chamfered plinth along the west wall only. The north-west quoin, of mixed face- and side-alternate arrangement, is of rather small yellow sandstone slabs in the lower part but rather larger above; the bottom stone is a square clasping stone, longer each way than the others but no thicker. The south-west quoin is hidden by a modern buttress except the top three stones which look like renewals; they are of whiter stone and in better condition than the others. Both these quoins are visible too on the interior. The north-east and south-east quoins are hidden by modern buttresses. Much of the old, not necessarily original, plaster has peeled off, especially from the tower. The chancel is covered with modern rough-cast.

High up in the nave north wall, just west of the blocked north doorway, are the remains of an early window (referred to by Godfrey) visible on both exterior and interior. It was discovered in the 1916 restoration. It was perhaps originally one of three in each wall. It was unsplayed but the jambs narrowed slightly upwards, an indication of early date. It had an arched lintel on the exterior and jambs of four smallish slabs each. On the interior the round head had five voussoirs, the top three very narrow; the two springers, each as long as the top three stones together, are on end and cut to curved shape. The east interior jamb is of four stones of similar size, on their sides; only the top stone of the western jamb remains.

High up in the north-east corner is a short length of roughly formed string course, or interior cornice, of inverted L-shaped profile; it 'seems almost certainly pre-Conquest'.

Another early window (twelfth century but, according to Godfrey, a little later than the north one) is in the south wall near the west end. In the VCH plan it is shown as a single-splayed twelfth-century insertion in the eleventh century wall. On the exterior it had a double-arched lintel, imposts of thin slabs, jambs of two tall stones each on end, and a short sill, not turned up at the ends. Lintel and jambs are chamfered. The aperture is 7in wide and about 3ft high. On the interior it is widely splayed, the head has rather long narrow voussoirs, the jamb stones of 9 to 15in long are on end; there are no imposts.

The jambs of the original north doorway are visible below a modern window, almost opposite the existing fourteenth-century south doorway, which may have replaced an earlier one contemporary with the north doorway. The north doorway is 9ft 9in from the west wall on the exterior and 7 or 8ft on the interior. Only two western and one eastern jamb stones remain; they are similar in size to those of the blocked window above. The opening was about 2ft 7in wide.

The south porch may be sixteenth century. The two two-light windows in the south wall are fourteenth century; the middle one, a single light, is modern. In the north wall the two western windows, single lights, are modern; the eastern one (perhaps removed from the north aisle) is thirteenth century.

During the 1916 restoration traces of colour were discovered below whitewash and plaster.[77] These paintings were uncovered and treated by E. C. Rouse in 1934–5. They were extensive round much of the north and west walls, a complete series representing the life of Christ. Rouse dated them to c 1250–1300. Tristram dated the Passion on the north wall to c 1250, and the Christ in Majesty on the west wall (an unusual position for other than minor paintings) probably slightly later.

The *western round tower* (plate p 89) is one of three in Sussex; the other two are at nearby Piddinghoe and at St Michael's, Lewes. Its walls, of mainly unknapped flints, are 2ft 9in thick, only 4in thicker than the nave walls. VCH considered it to be twelfth century and later than the nave; Godfrey as twelfth century and contemporary with the nave. There are no angle pilasters between nave west wall and tower such as are to be found in many East Anglian round-towered churches. The tower east wall, lower part, is flattened to fit the nave. This flat part narrows upwards above the tower arch so that the nave roof is shaped to fit the tower round wall.

The only exterior opening in the ground floor is a round-headed western window. The aperture is 10in wide and about 20in high. Originally it had a very narrow single splay but the exterior has been re-made in modern brick and there is now no splay. Above and a little to the north of this window are remains of a blocked opening: a short sill and a north jamb of five stones, four small ones and a massive one below. In the north wall is a large, tall blocked window, a little east of central; its head is about on a level with the nave roof ridge. Its round head is of two long thin stones cut to curved shape. The imposts are plain; the western one is at a lower level than the eastern, a small upright stone being between the impost and the head. The rather ill-defined jambs are of four or five stones each; there is no apparent sill.

Further reading: W. H. Godfrey (d), plan; H. Poole; E. C. Rouse (a); VCH, VII, pp 74–5, plan.

SOUTH STOKE: *St Leonard's Church*

The village is on the west bank of the River Arun, less than 2 miles north of Arundel. It is little more than half a mile south of North Stoke but there is no connecting road, only a right of way across a field, a coppice and two bridges, one over the Arun. Both manor and church are mentioned in Domesday Book as Stoches. It consisted of 4 hides and was worth £4.

It is only doubtfully Saxon though it has some Saxon features. It is reputed to be probably thirteenth century. It consists of nave, chancel and a particularly narrow western tower. All walls are of plastered flint; the plaster hides the herring-boning reported by Barr-Hamilton. The walls are high and only 2ft 4in thick at the south doorway. The nave is about 46ft long and 20ft 6in wide. The side-alternate nave quoins are of fair sized slabs.

There were two doorways, north and south, opposite each other and about 10ft from the west wall. The north door is blocked. On the interior the head is of seven voussoirs with rough horizontal tooling. It is 4ft 9in high to the springing and 2ft 9in wide.

The south door is the present entrance. The outer frame is 9in thick and has a head of eleven voussoirs with a projecting hood-mould of torus profile; the head is 9in wide and the hood 5in. The opening is about 3ft 9in wide and 4ft 6½in high to the 4in imposts above the porch floor, which is 10in above the nave floor; the height from nave floor to crown of arch is therefore about 7ft 7in. The inner frame 1ft 7in deep and 5in wider than the outer which acts as a 2½in rebate for the door. The head, of yellowish sandstone, is segmental and chamfered. The opening is 4ft 1in wide and 7ft 10in high.

The tower is very narrow, only 8ft 6in wide on the exterior. The quoins are similar to those of the nave, fairly large, some 22in by 16in by 12in. There is some diagonal tooling.

Further reading: A. Barr-Hamilton; H. Poole; J. H. Round; see also above, under North Stoke, p 149.

STOPHAM: *St Mary's Church*

The village is a mile west of Pulborough. It, but not its church, is mentioned in Domesday Book as Stopeham.

Baldwin Brown dated the church to 1040–1100, ie in his period C3. Poole considered it to be post-Conquest Saxon, but seemed to think the two—north and south—doorways as

equally doubtfully post-Conquest Saxon or early Norman. To
the present writer there are three definitely Saxon features in
the church: 1: the nave wall thickness—2ft 8in at the south
doorway and 2ft 5½in at the chancel arch; 2: two nave doorways, opposite each other and near the west end; 3: the inner
frames of these doorways are narrower and considerably higher
than the outer. Apart from these features it is not possible to
say how much or how little, if anything, is Saxon. The church
is of great interest, and some beauty. The interested reader,
after examination of the building, must form his own opinion
of the probable date.

The church consists of nave, chancel and Norman western
tower. A modern south porch and north vestry have been built
round the ancient north and south doorways.

The nave walls are of sandstone rubble with some flint. The
chancel is of smallish sandstone rubble with many very large
irregular stones, especially near the base. It is not plastered on
the exterior; the nave is, with old but not necessarily ancient
plaster, much of which has peeled off. All nave and chancel
quoins are similar: of large but not massive stones, becoming
smaller higher up, of mixed face- and side-alternate arrangement. In each quoin, near the base, is a very long quoin stone
on end, up to about 2ft 6in by 16in by 12in. The nave walls
are about 17 to 18ft high. The north and south doorways are
alike.

The south doorway (plate p 107) appears to be built in three
sections (cf Bolney, p 51). The inner opening is taller and
narrower than the outer. It is plain, square-cut, the head of one
order is of five stones, the key very narrow, the other four
stones very long, on end and cut to appropriate curved shape—
not real voussoirs. There are no imposts. The jambs are of thirteen slabs on their sides, but not side-alternate, and are 15in
deep to the interior face of the central rebate. The opening is
5ft 3in wide and 9ft 2in high to the springing, or about 11ft
9in to the crown. The outer opening is of more complex design.
It is 10½in thick. The round head (Baldwin Brown, fig 184) is

of voussoirs and is moulded with a ¾-round roll round the lower edge and two smaller ½-rounds above, round the face. The head is supported on plain chamfered imposts, 7in thick, below which are plain, square-cut 2in abaci which form part of the jamb facings; ie the top jamb stone and abacus are cut from one stone. Below are angle columns, one to each jamb, with capitals and bases. The bases, 6in high, are slightly flattened bulbous with rather large plain neckings (not unlike the bulbous bases, but more squashed) above; they are not unlike those in the belfry openings at Bolam (Northumberland).[78] The capitals, 6½in tall, have a Saxon appearance like the bases, but are ornamented with 'a pile of three sharp-edged disks with grooves between', or deeply serrated with three Vs with their points facing outwards.[79] The shafts are built up of drums: the eastern shaft is of two drums, the upper one being 10in and the lower 3ft 11in tall; the western shaft is of three drums, 15in, 2ft 8in and 10in tall respectively. The bases and capitals are cut from separate stones. The shafts, with joints, are 4ft 10in high; including capitals and bases they are 5ft 10½in high. The total height of the opening to the springing (ie including base, shaft, capital, abacus and impost) is 6ft 7½in. The width between jamb faces is 6ft 3in and 5ft between the columns. The overall height to the crown of the arch is 9ft 1½in, about 2½ft lower than the inner opening. The middle section is only 7in thick and the opening is 8½in narrower than the inner opening—6in on the west and 2½in on the east. It acts as a rebate against the inner face of which the door shuts. It does not appear to be entirely original: the head is pointed and of yellow sandstone, the jambs are grey. It has horizontal tooling; the other frames have vertical, not Norman diagonal, tooling.

The north doorway is structurally similar to the south, but differs in some details. On the north (formerly exterior but now within the modern vestry) face the angle columns are built up of drums, the eastern one of 6 drums the western of 5, the bottom one in each being 20in tall. The western drums correspond to (ie are cut from the same stones as) the jamb stones;

this is not so on the east. The bases are bulbous, as on the south doorway; the 9in capitals are of cushion type with wide 2in plain necking below. The total height of the columns, including base, shaft, necking and capital, is 6ft 6in. The tooling is vertical.

The chancel arch is very fine, plain, square-cut and of one order on the east, but with a ¾-round roll along the lower edge on the western face. This west face is very thin; it was built separately from (and possibly, at least arguably, later than) the main arch head behind and attached to it; a straight joint is all round the soffit. The head on the east has twenty-one voussoirs, two of which are through-stones as far as the thin outer western face. The jambs on east and west are faced with thin, large, well dressed slabs, with vertical tooling, and with small square and rectangular slabs, three or four per course, between the facings. The jambs, ie the wall, are 2ft 5½in thick. The opening is 9ft wide and 9ft 6in high to the plain-chamfered imposts which are 7–8in thick; the height to the crown is more than 14ft.

The altar recess, behind the altar rails, is narrower by 25½in than the chancel (which is 5ft 9in narrower—2ft 10½in on each side—than the nave); it is 6ft 1½in deep. It has its own arch, round-headed, slightly flattened, of twenty-one voussoirs. The jambs are of rather small (about 10in by 10in by 8in) slabs, eleven to each jamb. This altar recess does not show on the exterior; its north and south walls are thicker, on the interior, than the chancel main walls. It has been stated that this altar recess replaced an earlier apse in the fourteenth century when the east window was inserted. There is a piscina in the south wall.

The tower arch is of quite unusual interest. It is gabled, but not in true Saxon manner. The sides of the gable are curved, the curvature increasing towards the springing. Each gable face is of three shaped slabs; the apex is of one narrow stone cut to appropriate inverted—V shape. The imposts are plain—chamfered on the respond faces but cut off flush with the tower walls on east and west. There are 2ft high plain plinths—chamfered on respond faces only. The jambs, ie the wall here, are 3ft 2½in thick; this is about 6in thicker than the nave south wall, and hardly a Norman thickness for a tower wall. The opening is about 6ft 9in wide and 7ft 5in high from floor to the 7in imposts, ie about 11½ft to the gable apex. The tooling is vertical as elsewhere in the church; this may be modern: the tiny grooves appear to be of lighter colour than the rest of the face.

In the tower west wall is a blocked doorway. On the interior its plain round head is of three long curved slabs with three short ones at the crown. There are no imposts. The opening is 4ft 6in wide and 5ft 6in high to the springing. On the exterior, the head is a flatly elliptical single-arched lintel made of two stones. The jambs have three stones each above the tower plinth, in upright, flat, upright arrangement, the lowest stone being massive. The opening is about 3ft 10in wide and 4ft 5in high to the lintel, ie lower and narrower than the interior. There is no tooling. It looks characteristically Saxon. It may be the original Saxon west doorway to the church, moved to its present position when the tower was built; or, contemporary with the tower but made of re-used Saxon material. In the latter event where did the re-used material come from? Would there have been a west doorway, in view of the existing north and south doorways? Or, are the latter early Norman, contemporary with the tower, and in replacement of the original west doorway? These questions are pertinent but cannot be answered. Certainly the tower is not highly finished. It is of four stages with no exterior string courses. The belfry openings and those in the stage below are alike, single, with chamfered edges, but have a rough Saxon look about them as though perhaps made by Saxon masons working under Norman supervision.

Further reading: G. Baldwin Brown; H. Poole.

STORRINGTON: St Mary's Church

The town is 2 miles west-north-west of Washington and 4 miles south-east of Pulborough. It and its church are mentioned in Domesday Book as Estorchestone, Estorchetone and Storgetun.

Poole considered the church to be of the Overlap period with some Norman features. However, of the original Domesday Book church, of nave and small square chancel, only the greater part of the nave north wall and part of its doorway remain. In the thirteenth century a new nave and chancel were built against the old church, the nave of which became the north aisle. The old chancel (and chancel arch) were rebuilt as a Lady chapel, and the western tower added.

The old north wall is of irregular stone rubble. The blocked north doorway, centrally placed, has its head cut off by the large modern lancet window above, and its lower part by a later plinth. The jambs are of small stone work. It is 3ft 4in wide. A drawing from the north by S. H. Grimm (reproduced by Hayward) in 1789 shows the doorway without the lancet window above or the plinth below. It shows the doorway with a pointed head. But not much reliance need be placed on the accuracy of such details in early prints.[80]

The old nave was about 42ft long and about 16ft wide, a length-breadth ratio of about $2\frac{1}{2}:1$, a not uncommon ratio in Saxon Sussex.

Further reading: R. L. Hayward (a); H. Poole.

STOUGHTON: *St Mary's Church*

Stoughton together with a church and a priest are mentioned in Domesday Book as Stoctone, Estoctone, and Estone. Earl Godwin held it. It is 5 miles north-west of Chichester.

The church stands in an originally circular graveyard, a possible indication of early date.[81] Baldwin Brown and Poole dated it to post-1066, Baldwin Brown as Norman (on account of the volutes and Ionic bases of the chancel arch) with some Saxon features. Close examination of the fabric suggests that it is a Saxon church with some Norman—and later—features and restoration work. It is cruciform, consisting of nave, chancel

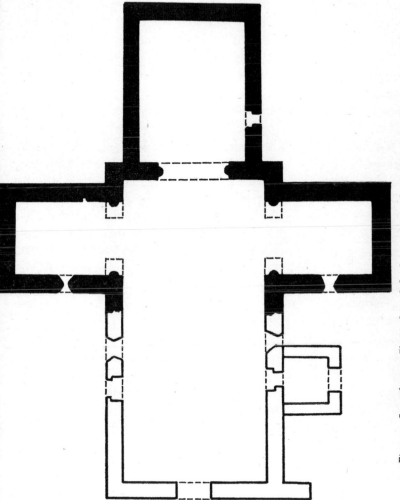

Fig 13. Stoughton. Chancel and both porticus, eleventh century; nave, thirteenth century; porch, modern

and north and south porticus or transepts, all probably parts of
the Domesday Book church with considerable later restoration
and rebuilding, especially of windows. The upper part of the
tower is fourteenth century; the south porch seventeenth century.

The nave is of flint, roughly plastered on the exterior. The
quoins are partly hidden by plaster and later buttresses. In the
north wall at the west end and just below the roof is a fairly
large rectangular section of walling of very thin regularly laid
Roman tiles; the plaster has been cut away to show them.

The chancel is of knapped flints, unplastered, with much
herring-boning in flints, and with many stone blocks here and
there among the flints.

The nave north-east quoin and the upper part of the north-
west (the rest are hidden) are of large well dressed slabs in side-
alternate arrangement and of similar heights. The chancel
north-east and south-east quoins are similar to those of the
nave; so also are the north porticus quoins though rather larger;
the south porticus quoins are covered with modern plaster.

The nave walls are about 30ft high. The chancel walls originally were only about 3 or 4ft lower. In the fourteenth century
the chancel walls were lowered, but not the roof ridge; this
resulted in a sharper angle to the gable. This lowering of the
side walls cut off the heads of two fine north and south windows
which were of the same size as the contemporary east window,
and had pilasters at the angles of the single splays. The now
flat heads of these windows are at eaves' height. Their inner
splays were widened and converted to Early English type when
the existing Early English east window was inserted.

The reputed twelfth-century rebuilding of the chancel may
not have been more than the lowering of the walls (which are
of Saxon thickness) and the insertion of the Early English
windows. The modern roof is of red tiles. The nave is reputed
to have been rebuilt in the late twelfth or early thirteenth century. Here again the rebuilding probably consisted only of the
insertion of new and larger windows and new style north and

south doorways to replace earlier ones. The west window is fourteenth century. There are few other signs of genuine rebuilding. The roof is low pitched and of Welsh slates, as are those of the porticus.

The nave is 50ft 6in long by 23ft 10in wide on the interior. The chancel is 23ft 7in long by 18ft 4in wide. The south porticus is 17ft 11in by 13ft 4in, and the north porticus is 17ft 11in by 13ft 1in at the north end and 13ft 2in at the nave end. The total width across porticus and central crossing is 59ft 8in. The walls are of different thicknesses: nave west wall is 2ft 6in, the north wall 2ft 4in and the south wall 2ft 2½in. The chancel east wall is 2ft 3½in, and the west wall (at the chancel arch) is 2ft 7in. The north porticus wall is 2ft 2½in thick.[82]

The nave has one tall, wide, single, round-headed, single-splayed window in each, north and south, wall. They are high up which suggests they may have replaced Saxon windows, and are east of central, rather near the porticus. The apertures are 8ft 9in high by 2ft 1in and splayed to a width of 4ft 1in. Their structure is hidden by plaster on the exterior. On the interior their heads have seven voussoirs of even width, jambs of seven stones each of roughly upright and flat arrangement, the top stone but one and the bottom stone of each (flats) being longer laterally than the others. There are no through-stones; jambs are of two stones per course. The sills are of two very thin slabs each and only very slightly longer than the aperture width; they look like renewals. There are no imposts. Though of the twelfth century they may have been influenced by earlier forms, or (like a window at Singleton) made of re-used older materials.

The nave north and south doorways are about centrally placed opposite each other. They are thirteenth century but probably replaced earlier ones. The north one is 9ft 2in high to the springing, the south one 7ft high. They have flat segmental heads.

The porticus are high, almost transepts: the roof-ridge of the north one is just above the nave eaves. The south porticus was carried up as a tower as far only as the nave eaves, ie the walls were extended upwards as far as the porticus roof ridge and surmounted by a very flat pyramidal roof of slates. The tower in consequence is relatively very low and squat and wide. On the interior the floor of the low upper stage is supported on massive oak verticals and struts.

The porticus arches, the entire width of the openings, are thirteenth century. It is stated that the originals were little more than half the width.

The north porticus north window and the south porticus south window are thirteenth century. In the west wall of each porticus is an original window, round-headed and double splayed. The glass line is nearer the outer wall, but the outer, shallower splay is the wider: 2ft 6in across, the inner one being 2ft 4in. The apertures are 14in wide and about 3ft 8in high. The interior heads are of seven voussoirs, through-stones of various thicknesses but all slightly wider than the jamb stones, which are not through-stones. The jambs have four stones each, the top and bottom ones much wider than those between. On the exterior the jambs have three stones each of equal widths; they are in better condition and were probably reconstructed at some time.

The Chancel Arch. This is original, very fine and of two orders (plate p 107). It is rather like that at Bosham which Baldwin Brown dated to 1045–65, but which may be considerably earlier. Perhaps Stoughton is of similar date. It has three-quarter round soffit rolls round head and down jamb reveals, and similar rolls down the east and west faces and round the head of the inner order, as at Bosham. The face rolls form the lower supports of the outer order; ie they support the imposts of the outer order and face rolls above. Each roll stands on a two-membered low plinth, the square-cut upper member of which is 4in high and the hollow-chamfered lower member 5in. The members project, east and west respectively, 7½in from the central plinth, which is of the same length 16in (east-west) as the thickness of the inner order which it supports, and which projects north and south respectively 10½in from the side members, each of which has a projection of 10½in from the wall face. The rear part of

the plinth—31in wide, east-west—ends flush with the wall
faces, so the wall here is 2ft 7in thick. The arch is 10ft wide
and 13ft 9in high to the imposts, ie the abaci of the capitals.

The column bases are of Ionic form consisting of three segmental receding rolls each, the smallest at the top, the thickest
and most projecting at the bottom.

The capitals of the soffit rolls are similar to each other, though
the south one is badly worn. They are not crudely Corinthian,
nor do they have foliage, even stylised, as stated by some writers.
Baldwin Brown called them voluted, which they are in a peculiar

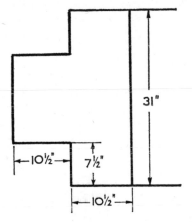

Fig 14. Stoughton, plan of
chancel arch south jamb

way. They have rather primitive volutes; on the soffit face there
is a pair of small volute patterns, side by side, between the
corner volutes. The lower ends of the corner and side volutes
expand sideways and outwards and are slightly hollowed out at
the base, which makes them look like skirts; they have indeed
been described as 'drapery'. However, there are no projecting
feet, and closer examination reveals them to be the three-
dimensional expanding ends of trumpet spirals, the upper, spiral
end being the volute. This is interesting, not only on account
of the rarity of the trumpet spiral in Saxon sculpture (the only
other example known to the writer is at South Kyme (Lincs);
(see Clapham (a), pl 28), but here at Stoughton it appears to be
represented 'in the round' and not, as is usual, in shallow relief.

H. M. and J. Taylor described this ornamentation as a bishop's crozier, the volutes representing the crook. This seems a singularly unacceptable description: no bishop's crozier would expand below the crook into a positively voluminous skirt-like arrangement, or as the trumpet end of a trumpet spiral, as here.

The capitals of the outer order, ie of the face rolls, are simpler; they are face and edge chamfered to make the square shape above meet the round shaft below. All capitals have plain neckings below. The abaci above the capitals are widely hollow-chamfered below and are continued along the wall faces, east and west, as strings as far as the chancel north and south walls, and the nave wall as far as the porticus wall faces.

Immediately outside and above the outer order of the head is an apparent hood mould, flush with the wall face but with a hollow segmental depression all round it, on both east and west faces. The arch head is slightly stilted or horse-shoed.

It will be noticed that there is no true crossing. An earlier type of Saxon winged church, ie with north and south porticus, had a crossing at the east end of the nave, sometimes surmounted by a central tower of stone or timber, and a single portal in the nave west wall. This was the usual form of Saxon monastic church. Brixworth, late seventh century, and Deerhurst, perhaps early eighth century, were of this form though there is no monumental evidence that these two churches had central towers. Repton, perhaps mid-tenth century, had a central tower, though nothing is known of its early nave. Later, smaller, parish churches were erected on the same model, as at Breamore (Hants) c 1000, Hadstock (Essex) c 1020–50, perhaps Britford (Wilts), St Mary-in-Castro, Dover (though this might be called a greater church). About early or mid-eleventh century a change of plan developed in parish churches, especially in the south. The central tower was omitted and, having now no tower to support, the western wall (and arch) of the crossing was also omitted, the crossing space being thrown into the nave. The single western portal was replaced by a pair of doorways opposite each other in the north and south walls, usually near the west end, as at Worth, though sometimes more centrally placed, as at Stoughton. The association of north and south doorways with the absence of a crossing is curious, but perhaps may mean no more than that two side doorways were more convenient in parish churches than a single western portal. (North and south doorways were a common Saxon feature in churches other than winged ones; they were particularly common in Sussex.)

H. Braun (op cit pp 117–19) called these two varieties of winged churches *crypto-cruciform* and *pseudo-cruciform* respectively. These are not very satisfactory terms; they seem harsh, ultra-modern, even anachronistic. There is nothing *crypto-* about a winged church with a crossing: it is clearly cruciform, though not transeptal. The term *pseudo-cruciform* might be useful as a convenient one to indicate a winged church with no crossing. It may be preferable however to use the terms *monastic* and *parochial* for these two types of church, terms which are rich in historical associations and significance.

Further reading: H. Braun; G. Baldwin Brown; H. L. Jessep; H. Poole; VCH, IV, pp 124–5, plan.

SULLINGTON: St Mary's Church

Sullington is situated mid-way between Storrington and Washington, roughly a mile from each, and 5 miles south-east of Pulborough. It, but no church, is mentioned in Domesday Book as Semlinton.

The church consisted originally of a nave, and probably a square chancel and western tower. Poole considered it to be pre-Conquest but not much earlier than 1066. The walls are only 2ft thick and nearly 20ft high, characteristic Saxon dimensions; the nave roof ridge is above the tower eaves. Such dimensions are unlikely to occur after the eleventh century. The nave exterior length of 27ft and breadth of 18ft 8in are not characteristically Saxon.

The nave is built mainly of stone rubble with some flints; the tower is mainly of flints, but the later upper stage is of mixed rubble blocks and flints. The later chancel, much lower than the nave, is entirely of flints.

The nave south-west quoin is largely hidden behind a later buttress; the short portion above is of small stone work. The south-east quoin is irregular: one slab on end, one on its side, two flats on their faces, narrow slabs above.

The thirteenth century north arcade is of two bays. The western one near the tower has a flat original respond or reveal of rather indiscriminate tooling and is only 2ft wide, north-south. This appears to be a section of the original Saxon walling left as a plain respond without the addition of an attached column to match the arcade. The walling above the arcade is presumably original Saxon too.

The low tower is of two stages; the upper one is short and recessed but with no separating string course. The lower stage only is Saxon. The south-west quoin is of Saxon type (Poole, pl V). Stones nos 7 to 12 are 20 to 24in long and arranged in upright and flat manner; the stones above and below are in side-alternate arrangement. In the north-west quoin the bottom seven stones are upright and flat. The quoins of the upper, later stage are of small stone work. The tower is 18ft 8in wide, north-south, and 18ft 7in east-west, ie the same width as the nave. There is no opening in the north wall. The tall round-headed window in the south wall is similar in size to the nave south lancets and like them is modern. The west doorway, now the only entrance to the church (there is no nave south doorway) was a Norman insertion. It is in good condition and looks like a modern replacement.

The upper stage was originally late Norman, possibly of c 1175. The two round-headed blocked windows in the north wall are of the same date. The other openings are of later dates. There has been much restoration and repair work, especially in the west and south walls, at various times up to perhaps the eighteenth century. There is no clear evidence to show whether this stage was a Norman addition to a Saxon porch, or a replacement of a Saxon belfry. The latter however seems indicated by the width of the tower; no porch would be as wide as the nave.

The nave and tower roofs are of, presumably later, red tiles. The chancel roof is of Horsham slabs.

Further reading: R. L. Hayward (b); H. Poole.

TANGMERE: *St Andrew's Church*

Tangmere is about 3 miles east of Chichester and 7 miles west of Arundel. It is an ancient place. King Caedwalla of Wessex granted land at Tangmere and elsewhere to Bishop Wilfrid c 680.[83] It and its church are mentioned in Domesday Book as Tangemere. The manor was held by King Edward and, after the Conquest, by Archbishop Lanfranc in demesne.

The church is only doubtfully Saxon, though Poole considered it to be Saxon of Overlap date with some Norman features, the nave being original. Baldwin Brown rejected it as Saxon as he thought it had no distinctive Saxon features but considered it to have been built within fifty years or so after the Conquest. VCH dated the nave and the western two-thirds of the chancel to the early twelfth century in the plan, but in the text wrote: 'The eleventh century church which is mentioned in Domesday Book consisted of the present nave and a chancel; the latter was enlarged to its present dimensions in the thirteenth century.' The chancel arch is thirteenth century.

The walls are of flint, with a few Roman bricks here and there. Much of the plaster has peeled off. The nave quoins are much alike: they are of small stone work, of mixed face- and side- (though mainly side) alternate arrangement with some duplications. The nave is about 39ft long by about 20ft wide; the old part of the chancel is about 16ft square.

Near the east end of the nave north and south walls are two narrow, round-headed windows in each wall. They are single-splayed but rather widely; a twelfth-century date has been suggested for them. The most easterly one on the south has jambs of red sandstone, two slabs to each jamb, and an arched lintel of grey stone. The lintel appears to be a re-used stone from else-where. It has on it a rude bas-relief of early type, probably earlier than the church. It has been suggested that it represents the beheading of John the Baptist. Poole (pl XI) described it as sculptural beasts. It is very badly worn and the figures are far from clear. They appear to the writer to be men (they are stand-ing on two legs) with animal heads, a by no means rare motif in early Saxon sculpture.[84]

Further reading: G. Baldwin Brown; H. Poole; VCH, IV, p 238, plan.

UP MARDEN: *St Michael's Church*

Up Marden is 6 miles south-south-east of Petersfield and less than 2 miles north of Stoughton. It is an ancient place. Land at a place 'which the yokels call Upmarden' *(in loco quem solicolae Upmerdene vocitant)* is mentioned in a grant made in c 918–25.[85] Four Mardens are mentioned in Domesday Book as Mere-done: Up Marden, North, West, and East Marden. All existed in King Edward's time, but no church is mentioned in Domesday Book at any of the Mardens.

According to VCH, nave, chancel and western tower are of the thirteenth century. Parts may however be earlier; the nave east wall is only 2ft 2in thick, a Saxon feature. The church is built of knapped flints. The nave quoins are very irregular mixtures of large slabs on their sides, smaller slabs approximat-ing to side-alternate, tall slabs on end, some very long flats.

The chancel is very long, almost as long as the nave but narrower. All the windows, in nave and chancel, are lancets.

The chancel arch is peculiar and most interesting. It is gable-headed and within and below a bluntly pointed thirteenth-century arch head. The gable head is rather flat. There are two double 10in imposts with the lower members convexly cham-fered below. The impost ends are flush with the east and west wall faces, and the arch head is set back somewhat behind the jambs. The head is not of through-stones. The jambs are square-cut and are of through-stones, except one stone in each jamb near the top. The tooling is random. The upper part of the opening is about 6ft 8½in wide and 3ft 7in high on the north and 4ft 4in on the south. The lower part of the opening is 2ft 6in high on the north and 2ft on the south. This lower part has been narrowed to 4ft 8in (ie 24½in narrower than the upper part) by the insertion of massive but well dressed stone work, which might almost be described as massive tall plinths. Below this is a real plinth projecting one to two inches on the reveal face only and chamfered on that side only. The jambs are flush with the east and west wall faces and are only 2ft 2in thick.

This arch, apart from the lower insertions, is of the eleventh century, and certainly Saxon. Up to 1923 it was regarded as the original Saxon chancel arch of the probably Saxon church. In that year, during repairs, the interior plaster was stripped off the walls and the wider, later arch head was discovered and opened out. The fact that it was outside the gabled arch showed it to be earlier and the gabled one (though certainly older) a later insertion. It may be that the insertion of a wide, tall, thirteenth-century arch in an earlier (perhaps eleventh century) thin wall caused some bulging; the south wall is out of plumb. Some strengthening was needed which was effected by bringing from elsewhere the lower, narrower gabled arch thereby making the opening smaller. The inward extensions to the lower parts of the jambs would have served as further strengthening. The gabled arch may have come from the small church of West Marden. This church had become subsidiary to Up Marden, the mother church, at an early but unknown date and was apparently secularised before 1585; it no longer exists.

Further reading: W. D. Peckham; VCH, IV, pp 112–13, plan.

WALBERTON: *St Mary's Church*

Walberton is 3 miles west-south-west of Arundel. It is mentioned in Domesday Book as Walburgetone; a church and priest are also mentioned.

Baldwin Brown rejected the church as Saxon as it has no distinctive Saxon features but thought it was built within fifty or so years after the Conquest. It was rebuilt drastically in 1903. The north and south arcades are Norman but probably of two dates. It has been stated that the west wall and the western ends of the nave north and south walls are pre-Conquest but much altered, in fact largely rebuilt in 1903. It has also been stated that the original west wall and quoins were largely of Roman bricks. The west doorway was blocked in flints; the rectangular outline is visible on the exterior, so presumably some part of the original wall remains. Above the blocked doorway, in the gable, is a round-headed window, of probably Norman date. It has an arched lintel, jambs of five stones each of similar heights but in upright and flat arrangement, and a sill of one stone turned up at the ends.

During the rebuilding a crudely sculptured gable cross was found in the west wall; it had been re-used as building material in some earlier (but modern) repair work. Some writers have called it Saxon, but Johnston insisted that it was a crude modern piece of work carried out by the daughter of a former vicar. It is now lost; it was last seen in the rockery of the vicarage garden.

The font is early, probably pre-twelfth century—Johnston thought it probably Saxon. It is tub-shaped of rough finish with random tooling; it is really just deeply pick marked. The bowl is 22in high, tapering below. It is 2ft 5in across at the top; the lip is 2½in thick and has a quirk all round its top, horizontal face. There is no other ornament. The bowl stands on a similarly roughly finished cushion stone base. This is of slightly less diameter than the top of the bowl, is about 15in high, and its rounded edge slopes inwards rather more below than above. The stone stands on a large circular base made in sections, in voussoir fashion, which is probably modern.

Further reading: G. Baldwin Brown; P. M. Johnston (u), note on pp 187–8; H. Poole.

WESTDEAN: *All Saints' Church*

Westdean (East Sussex) should not be confused with West Dean (West Sussex). It is some 5 miles west of Eastbourne and 2 miles east of Seaford.

In early Saxon days it was a prosperous place of some importance. Though predominantly agricultural it was also a small port. Small ships could sail up the Cuckmere river as far as Dene. Villagers also worked in the local salt pans. Asser stated that Alfred the Great had a residence here but does not say which Dene; four Denes are mentioned in Domesday Book. Hussey thought West Dean, in West Sussex, more likely. Actually neither Dene was owned by Alfred. In his very orderly and detailed will[86] no Dene is mentioned among his Sussex manors. The only Dene mentioned is land at 'the Dene', in the same paragraph with manors at Sturemynster, Kruerne, Whytchyrch, Aramuntham, Exanmynster and Lyntum—all in Wessex beyond Selwood, ie Somerset and North Devon.

Westdean however may have been a very ancient place. Land at a Dene, though which Dene is not known, was granted by Nunna, King of the South Saxons, to the Bishop of Selsey c AD 725.[87]

Dene, in Willingdon Hundred, but no church is mentioned in Domesday Book. It was assessed at 9½ hides of land and worth more than £8. It was held by Azor of King Edward. Countess Gida, a sister of King Edward, held a moiety. Later, it was held by Ralph, of the Count of Mortain, who took the name of de Dene (L. F. Saltzman (*a*)). Later, the son of the Count of Mortain gave the manor, and neighbouring Exceat, to the Norman monastery of Grestein, the mother-house of Wilmington Priory.

The church is dated by VCH to the eleventh century. W. H. Godfrey[88] described it as an aisleless nave of the twelfth century, and a later, early fourteenth century, chancel of the same width as, and with no structural division from, the nave. As evidence he mentions quoins or quoin stones in the north and south walls, just to the east of the blocked fourteenth century doorway and about 10ft or so from the east wall. These quoin stones, if that is what they are, are few; four on the north, two near the base and two (one duplicated and a single one above) near the top of the wall; and three stones close together on the south. These may or may not be quoin stones; they look as though they are merely odd stones in the flint walling, though they are approximately vertically disposed; there is no evident difference in the walling on either side.

The church is built of knapped flints with dressings of East-bourne rock. There is a 3ft high thickening of the wall along the chancel east wall and for a little way along the north and south walls, acting as a plinth. The wall at the south door is 2ft 11½in thick and at the tower arch 3ft. All quoins are of fairly large slab work in side-alternate arrangement, with some renewals. There is some diagonal tooling but it is mostly irregular.

It is stated that the western oblong space, now the ground floor of the later tower, was at one time under the same roof as the nave and represented, or was, an original feature. There are, or were, similar features at Boarhunt (Hants), Dagling-worth (Glos) and possibly South Elmham (Suff). The church is 42ft long, (including the, now, ground floor of the tower which is about 7ft east-west by 16ft 6in north-south) and 16ft 6in wide, a length-breadth ratio of about 2½ : 1.

Near the west end of the north wall is a small, narrow, loop window opened out in 1961. It has a tall, double-arched lintel, taller than it is wide and apparently very roughly pointed; the point is 'rounded', but whether intentionally pointed or just poor work is not clear. The jambs are of one slab each on end, the sill of two rectangular slabs side by side. On the interior is a narrow single splay, the jambs of which are of two stones each, on end. A third stone on the west is cut to curved (arch) shape and is a springer; the rest of the head is plastered.

The tall narrow blocked window in the north wall, to the west of central, is of the fourteenth century. The south porch is fifteenth century. The south doorway is fourteenth century; it is not known whether it replaced an earlier one; there is no ancient work in it. It is rebated for a door. It is 3ft 11in wide and 7ft high. The roofs are high pitched and of red tiles, not ancient.

The tower is early fourteenth century. It is strikingly rectangular in plan with its much longer axis running north-south. This is due to the fact that it was raised over the rectangular western adjunct of the nave. The curious spire is low and is more like a cap than spire: it does not stand on the tower; it covers it like a cap with projecting eaves. Moreover, the north and south faces pass downwards several feet further than the east and west faces. It has been described as looking, at a distance, like a monk's cowl, the three small western windows, two above and one below, giving some resemblance to a face.

The tower is of two stages with strings only on the north and south walls, the upper stage being recessed only on these two sides. There are no openings in the north and south walls of either stage. In the upper stage in the west wall are two windows near the eaves and laterally disposed but far apart. Similar windows are in the east wall, one on each side of the nave roof ridge. They are all rectangular, with flat lintels which are turned down at the ends, like reversed Norman-type sills. The jambs have three slabs each on end, the sills are thin.

The moulded parts of the tower arch, cut through the earlier nave west wall, are of the same date as the tower upper stage. The type of original opening from nave to western adjunct, whether doorway or open arch, is not known.

Further reading: Anon (b), plan; A. Hussey; VCH, IV, pp 99–100, plan.

WEST DEAN: St Andrew's Church

The village is 5 miles north of Chichester and 6 miles south-south-west of Midhurst. It is not mentioned in Domesday Book. Poole considered the church to be pre-Conquest as there are through-stones in the old doorway. The nave was dated to the eleventh century by VCH.

The present church is a fine aisleless transeptal church of various dates, except the nave, from the thirteenth to eighteenth century. It was extensively rebuilt after a disastrous fire in 1934 which almost gutted the building.

The original Saxon church consisted of nave and probably square chancel; the latter was on the site of the present crossing. The nave is 39ft long and 19ft wide; the crossing, probably of similar dimensions to the original chancel, is 16ft east-west by 14ft. There is no evidence of an early tower; the existing one is eighteenth century. The walls are of stone rubble, now completely covered with modern plaster. They are stated to be 2ft 2in thick; the writer's measurement was 2ft 4in including the plaster.

There is an early blocked doorway (plate p 108) in the north wall. Its round head, of one order, has seven voussoirs, the top one narrow. The imposts, badly worn, are chamfered and are not returned. The square-cut jambs have six stones each, all through-stones and in approximately upright and flat arrangement. The opening is 9ft high and 2ft 8in wide. There is no rebate for a door. It is definitely of Saxon technique. On the interior the jambs are very badly worn and damaged, and jambs and head show extensive redness resulting from fire damage. The sill is now 20in above the nave modern wooden floor, but is at ground level on the exterior.

A similar eleventh-century doorway was reputed, before the 1934 fire, to be in the south wall and opposite to the north door. If still there it is beneath the interior and exterior plaster and so not visible.

Further reading: P. M. Johnston (l); H. Poole; VCH, IV, pp 99–100, plan.

WESTHAMPNETT: St Peter's Church

Westhampnett is about a mile north-east of Chichester. It

and its church are mentioned in Domesday Book as Hentone. It may be a very ancient place. It is just off the edge of Stane Street, the Roman road from Chichester to London. At this point is a divergence or 'elbow', probably an early Saxon divergence to bring the road to the water-mill on the River Lavant, a little west of the church. This mill is mentioned in Domesday Book, one of two in the manor, valued at five shillings. Alternatively, the paved road here, which was on lower ground, may have become boggy through inattention, so the Saxons may have made a diversion on higher ground.

There was no real village. The church served, and still serves, the four hamlets of Westerton, Woodcote and Waterbeech on the north and Loddesdown (now called Maudlin) on the east. This may suggest that the church was an ordinary minster, the secular priests of which served the surrounding area. Baldwin Brown rejected it as Saxon as he thought, incorrectly, that it had no distinctive Saxon features but that it was built probably within fifty years after the Conquest. Poole thought it the Domesday Book church but post-Conquest, which seems a reasonable date. Johnston thought the chancel was Saxon.

Originally it consisted of a nave and chancel. Part of the nave east wall (including perhaps the north-east corner of which three quoin stones remain in situ), the western two-thirds of the chancel south wall and about one-third of the chancel north wall are original Saxon. The church was badly set-out: the nave east wall diverges very slightly and the west wall considerably to the west, the chancel is orientated markedly to the south. The nave is 47ft long and about 18ft wide on the interior. The chancel was about 16–17ft long by about 13ft; it was lengthened to about 24ft in the thirteenth century. The walls were barely 2ft 2in thick. The nave was rebuilt c 1190–1200; it was restored further in the fifteenth century when the south aisle was built, and there was a drastic restoration in 1867 when the north aisle was added and the nave west wall, chancel east wall and chancel arch were rebuilt. Three stones were left in the nave north-east quoin. Whether these are

N

original or of the late-twelfth-century rebuilding is not known.
They look old. One is small and flat, 14in by 8in; above this is
a massive one on end, 2ft 1in by 14in, and a small flat higher
up. The Norman tower is attached to the south of the east end
of the nave, the fifteenth-century south aisle being to the west
of it. Though Norman in date, the tower is of Saxon proportions and wall thickness. It is relatively tall and slender, only
about 11½ft square on the exterior and about 6½ft on the
interior; the walls are 2ft 6in thick, little thicker than the
original nave walls. However the single belfry openings, one in
each face, are not of Saxon type. The tower is plastered all over
on the exterior, including the quoins, so no structural details
are visible.

The old part of the chancel south wall is mainly of roughly

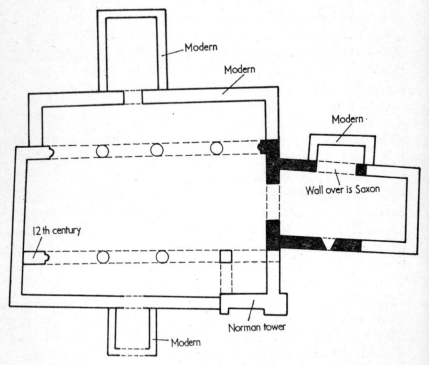

Fig 15. Westhampnett

broken flints with wide 'joints' and much mortar. There is much herring-boning in Roman bricks (plate p 108). Not all these bricks may be Roman. Some are only 9–12in long by 2in thick, others 5½in long by up to 6in thick; these may be broken pieces of perhaps medieval bricks used in later repair work; they are rather more red in colour than the others. There is no Roman material in the chancel later walling and the flint work here is better and more regular. The differences in masonry show clearly on the two sides of the exterior straight joint. The chancel quoins are well squared but look early. They are of large slabs, some up to 2ft by 15in by 12in, in upright and flat (short flats) arrangement. Possibly they are early quoin stones re-used.

A blocked Saxon window is in the chancel south wall between the two western lancets, about 6ft above ground. It is visible only on the exterior. The aperture is 8in wide below tapering to 7in above, and is 2ft 6in tall. The jambs are partly of Roman bricks; no provision for glazing or for a light slab or shutter is visible. The single stone arched lintel is of white stone and may be a replacement; it shows diagonal tooling. A similar window exactly opposite in the north wall was removed when the organ chamber was built in 1867; the arched lintel of this one, 6in by 20in, is built into the exterior east wall of the organ chamber.

When some masonry and the plaster were removed in 1867 (when the present arch was inserted) from both sides of the old chancel arch, much Roman material was found in the wall including hollow tiles, mostly broken. One, entire, is now on the sill of the east window of the north aisle (Hills, fig 5). These were curiously, perhaps uniquely, shaped as hollow voussoirs. They were 8⅞in long at the base (intrados), 10¼in at the top (extrados), 11⅝in high or long, and 5¾in wide at the cavity side. The cavity, flatly rounded or segmental at the interior end, is about 3in by 9in, leaving thin walls of about 1½in thickness. Hollow tiles, as is well known, were used by the Romans for three purposes: as flues of hypocausts, for hollow flooring to promote dryness and ventilation; and as supporting pillars for floors. But why were these at Westhampnett voussoir-shaped? Hills suggested that they were made specifically for use in an arch head. Thirteen were discovered in the wall, sufficient for an arch head 6ft 8in wide (allowing for fine joints of about ¼in). The faces were decorated with lozenge patterns which would give a good hold for mortar or plaster; the tops, which would support the walling above, were plain. In the narrow side of each end is a semi-circular opening making, when two voussoirs were joined together, a circular hole of about 2½–3in diameter. The reason for this is obscure. These tiles may have been used in an arch head elsewhere and re-used at Westhampnett as building material. It is unlikely that they were used in an arch head here, for the chancel arch removed in 1867 was of ordinary flat Roman tiles (like that at nearby Rumboldswyke). In the arch, according to F. C. Hayden's drawing (in A. A. Evans (a); also in A. M. Hills), the lowest tile on each side, instead of lying flat on the impost, was inclined with half tiles propping them up on the outer edges. The jambs were of upright and flat work, the uprights and flats being of similar heights; the imposts were plain.

Further reading: G. Baldwin Brown; A. A. Evans (a); G. M. Hills (a); P. M. Johnston (a 2), p 150n; and (b), p 155; H. Poole; VCH, IV, pp 177–9.

WEST HOATHLY: St Margaret's Church

The village is some 4 miles south-south-west of East Grinstead and about the same distance south-east of Worth. Neither the place nor the church is mentioned in Domesday Book. It is however only doubtfully Saxon.

The nave north and west walls are all that remain of the original church which is dated by VCH to c 1090. They are built of local, coursed, sandstone rubble with wide joints. The north-west quoin is of dressed stones with diagonal tooling. The north wall is about 37ft long and the west wall about 18½ft.

There are no original openings in the body of the church, though a small early thirteenth-century lancet in the north wall may be an enlargement of an earlier smaller opening; the head is of one stone and the west jamb is rough and badly jointed compared with the east jamb. It seems likely too that two original round-headed windows in the west wall were removed when the tower (c 1400) was built, and built into the north and south walls of the belfry, beside two pointed contemporary windows.

The chancel arch was removed and the chancel rebuilt c 1200; the chancel was extended to its present length, which makes it longer than the nave, c 1250. The remainder of the church—south arcade, south aisle and south-east chapel—is later and of various dates.

Further reading: I. C. Hannah, plan; VCH, VII, pp 169–71, plan.

WEST STOKE: St Andrew's Church

The village is some 3 miles north-west of Chichester. It is not mentioned in Domesday Book though North Stoke and South Stoke are, as Stoches. Some writers have stated that South Stoke was West Stoke. This seems most unlikely. North and South Stoke are less than a mile apart, each with a church; West Stoke is 12 miles to the west. Moreover, L. F. Salzman (op cit, (b)) in his notes on Domesday Book stated that the second church at Bosham was at West Stoke. The main Bosham church was held by Bishop Osbern; the second one by King William in demesne. Bosham was a large and rich manor with a number of outlying possessions; West Stoke was only about 4 miles to the north east.

West Stoke may be a very ancient place. It is stated to have had a flint manufacturing, ie mining, industry before Roman times.

The original nave and chancel were probably eleventh century; Poole thought them pre-Conquest. The chancel was rebuilt, narrower than the nave, in the thirteenth century. The nave is original. The eastern quoins of the chancel appear to be Saxon stones re-used: they are side-alternate and resemble the nave quoins but have closer joints. The nave quoins are of mainly side-alternate slabs of various sizes. It has been stated that, though on their sides, all point in one direction, ie not side-alternate. This is not so: one group of three stones only in the north-east point east, and one group of three in the north-west point south; one long (about 16in) in the north-east and one (24in) in the north-west are on end. The south-east quoin stones are side-alternate.

The nave walls are high and of plastered stone rubble with some Roman bricks in groups showing beneath the plaster. The later two-staged tower is a lateral one, off the west end of the south wall; it is no higher than the nave roof-ridge. The roofs are of red tiles; the chancel is lower than the nave. The nave is 29ft 3in long and 18ft 10in wide on the exterior. The wall at the south doorway is 2ft 7in thick.

The south doorway, through the tower, is probably thirteenth century, is pointed and of one order, with plain-chamfered jambs; the inner part of the west jamb seems to be original, ie of the eleventh century: it has no chamfer and shows random tooling.

The north doorway, exactly opposite the south, is about 8ft from the west wall and now leads into a modern vestry. It is probably original. It has a round head of ten voussoirs, no imposts, and jambs of six slabs each, not through-stones. There is a Roman tile in the east jamb exterior (ie within the vestry) where an impost should be. The interior (nave side) has a narrow chamfer all round and a later 3in by 3in rebate for a door. The tooling is random. The nave wall here is 2ft 4in thick. The opening is 2ft 9in wide between jambs and 6ft high to the springing above the nave floor, ie about 7ft 4in to the crown of the arch. On the exterior (ie within the vestry) the jambs are roughly plastered. In the wall is stated to be a mixture of broken Roman bricks, not visible.

A round-headed opening with Roman bricks in it was discovered, during restoration, high up above the chancel arch—a distinctively Saxon feature. It is not visible from the nave; it is either above the interior roof or, perhaps, plastered over.

Further reading: H. Poole; VCH, IV, pp 193–4, plan.

WIVELSFIELD: *St Peter and St John the Baptist Church*

The village is 2 miles south-south-east of Hayward's Heath. It was originally a chapelry of Ditchling, 4 miles to the south, but was made an independent parish between 1438 and 1445. It is not mentioned in Domesday Book.

A nave, 27ft long, and a chancel, both earlier than the present church, have been dated to c 1120. They may have replaced an earlier church for in the plan in VCH, though not in the text, the nave north-east quoin, hidden by the modern north aisle, is indicated as eleventh century. The present elaborate church has resulted from a number of rebuildings and extensions between c 1250 and 1869. The only remnant of the original church left is the north doorway built into the new north aisle wall in 1869. The doorway is tall and narrow, with square-cut jambs and a round head of voussoirs. On the interior, the jambs have eleven slabs each in side-alternate arrangement, there are no imposts or through-stones, and the round-head of nine voussoirs is plain and of one order. On the exterior the jambs are of eight stones, side-alternate, and there are plain-chamfered imposts, not returned. The round head is of two very slightly recessed orders, the inner one of seven voussoirs, the outer of eight including a very thin (about 1½in) one as keystone. The inner order is 9in wide, the outer 8in. The opening is 2ft 7in wide and 5ft 5in high to the 7in imposts, making an overall height to the crown of about 7ft 4in.

The V-type ornamentation on the exterior face of both orders is closely similar to that at Bolney, about 5 miles to the west. Apart from slight differences in dimensions the two ornaments are facsimiles; they are certainly of the same date and must have have been cut by the same mason. The detailed description and discussion given above for Bolney applies exactly to Wivelsfield ornament and need not be repeated.

Further reading: G. Baldwin Brown; H. Poole; H. J. Rush, plan; VCH, VII, pp 122–3, plan.

WOOLBEDING: *All Hallows' Church*

This is about a mile north-west of Midhurst. The manor and a church are mentioned in Domesday Book. Fulcui held it of King Edward. Later it was held by Odo, Ode or Oda of Winchester. This Odo was not the bishop but a Saxon thegn styled 'de Wincestre'. He and his brother Eldred held lands in Sussex apparently as tenants-in-chief directly of King William.

The nave is 34ft 8in long and 19ft 3in wide on the interior. It is built of stone rubble, rough cast all over the exterior except the north quoins and the pilaster strips. These strips (plate p 125), five on the south and three on the north wall exteriors, are 13in wide and of slight (2in) projection. Though of 'long and short' work nearly all the strips are long ones of slightly different heights, averaging about 2ft 4in. They extend to the eaves, except one on the north, the upper part of which has disappeared. On account of the pilaster work Baldwin Brown dated the church to post-950, but stated incorrectly that the church has no other specific Saxon feature (cf the quoins and blocked doorway). Poole called it pre-Conquest.

The nave south quoins are hidden by the rough cast. The north quoins are of Saxon type. The north-east quoin has eight very large slabs below and seven much smaller above, all side-alternate. The north-west quoin has twelve large slabs below and four slightly smaller above.

There is a Saxon blocked doorway in the south wall, rather west of central, visible only on the interior. Only the inner jambs remain. These are of thin (about 3in wide) slabs on end, true 'long and short'; some are through-stones as far as the blocking, only 8in from the face. The head is a flat, thin, short (shorter than the interior width of the opening) lintel which rests on the ends of two very large cubical blocks (imposts), hollow chamfered on their lower, inner edges. The head (lintel and imposts) appears to be later than the jambs; they have vertical and very regular, perhaps modern, tooling. The opening is 2ft 9in wide and about 7ft 8in high from the nave floor.

The font may be Saxon. It is circular, tub-shaped, with straight sides inclined sharply inwards and downwards. It has vertical tooling. It is 2ft 2in across the top, 2ft 3½in high and 2¾in thick at the lip which has no fillet. The base may be later.

Further reading: G. Baldwin Brown; H. Poole; VCH, IV, pp 86–7, plan.

WORTH: St Nicholas' Church

Worth is 9 miles south of Redhill and about 2 miles east of Crawley.

The county boundary was vague and unsettled in Saxon times. Worth, known as Orde, was in Surrey: the place but not the church is mentioned in the Surrey Domesday Book. It was in the Hundred of Cherchefelle, later Reigate, and about 9 miles south of the manor of Cherchefelle (Reigate). It appears to have been a small, poor, isolated settlement, perhaps hardly more than a clearing in the forest. In an area around of about 30 miles wide, east-west, and 20 miles north-south only one other small settlement (Ifelt, modern Ifield, some 3 miles to the west) is recorded in Surrey or Sussex Domesday Books; all around was merely forest. It is still hardly a village: a few houses only. As a reminder of its former isolation the parish includes the forests of Worth and Tilgate, covering more than 13,000 acres. The Domesday Book entrance reads: 'There is 1 villein with half a plough [ie sufficient land to be ploughed by a single plough in half a day]. In the time of King Edward it was worth 30 shillings, and afterwards 2 shillings, now (in 1086) 20 shillings'. The question arises

—there is no answer—why was so fine and large a church built in so small and unimportant a place? Hardly to meet the spiritual needs of one villein and his family. Who built it is also not known. Worth was part of the King's demesne land, as was also the neighbouring large and wealthy manor of Reigate. The church may have been built by the king (not necessarily by the Confessor) or by a member of his family. Another possible founder was the rich abbey of Chertsey, which owned, wholly or in part, 21 manors in Surrey. Oswol or Oswold who held Worth (and five other manors) under King Edward was a brother of Wulfold, abbot of Chertsey; this family or personal connection may have been of some long standing.

Worth church is very different from other Sussex churches (plate p 126). It has apse, north and south porticus, pilaster strips, and windows of quite exceptional type for the area; it is also more substantially built and better finished than most Sussex churches. From this, and its former isolation from its southern neighbours, it may be inferred that it was not the work of Sussex masons. Its builders must have come from Surrey or further north.

The nave, north and south porticus or wings, and apsidal chancel are all of one period but probably not earlier than the first half of the eleventh century. Bloxham, Sharpe, Walford, P. Eden, Fletcher and Jackson all agree. Clapham and Godfrey thought it tenth century. Baldwin Brown put it in his period C3—post-1040—as it has no Norman features and the heads of the nave double windows are of voussoirs (not arched lintels) like those of the Lincolnshire bell-towers which he considered (incorrectly) to be of post-Conquest Overlap date. A late date is also suggested by the advanced type of porticus arches—almost as wide as the porticus—and the absence of a western arched wall to the central crossing.

There was much repair work in earlier centuries. The north and south walls of the porticus are probably thirteenth century and are of large rubble blocks more regular in size than the rest of the fabric. The nave north wall below the string course was refaced with regular rectangular rubble blocks, very different from the irregular rubble above the string. (Eden stated the wall to be original which seems most unlikely; it is quite different from the wall above, and has no pilasters; Eden gives no evidence.) The north buttress at the north end of the west wall is fifteenth century. At some time the apse was heavily buttressed with six buttresses, three of which were of brick, perhaps of different dates.[89] The north wing was given a hipped roof from which rose a timber bell tower, with broach spire, from which a small gabled north annexe projected.[90] This tower was supported on a timber framework within the wing. All this was removed in the 1871 restoration. The nave roof and that of the north wing are modern. The existing tower to the north of the chancel, the organ chamber with the entrance thereto, and the newel stair turret to the west of the tower are of 1871. The south porch is of 1886.

The Nave. This is 60ft long by 27ft wide. The south and west walls are of rubble, similar to the largely rebuilt chancel. It has been stated that in the west part of the south wall are two short courses of herring-boning. This is not so; the courses are just bits of rough work of much smaller rubble than elsewhere. There are pilaster strips on the south and west walls reaching only to the string courses, about 15ft above ground (plate p 126). There are three in the south wall, two to the west of the porch and one to the east; the latter is cut short by the large three-light fifteenth-century window, which also cuts into the string course above; a mere scar remains of a fourth pilaster, formerly near the south doorway. The west wall now has two pilasters, one on each side of the west doorway, and traces (two stones only) near the crown of the doorway and slightly to the south of it, of another. There are also two projecting corbels, one to the north and one to the south, about 5ft above ground, the south one being in line with the pilaster trace.

The south-west and north-west quoins are similar to the pilasters but extend upwards to the eaves, and diminish in width towards the tops. All are about 14–15in wide and project 2–4in.

The edges are cut back to the wall surface. They are mainly of 'long and short' work; but a few shorts are really flats, ie among the true longs and shorts are a few short stretches of 'upright and flat' work.[91]

The pilasters in the north wall were presumably removed when the wall was refaced. There is some ashlar refacing in the west wall especially between the level of the south eaves up to below the circular window in the gable. A part of the west wall to the north of the doorway is stated to be modern (Godfrey (f); Eden, his p 240) but doesn't look like it. Originally there was probably a parapet above a corbel table; four of the projecting corbels are still in place below the eaves of the modern roof. The west and east gable heads have modern copings.

There is a bold two-membered plinth along the south and west walls, of square sectioned large rectangular slabs, and also along the north wall of the north porticus, both presumably original; each member is 9–10in high. No plinth is visible along the south porticus; the ground here however has risen and may hide the plinth which Godfrey stated is there. The nave north wall has a single-membered chamfered plinth which extends round the fifteenth-century north-west buttress; this suggests a possible date for the refacing of the north wall.

The original north and south tall and narrow doorways are blocked. They are opposite each other but further from the west wall than is usual in Saxon churches, about 20ft or one-third of the nave length, and about half way between the west wall interior and the west jambs of the porticus arches.

The north doorway on the interior is fully blocked to about 4ft above the nave floor; above this it is a recess about 14in deep. Above the full blocking the square-cut jambs have five slabs in the east one and seven in the west, the bottom one on the east is about 18in high; the others are shorter and all are through-stones. The square imposts project only on the reveal sides. The head is of nine rough voussoirs of irregular widths. The interior width between jambs is 3ft 7in and the height is about 12ft to the imposts and about 14ft to the crown of the arch. On the exterior only the western halves of the head and strip work round it remain in situ.

The south doorway (plate p 143) is similar, though most jamb stones are renewals. The head is of seven rough voussoirs. It is 3ft 9in wide between jambs and about 14ft high to the crown of the arch. The present fourteenth-century south doorway has been cut through the blocking. There are no visible remains of the old doorway on the exterior wall. Before the 1871 restoration the church was plastered thickly on both interior and exterior; this hid all signs of the two original doorways. Walford stated that (in 1856) only the two low south and west doorways were there 'both are manifestly insertions'. He refers however to earlier rumours that remains of earlier doorways might be behind the plaster.

The west doorway is of the fourteenth century as is also the three-light window above.

High up in the nave north wall are two original window openings (plate p 143) and a similar one in the south wall opposite the western north one. The eastern south window was replaced by the existing large three-light fifteenth-century window. These three windows have double round heads and plain bulging baluster shafts, almost mid-wall, which stand on square slab bases exactly similar to the jamb bases and imposts; they have no capitals. There are long rectangular central impost blocks above the balusters to support the double heads. These openings in form are typical Saxon belfry windows found only in towers, though occasionally also in the lower stages of towers (as at Bardsey, Yorks WR, at Barton-on-Humber, Lincs, and St Michael's, Oxford). The triple opening at Brixworth (Northants) is in the third stage of the tower and overlooks the nave, and is of later date than the nave. One at Wing (Bucks) in the east wall above the chancel arch may have overlooked an inter-roof space. The windows at Worth seem to be the only example in England of normal nave lighting by such openings. The baluster shafts too appear to be the only example of plain, unornamented balusters, except a very crude one built up of flints and much mortar at East Lexham (Norfolk); all others have from one to six half-round, usually projecting, bands. The Worth windows however appear to have been blocked at some time and replaced by single round-headed openings. Walford does not mention any double windows, but describes the round-headed ones. In pictures of the church before 1871 (P. Eden, pl XXIX) a round-headed single window only is shown in the nave north wall above the string course and near the west end, where a double window now is. Presumably these early double windows were opened out in 1871. Presumably also the central shafts must have been removed to make way for the later single openings. The existing shafts may therefore be replacements and not necessarily copies of the originals, which may have disappeared. It is therefore not legitimate to assume (as some writers have done) that the present shafts are ancient, and unique in being unornamented.

The half-heads are of three or four stones each, plus a central one so shaped as to be common to both half-heads. The jambs are square-cut of two through-stones each (the south window has three in each, a long one on end below, and two short ones above), with imposts and bases which project slightly inwards (ie towards the shafts) but are flush with the wall face. There are no sills; jamb and shaft bases rest on the string course. The central shaft imposts project very slightly on the exterior; on the interior they are level with the wall face. The jambs (ie the wall) are 2ft 7in thick. The shafts are not quite mid-wall: the 'glass line' is 18in from the interior and 13in from the exterior wall face. The total width between jambs is 4ft 11in; the central impost is 18in wide; the western opening is 21in and the eastern opening is 20in between imposts (see measured drawing in Baldwin Brown, fig 14). The shafts and imposts and parts of the heads and jambs of the north windows, and most of the south window are plainly renewals.

The Porticus. The north and south wings, exactly opposite each other and only about 6ft from the nave east wall, though often described as transepts (being of substantial size and comparable with those at Stoughton are really large porticus.[92] Their roof eaves are on a level with the nave string courses, ie about 15ft from the ground, and their roof ridges only a few feet above the nave eaves. They are of a late type; their entrances from the nave are arched openings about 8½ft wide, wider than early porticus openings.[93] Earlier porticus, too, often abutted on to a central presbyterial space, or crossing, which had eastern and western arches—as at Breamore, and formerly at Brixworth, Deerhurst and probably Hadstock (Essex). At Worth the western wall of the crossing has been omitted, the crossing space being open to the nave. It is interesting that the earlier churches with four-walled crossings had their nave entrances in the nave west wall (as at Brixworth and Deerhurst) whereas these later ones with no separate crossings had two nave entrances often near the west end of the north and south walls, and no opening in the west wall, as at Worth (see also above under Stoughton, p 198–9).

The North Wing. This is 19ft long (north-south) by 14ft 10in wide on the interior. The north wall is of the thirteenth century and has no pilaster strip work. There are two pilasters on the west wall and there was a corresponding pair on the east wall, but the south-east pilaster with a bit of walling was removed in 1871 when the stair turret was built. The north quoins are of similar work to the pilasters, as in the nave. The pilasters extend upwards to the string course which is just below the roof eaves, on about the same level as the nave string. The porticus has no original windows. The upper lancet window in the north wall is contemporary with the wall. In the east wall is a tiny lancet set high up in a tall thirteenth-century altar recess.

The south wing is closely similar to the north wing, though about 1in narrower. The south wall is thirteenth century and is not at right angles to the east and west walls. That this deviation was original is indicated by the south quoins which are original. There are two pilaster strips on the east and west walls. Quoins and pilasters are of similar 'long and short' structure. The south window is a modern three-light one.

There is a blocked very wide and rather low (8ft 3in wide by about 9ft 3in tall) opening in the east wall visible only on the interior, round-headed and square-cut. There are no imposts; head and jambs are continuous and are of small roughly cubical slabs about 8–10in square. Within the blocking is a smaller pointed recess of thirteenth-century date, perhaps an altar recess. It is possible that the larger, earlier opening may have been of Saxon date, leading to an eastern apsidal chapel. Drawings by Sharpe (VCH, VII, p 198) in 1805 and by Walford in 1856 show pilasters on the east wall exterior only in the upper part of the wall. They have now been carried down over the blocking, presumably in the 1871 restoration.

The west wall has a modern doorway close to the south wall. To the north of this is a blocked single-splayed narrow window supposed to be of the thirteenth century. It has an arched lintel, jambs of three slabs—flat, upright, flat—of equal lengths, and no sill. It is chamfered on the exterior. It is not visible within the porticus being beneath the plaster. The roof is medieval, not Saxon.

The two arched porticus openings from the nave are closely similar: square-cut plain round heads of voussoirs and jambs, with plain square-cut pilaster stripwork round the heads (on one face only) and down the jambs (on both faces), and plain double imposts. They are 15ft high to the crown and 8ft 8in (the north one) and 8ft 7in (the south one) wide, about 7ft lower and 5ft 4 or 5in narrower than the chancel arch. They show much modern restoration work. At some time the imposts and jambs and stripwork of the south entrance were cut away for the convenience of the occupiers of pews in the porticus. Walford's drawing[94] of 1856 of the interior looking east shows no imposts or stripwork on the south arch. They appeared badly damaged in Walford's time. He wrote that the arches:

'are quite plain. The imposts should seem to have consisted of two members on each jamb, the upper projecting beyond the lower. They were in all probability both square and perfectly plain as if left in block; and a plain square moulding descended from them to the floor on the inner side in a corresponding

situation to the half-round on the eastern face of the chancel
arch. All these have been removed, with the exception of
small portions in the jambs of both transepts.'

They were restored in 1871. There are no through-stones in
the jambs of the south porticus arch. The head is original and
of nineteen very thin through-stone voussoirs; the two springers
are about twice the length of the others. The stripwork hood
mould on the north face (there is not one on the south), like the
vertical stripwork down the north jambs, is modern. There is
stripwork, though no hood, down the south face of the jambs
which looks original. The tooling is indiscriminate even on the
modern replacements. The vertical stripwork is about 2–3in outside, ie to east and west of, the hood mould. The vertical strips
are about 7in wide and the hood 6in.

The north arch is similar: the head is of nineteen voussoirs
with stripwork hood on the south face only. The jambs look
older than those of the south arch; the bottom stone on the west,
and the top stone on the east are through-stones; the others are
two to four per course. The stripwork, on both jamb faces, is
further east and west of the hood (on the south) than in the
south arch. It is of long and short work, 8–10in wide and projecting 3–4in.

The Chancel. This is 33ft long and 21ft 6in wide. It has the
form of a greatly stilted semi-circular apse, with stilts, ie the
straight north and south chancel walls, about 22ft long dying
into the wall of the apse. It was practically rebuilt in 1871. The
buttresses and the fifteenth-century east window were removed,
and fresh pilasters were inserted below the string course. The
walls are of irregular rubble, like the nave, with wide joints. The
rubble above the string is smoother, better faced than that below
and may be part of the restoration work. The roof is modern.
Six lancet-type windows were inserted above the string course:
three in the apse, two in the south wall and one in the north.
The two-light window near the west end of the south wall and
below the string is thirteenth century.

o

The chancel arch (plate p 144) is very fine, 22ft high to the crown, and 14ft wide. The square-cut round head is slightly depressed due to the spreading of the jambs which are not now strictly vertical (though the stripwork appears to be). The head has thirty-two thin voussoir blocks, all through-stones. There is a square-cut stripwork hood mould on each face; the one on the west was originally double, the lower member being of shallower projection than the upper; only a short strip of the upper member remains, above the north impost. On the east the hood is single and of about the same width as the double western one. The jambs have half-round reveals, 2ft 8in in east-west diameter; ie 4in (2in on each face) less than the thickness of the jambs, or wall, which is 3ft. There is stripwork, square-cut on the west and half-round on the east, down the jamb faces, vertically below the hood on the west but rather outside, ie somewhat to north and south of, the hood on the east (drawings in Walford, p 241; and drawing and plate in Nibbs). The square-cut stripwork on the west is of longs and shorts, about 18in and 6–7in long respectively, 7in wide and projecting about 2in. The half-round stripwork on the east face is attached to, but does not form an integral part of, the jambs; ie though the jamb and stripwork stones are of similar lengths—short longs—the joints of strip and jamb do not correspond; a strip stone and a corresponding jamb stone are not cut from a single stone, but from two. The imposts, or square capitals, are double. The upper half, of greater projection than the lower, is square-cut above and moulded below; the lower member is square-cut above and moulded to a flat square cushion shape below. The two imposts are not quite identical, being slightly dissimilar in projection and profile.

Further reading: H. Braun; G. Baldwin Brown; A. W. Clapham (a); P. Eden, plan; W. H. Godfrey (f), plan; E. G. M. Fletcher and E. D. C. Jackson; R. H. Nibbs; H. Poole; E. Sharpe; VCH, VII, pp 197–9, plan; W. S. Walford.

List of Saxon Churches, Existing and Recorded, in Sussex

At the time of the Domesday Book, Sussex was divided, north-south, into five 'administrative' units called Rapes. Each of these was held by one of the Conqueror's barons, who held as tenant-in-chief under the king. Many manors were held by sub-tenants under the tenant-in-chief, and some might be held by sub-sub-tenants under the sub-tenants. Each rape was named after the chief town or township or borough where the tenant-in-chief had his castle. Passing from east to west of the county the rapes were:

Rape	Chief town	Tenant-in-chief
Hastings	Hastings	Count of Eu
Pevensey	Pevensey	Count of Mortain
Lewes	Lewes	W. de Warene
Bramber	Bramber	W. de Braose
Arundel	Arundel	Earl Roger,
(and Chichester)	(and Chichester)	(of Shrewsbury, Montgomery and Arundel, one of the Conqueror's greatest barons)

The map on pp 232–3 shows the distribution of Saxon churches throughout the county. It will be noticed how the concentration of such churches increases markedly from east to west and from north to south.

The churches are listed separately in each rape. Within the rape they are arranged in three groups:

A. Both manor and church are mentioned in Domesday book;

227

B. The manor but no church is mentioned in Domesday Book, though a Saxon church, entire or in part, exists there;

C. Neither manor nor church is mentioned in Domesday Book.

Within each rape, too, the churches are given in alphabetical order, independently of the grouping, so that they may be readily identified on the map. Those places where there are existing Saxon churches, entire or fragmentary, are given in capital letters. At the other places the original churches have disappeared or have been replaced by later medieval or modern churches. The names in brackets are those in Domesday Book.

I. THE RAPE OF HASTINGS

A. *Manor and church mentioned in Domesday Book:*
1 Ashburnham (Esseborne)
2 BEXHILL (Bexelei), two churches
3 Brightling (Brislinga)
4 Catsfield (Cedesfille), an *ecclesiola*
5 Fairlight (Ferleg)
6 Filsham (Wilesham)
7 Hazelhurst in Ticehurst (Haslesse)
8 Herstmonceaux (Herste)
9 Hooe (Hou), an *ecclesiola*
10 Ninfield (Nerewelle)
11 Playden (Pleidenham)
12 — (Rameslie), five churches, sites unidentified
13 Salehurst (Salhert)
14 Sedlescombe (Saliscome), an *ecclesiola*
15 Udimore (Dodimore)

B. *Manor but no church in Domesday Book:*
16 GUESTLING (Guestelinges)

C. No manor or church in Domesday Book:
    None

II. THE RAPE OF PEVENSEY

A. Manor and church mentioned in Domesday Book:
    1   Beddingham (Bedingham) Church presumed: 'Ulnod a
        priest held land here under King Edward'.
    2   Brambletye (Branbertie) Church presumed: 'there is a
        priest here'.
    3   Selmeston (Selmestone)
    4   South Malling (Mellinges) Church presumed: 'the canons
        of St Michael's [Malling] hold 4 hides'.
    5   Willingdon (Willendone) Church presumed: 'Godfrey
        the priest [holds] 1 hide and 1 virgate.

B. Manor but no church mentioned in Domesday Book:
    6   ARLINGTON (Herlintone)
    7   BISHOPSTONE (Biscopestone)
    8   EASTDEAN (Esdene, or Dene)
    9   EXCEAT (Essete)
    10 HORSTED KEYNES (Horstede)
    11 WESTDEAN (Dene)

C. Neither manor nor church mentioned in Domesday Book:
    12 FRISTON

III. THE RAPE OF LEWES

A. Manor and church mentioned in Domesday Book:
    1   Balmer (Burgemere), an ecclesiola
    2   Barcombe (Bercham)[95]
    3   Brighton (Bristelmetune)
    4   CLAYTON (Claitune)
    5   Ditchling (Digelinges, Dicelinges, or Dicenlinges)[95]
    6   Falmer (Falemere)

   7   Hamsey (Hame)
   8   Hurstpierpoint (Herst)
   9   Iford (Nivorde)
 10   Keymer (Chemere)
 11   OVINGDEAN (Hovingedene), an *ecclesiola*
 12   PATCHAM (Piceham)
 13   Plumpton (Pluntune)
 14   Poynings (Poninges)
 15   Preston, or Bishop's Preston (Prestetone)
 16   Rodmell (Ramelle)
 17   Saddlescombe (Salescome)
 18   SOUTHEASE (Suesse)
 19   Street (Estrat), two *ecclesiolae*

B.   *Manor but no church mentioned in Domesday Book:*
 20   HANGLETON (Hangetone)
 21   LEWES (Lewes, Lawes, or Laquis), 9 churches mentioned
       in ancient charters (see above p 136)
 22   ROTTINGDEAN (Rotingedene)
 23   WORTH (Orde)

C.   *Neither manor nor church mentioned in Domesday Book:*
 24   BOLNEY
 25   Newick
 26   SLAUGHAM
 27   WEST HOATHLY
 28   WIVELSFIELD

IV. THE RAPE OF BRAMBER

A.   *Manor and church mentioned in Domesday Book:*
  1   Beeding (Beddinges) two churches[96]
  2   BOTOLPHS or Annington (Haningedune)
  3   Broadwater (Bradewatre)
  4   COOMBES (Cumbe)
  5   Durrington (Derentune)

   6 Findon (Findum)
   7 Henfield (Hamfelde)
   8 KINGSTON BUCI (Chingestone), two churches
   9 Shermonbury (Salmonesberie), an *ecclesiola*
  10 SHOREHAM (Soresham)
  11 SOMPTING (Sultinges)
  12 Steyning (Staninges) two churches[97]
  13 Thakeham (Taceham)
  14 West Tarring (Terringes), two churches
  15 Wiston (Wistanestun)
  16 Woodmancote (Odemanscote)

B. *Manor but no church mentioned in Domesday Book:*
  17 BUNCTON (Bongetune)
  18 SULLINGTON (Sillentone, or Semlinton)

C. *Neither manor nor church mentioned in Domesday Book:*
     None

V. THE RAPE OF ARUNDEL

A. *Manor and church mentioned in Domesday Book:*
   1 ALDINGBOURNE (Aldingeborne)
   2 Barnham (Berneham)
   3 Bepton (Babintone)
   4 BIGNOR (Bigneure)
   5 Binderton (Bertredtone)
   6 BOSHAM (Boseham), three churches[98]
   7 Boxgrove (Bosgrave). Church presumed: 'the clerks of
      the church held 1 hide'.
   8 BURPHAM (Bercheham)
   9 Bury (Berie)
  10 CHICHESTER (Cicestre), two churches. One church only
      is mentioned
  11 CHITHURST (Titeherste) an *ecclesiola*
  12 COCKING (Cochinges)

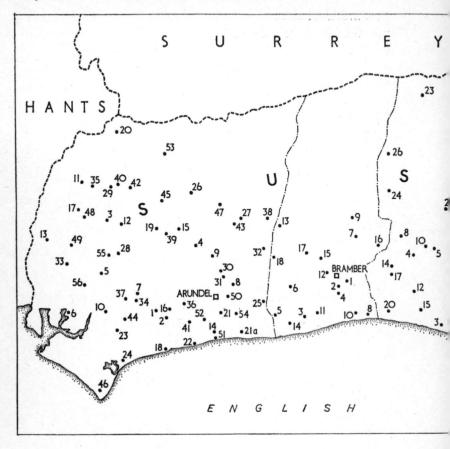

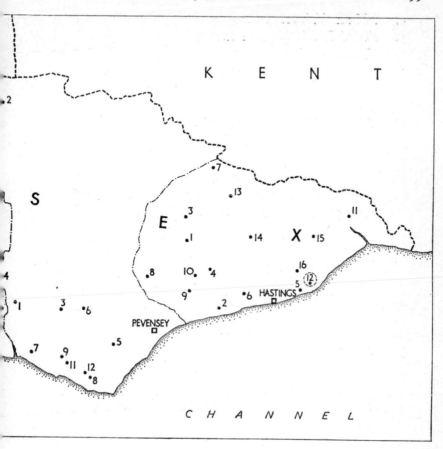

22 Middleton-on-Sea (Middeltone), one church. Now under the sea
23 Mundham (Mundreham)
24 PAGHAM (Pageham)
25 Patcham (Petchinges)
26 Petworth (Peteorde)
27 Pulborough (Poleberge), two churches
28 SINGLETON (Silletone)
29 Stedham (Stedeham)
30 STOKE, NORTH (Stoches)

31 STOKE, SOUTH (Stoches)
32 STORRINGTON (Estorchestone)
33 STOUGHTON (Estone)
34 TANGMERE (Tangemere)
35 Trotton (Traitone)
36 WALBERTON (Walburgetone)
37 WESTHAMPNETT (Hentone)
38 West Chiltington (Cilletone)
39 Woolavington (Levitone)
40 WOOLBEDING (Welbedinge)
41 Yapton. Unnamed, but is probably the church mentioned in Binsted (Benestede) Hundred

B. *Manor but no church mentioned in Domesday Book:*

42 EASEBOURNE (Tadeham)
43 HARDHAM (Heriedham, or Eringeham)
44 RUMBOLDSWYKE (Wiche)
45 SELHAM (Saleham)
46 Selsey (Selsige), now under the sea
47 STOPHAM (Stopeham)
48 Treyford (Treverde), now a heap of rubble
49 UP MARDEN (Meredone)
50 Warning Camp (Warnecheham, or Garnecampo), no remains

C. *Neither manor nor church mentioned in Domesday Book:*

51 Atherington, now under the sea
52 FORD
53 LURGASHALL
54 POLING
55 WEST DEAN
56 WEST STOKE, see also under Bosham

Notes

PART I

INTRODUCTION

1 Or, probably, Romano–British; true Romans were probably few, mainly official and military
2 Tufa is very light and porous; travertine is the name given to a harder and heavier (because less porous, or almost non-porous) kind of tufa

PART II

3 *Cart Sax*, No 64; E. Barker, No II
4 *Cart Sax*, No 78; E. Barker, No IV
5 *Cart Sax*, No 79; E. Barker, No V
6 Probably Bishop Eadberht, Wilfrid's successor, is meant; Wilfrid returned to Northumbria in 686
7 *Cart Sax*, No 553, English and Latin translations in Nos 554 and 555
8 He calls the nave Transitional and the arcading late Norman. This could not be: Norman Transitional was later than late Norman; the nave could not be later than the aisle
9 André et al
10 The phrase *in prebenda* is consistent with the church being a minster
11 *Cart Sax*, I, No 208; also quoted by J. Romilly Allen, p 275, and by P. M. Johnston (*h*), p 155; also E. Barker, No XIV; and W. H. Mullens, pp 5–7
12 Quoted by J. Romilly Allen, op cit, p 274 and by P. M. Johnston (*h*), p 154n
13 An interesting example of the shoddy work which Norman masons sometimes indulged in; see E. A. Fisher (*a*), p 37, and (*b*) pp 33, 197
14 The word porticus has had a curious and complicated derivation. In early medieval times it was used generally to indicate any adjunct opening from the main body of a church (or other building) normally not forming part of the main body, as a transept is by means of wide

arches, but kept separate from it by small narrow doorways. They derived probably from the prothesis and diaconicon of Syrian churches (Clapham (*a*), pp 26–8), but in western Europe and especially in Saxon England usually had altars (secondary altars at which masses could be said), or were tomb chambers (as at SS Peter and Paul, Canterbury). Porches were styled *porticus ingressus*. Porticus with or without altars, whether or not tomb chambers, may be called ecclesiologically 'side—or lateral chapels', or architecturally 'wings', but not transepts (See also E. A. Fisher (*a*), pp 56–7)

15   D. Whitelock, op cit, p 105; F. E. Harmer, op cit, pp 33, 116–19
16   See A. W. Clapham (*a*), p 34, fig 11 and p 48, fig 16; E. A. Fisher (*b*), p 172, fig 13 and p 202, fig 15
17   Cf the ornamentation on the west face of chancel arches and the east face of tower arches, as at Barton-on-Humber and Broughton-by-Brigg (Lincs), see E. A. Fisher (*b*), pp 260, 268
18   Not shown in Godfrey's plan
19   Shown in Sharpe's drawings, Nos 37 and 38
20   See T. G. Jackson, II pl CXLIII; or R. Birt, pl on p 71; or M. Hurlimann and P. Meyer, pl 63
21   Jackson and Fletcher (*d*), pl c and d
22   Salzman, Charter No 1, and p xviii
23   See also VCH, I, p 444
24   E. A. Fisher (*c*), pp 120–3
25   See Blaauw, op cit; also *Cart Sax*, I, No 261; Eric Barker, No XVII. Only Blaauw uses the term 'heretoga'; the others use 'dux'
26   E. Barker, No VII
27   See F. Stenton, p 262
28   For description of the painting see André et al; P. Freeman; E. W. Tristram (*b*), p 307, 525
29   Perhaps by Trevet, as a support for the raised chancel floor
30   Presumably he meant the undercroft: the two openings could not be at the same level if one was in the chancel
31   It is fair to say that he was puzzled and put forward these suggestions as conceivable only; he had rejected a Roman date for the undercroft and church
32   See A. M. Hills (*b*); P. M. Johnston (*b*); R. J. Penny, p 59
33   For all these, except Ford (for which see p 117), see: C. E. Powell; R. E. Turner; R. N. Dennis; P. M. Johnston (*c*); T. R. Turner
34   P. M. Johnston (*n*), drawing in pl 10. Poole wrote that it was in the nave, Johnston in the chancel; it is definitely in the chancel
35   Johnston (*m*), drawing on p 104
36   Johnston (*n*), drawings on p 104

37 See drawings in J. E. Butler, pl facing p 20

38 Drawings in P. M. Johnston (*p*), p 150; and in A. Barr-Hamilton, p 93

39 Kendrick, pp 82, 86, pl LIV

40 There are similar openings, not recesses, at Bracebridge (Lincs), Scawton (Yorks, NR), Avening (Glos) and Castle Rising (Norf); See E. A. Fisher (*b*), pp 262–3

41 Among the studies of most general and (for Sussex) special interest are those of Dr Audrey Baker; Miss F. Byng-Stamper and Miss C. Lucas (introduction by Clive Bell); A. Caiger-Smith; Dr Joan Evans; P. M. Johnston (*b*), (*d*), (*f*), (*k*), (*m*); C. E. Keyser (*a*), (*b*), (*c*); and A. W. Tristram (*a*), (*b*). Other studies are by J. L. André (*a*); J. L. André et al; H. Campion; P. Freeman; E. C. Rouse; L. Vernon-Harcourt; J. G. Waller

42 P. M. Johnston (*q*), p 185, dr in fig 5; E. W. Tristram (*b*), pp 313, 531–2; also J. L. André et al, pp 231–2, coloured dr in pl 22, facing p 232

43 P. M. Johnston (*q*), dr in fig 1

44 Illustrated by P. M. Johnston (*a*)

45 These are not discussed by E. W. Tristram whose book appeared in 1944. They are referred to by J. L. André et al, op cit, 1900, p 232

46 J. H. Round and L. F. Salzman, in VCH, II, p 376

47 As discussed above (p 14) the presence of Caen stone cannot be accepted as evidence for a late date

48 J. L. André et al: P. M. Johnston (*b*), pp 142–51 and figs 17 and 18 on pp 140, 143, and (*c*); E. W. Tristram (*a*), p 124

49 Position indicated in P. M. Johnston (*b*), p 121, fig 6; see also above, under Chichester, pp 78–9

50 André et al p 235; P. M. Johnston (*d*), pp 82–115, drs of nave paintings pp 85, 91, coloured drs pp 88, 104, 110, of chancel p 106, coloured pp 104, 110; P. D. Mundy, pp 246–56; E. W. Tristram (*a*), pp 27–8, 128–33, pls 28–35, 89 k and l

51 Op cit pp 104–5, pls LXXII, LXXIII (2); see also D. Talbot Rice, pp 203–5, pls 68, 69 (*a*) and (*b*); Margaret Rickert, pp 57–8 notes 82, 83 (for dating), pls 44, 75a; and F. Byng-Stamper and C. Lucas, op cit

52 The sub-Castro of the dedication refers to this early encampment. It has no reference to the much later Lewes castle about a quarter-mile to the west

53 *Cart Sax*, No 421; E. Barker (*a*), No XXII. This appears to be a confirmation of an earlier grant by Baldred, King of Kent (who perhaps had no real authority over Sussex) in c 823. Barker thought that '*aet malingum*' refers to Malling in Kent. *Place Names of*

Sussex (p 354) however identifies it with South Malling near Lewes. Salzman (in his editorial note to Barker, p 132) pointed out that the Kent Malling was in the diocese of Rochester and therefore not directly under Canterbury, and that it is 'not impossible' that the Malling of the charter is the one in Sussex. There seems little real doubt of this. Aldulf, dux of the South Saxons, in 765 gave land at Stanmer and elsewhere in order to found a monastery of St Michael at South Malling, which he had apparently already established c 760 (*Cart Sax*, No 179). There is no later mention of this college until Domesday Book when it is stated that the *canons* held four hides at Malling and the estate of Stanmer, a large and very rich manor. Apparently at some time secular canons must have replaced Aldulf's monks. The college was re-founded by Archbishop Theobald c 1150. Malling was a large and rich manor. In King Edward's time; it was assessed at 80 hides, sufficient for 50 ploughs, and worth £40, later £30 and now (in 1086) £70. (See also J. R. Daniel-Tysson; E. Turner)

54   Poole, p 39, pl II; Johnston (I), good drawing, showing also sections of head and jambs

55   As shown in the plates of Burrell, Sharpe, and Horsfield

56   Camden, op cit; the chancel was standing in Camden's time, so he may have seen the monument in situ

57   See John Speed, Bk 8, Chap 7, pp 408–9

58   André et al; E. W. Tristram (b), pp 578–9; M. A. Lower (a), Vol II, p 36

59   *Cart Sax*, Nos 553, 554, 555

60   J. H. Round and L. F. Salzman in VCH, I, p 370

61   It is not mentioned in VCH, II, under Religious Houses, Priory of Lyminster, p 121

62   According to Round and Salzman there is no documentary reference before 1263 to any priory at Lyminster though later tradition is strong that Earl Roger founded one. Round and Salzman appear to accept the tradition as fact (VCH, I, p 429). The land grants were made to the Norman abbey, not to any local priory. Both the Saxon and the Norman priories may have been small. The Norman priory is stated to have had at one time (unspecified) only 26 nuns

63   Bailie's Court, the moated house of the bailiff with its little thirteenth-century chapel, still exists

64   As stated definitely by Salzman in VCH, Atherington church and most of the village, like the old church at nearby Middleton-on-Sea, have been covered by the sea long since. In 1832 Dalloway and Cartwright (op cit, II, pt 1, p 11) described Middleton Church as small and low, and that the south aisle, tower and half the chancel and

the whole south side of the church yard 'are now covered by the sea'. Bits are still visible at low tide

65 For further discussion of such very late post-Conquest Saxon work see above, pp 9, 65–6, and below, p 183

66 There was a port or harbour here, as there is still at New Shoreham. The church here, St Mary de Haura (of the Harbour), still existing in part, was built by the same monks between 1075 and 1103

67 See above under Clayton, p 85; and also Bracebridge (Lincs), E. A. Fisher (*b*), p 138

68 *Cart Sax*, No 50; E. Barker (*a*), No 1

69 André et al; C. E. Keyser (*b*); E. W. Tristram (*b*), pp 307–9; J. G. Waller

70 See also above under Lyminster, p 140ff

71 It is reported that the River Arun was navigable up to Poling and Angmering, 2 miles from the sea, in the fifteenth century. The Arun formed a delta, several miles wide, of gradually rising ground, dotted with pools such as the existing Poling Decoy for wild ducks. This rendered transport easy for Caen and Quarr stone

72 See J. L. André et al; S. H. Campion; E. W. Tristram (*a*), pp 30, 145–6

73 The charter is given in full in *Cart Sax*, III, No 1190

74 See T. D. Kendrick, pl II; D. Talbot Rice, pp 184–5 and pl 46; Margaret Rickert, pl 25

75 *Cart Sax*, III, No 1191

76 For this information the writer is indebted to Mr R. L. S. Bruce-Mitford and Dr C. E. Wright of the British Museum

77 J. L. André et al; W. H. Godfrey (*d*); C. E. Rouse (*a*); E. W. Tristram (*b*), pp 313, 599–600

78 See E. A. Fisher (*b*), pls 5 and 6

79 There is closely similar ornament on the imposts of the chancel arch at Boarhunt (Hants) and on the exterior pilaster strips round the blocked north doorway at Corhampton (Hants), both undoubtedly Saxon churches

80 Eg, there are many errors of details even in such accurate and beautiful engravings as those of John Britton

81 A. Hadrian Allcroft (*a* ii), p 306

82 All measurements of this church (except of the chancel arch, which are the author's) are taken from measured plans and drawings, by an unnamed architect, hanging in the south porticus

83 *Cart Sax*, No 50

84 See E. A. Fisher (*a*), p 84 and pl 29B

85 *Cart Sax*, II, No 640; E. Barker, No XXV

86 *Cart Sax*, II, Nos 553, 554, 555

87   *Cart Sax*, I, No 144

88   In Anon (*b*), of which he may be the author

89   See Sharpe, view (No 365) from SE in 1805; Walford, view from SE facing p 235; VCH, VII, plate facing p 198

90   See Godfrey (*f*), pl on p 14; a better view in Eden, pl XXIV, facing p 232

91   See Fletcher and Jackson, pl XXIII (*a*) SE quoin looking N and XXIII (*b*) same quoin looking west; also H. Braun, pl 46

92   Early porticus were small : at St Pancras, Canterbury, (dated to c 600) they are 10ft by 9ft; at Brixworth (late seventh century) c 9ft square; at Breamore, Hants (c 1000) 11ft by 8ft, at Deerhurst (eighth century or later) NE one 10½ft by 8ft and the north-central one 13ft by 11ft. At Worth they are about 19ft by 15ft, and at Stoughton about 18ft by 14ft

93   At Britford (Wilts) the N and S openings are 5ft 9in and 5ft 7in respectively; at Brixworth only about 3ft; at Breamore 4ft 11in; at Deerhurst, 2-storeyed north-central porticus, lower opening is 3ft 2in wide, the upper 5ft.

94   Walford, facing p 241; also R. H. Nibbs, plate; and also photo of a water colour, looking east, hanging in the church

95   Some parts of the flint walls exteriors are stated to be Saxon, but are indistinguishable from the rest

96   The existing church has nothing Saxon in it; the earliest part is the Norman tower of probably early Overlap date

97   One probably at Warminghurst, 5 miles to the NW; there are no certain remains of either

98   One probably at nearby Thorney (Tornei); the third was probably at West Stoke (which see)

Bibliography

Abbreviations used:

Ant J	Antiquaries Journal
Arch J	Archaeological Journal
Arch	Archaeologia
J Br Arch Ass	Journal of the British Archaeological Association
SAC	Sussex Archaeological Collections
VCH	Victoria County Histories: Sussex

Adam, M. B. 'Sompting Church', *Building News*, 26 Jan 1872

Allcroft, A. Hadrian.
    (a) 'The Circle and the Cross': (1) ch I–IV, *Arch J*, NS, xxvii (1920), 229–308; (2) ch XXII–IV, ibid xxxi (1924), 189–307
    (b) 'The Sussex War Dyke: A Pre-Roman Thoroughfare', *SAC* lxiii, (1922), 54–85
    (c) *Waters of Arun* (1930)

Allen, J. Romilly. 'On Recent Discoveries of pre-Norman Sculptural Stones', *J Br Arch Ass*, xli (1885), 267–77

Anon.
    (a) *Poling and the Church* (nd; guide)
    (b) 'Westdean: The Church of All Saints', *Arch J*, cxvi (1959), 235
    (c) 'Guestling Church', *J Br Arch Ass*, NS, 30 (1924), 23
    (d) *Notes on Arlington and the Church* (guide)

André, J. L.
    (a) 'Mural Paintings in Sussex Churches', *SAC*, xxxviii (1892), 1–20
    (b) 'Sompting Church', *SAC*, xli (1898), 7–24

André, J. L., Keyser, C. E., Johnston, P. M., Whitley, H. M. 'Mural Paintings in Sussex Churches, Report of Committee', *SAC*, xliii (1900) 220–48

Baker, Audrey. 'Lewes Priory and the Early Group of Wall Paintings in Sussex', *Walpole Society*, xxxi (1946), 1–44

Barker, Eric. 'Sussex Anglo-Saxon Charters'
    (a) *SAC*, lxxxvi (1947) 42–101
    (b) ibid, lxxxvii (1948) 112–63 [with translations and notes]

Barr-Hamilton, Alec. *In Saxon Sussex* (Bognor Regis 1961)

Bede, The Venerable. *History of the English Church and People*, trans by L. Shirley-Price, (1955)

Birch, W. de Gray (ed).

(a) *Cartularium Saxonicum:* A Collection of Charters Relating to Anglo-Saxon History, Vol I, AD 430–839 (1885); Vol II, AD 840–947 (1887); Vol III, AD 948–1075 (1893)

(b) *Index Saxonicum*, index of persons in *Cart Sax* (1899)

Birt, Raymond. *The Glories of Winchester Cathedral* (1948)

Blaauw, W. H. 'Buncton, The Grant of part of a Wood in Cealtborgsteal by Ealdwulf, Heretoga of the South Saxons, dated from the Hill of Biohchandoune, AD 791', *SAC*, viii (1856), 177–88

Bloxham, M. H. 'Buncton Chapel', *SAC*, xxxviii (1892), 203–5

Braun, H. *An Introduction to English Mediaeval Architecture* (1951)

Brown, G. Baldwin. *The Arts in Early England, Vol II: Anglo-Saxon Architecture* (2nd ed 1925)

Budgen, Rev W. 'Excete and the Parish Church', *SAC*, lviii (1916), 138–70

Butler, J. E. 'The Antiquities of Stedham Church', *SAC*, iv (1851), 19–21

Byng-Stamper, Frances, and Lucas, Caroline; introduction by Bell, Clive. *Twelfth Century Paintings at Hardham and Clayton* (Lewes 1947)

Caiger-Smith, A. *English Medieval Mural Painting* (Oxford 1963)

Camden, William.

(a) *Britannia* (in Latin), (1st ed 1586)

(b) Trans by Philemon Holland and finally revised and enlarged by the author (1610; 2nd ed 1637)

(c) Revised and enlarged edition of the original, by Edmund Gibson, Bishop of Lincoln, 2 vols (4th ed 1772)

Campion, C. H. 'Mural Paintings in Slaugham Church', *SAC*, xiii (1861), 237–9

Cartularium Saxonicum, see under Birch, W. de Gray

Cavis-Brown, Rev J. *An Old English Hospital* (1894)

Cheal, Henry. *The Story of Shoreham* (Hove 1921)

Clapham, A. W.

(a) *English Romanesque Architecture before the Conquest* (Oxford 1930)

(b) 'Bosham Church', *Arch J*, xcii (1935), 411

(c) 'Sompting Church', *Arch J*, xcii (1935) 405–9

Clayton, C. E. 'Hangleton and its History', *SAC*, xxxiv (1886), 167–84

Clifton-Taylor, A. *The Pattern of English Building* (1962)

Cole, T. W. 'Church Sundials in Mediaeval England', *J Br Arch Ass*, 3rd ser, x (1947), 77–80

Collingwood, R. G. *Roman Britain* (Oxford 1945)

Dale, J. 'Notice of the South Doorway at the Church at Bolney', *SAC*, x (1858), 59–62

Dalloway, John.
  (a) A History of the Western Division of the County of Sussex, Vol
      I (1815)
  (b) with Edmund Cartwright, Vol II, pt 1, The Parochial Topography
      of the Rape of Arundel (1832)
  (c) with E. Cartwright, Vol II, pt 2, The Parochial Topography of the
      Rape of Bramber (1830)
Daniel-Tyssen, J. R. 'Survey of the Church of the College of Malling,
  near Lewes', SAC, xxi (1869), 159–90
Dengate, Rev W. A. Slaugham: A Parish in Sussex (1829) pp 45–61
Dennis, R. N. 'Urns found in East Blatchington Church', SAC, xiii
  (1861), 319
Domesday Book of Sussex (Sudsexe), ed J. H. Round and L. F. Salzman,
  VCH (Sussex), i: introduction by J. H. Round and L. F. Salzman, pp
  351–86; translation and notes by L. F. Salzman, pp 387–452
Drummond-Roberts, M. F. Old Sussex Fonts (1935)
Earwaker, C. The Story of St Peter's, Bexhill (Bexhill 1959)
Eden, Peter. 'Worth: Church of St Nicholas', Arch J, cxvi (1959), 240–1
Evans, A. A.
  (a) Westhampnett, the Parish Church of St Peter; Some Notes, Histori-
      cal and Architectural (Eastbourne, nd, guide)
  (b) Eastdean Parish Church (nd, guide)
Evans, Joan.
  (a) The Romanesque Architecture of the Order of Cluny (Cambridge
      1938)
  (b) Cluniac Art of the Romanesque Period (Cambridge 1950)
Figg, W. H. 'On Bishopstone Church, with Some General Remarks on the
  Churches of East Sussex, SAC, ii (1849), 272–84
Fisher, E. A.
  (a) An Introduction to Anglo-Saxon Architecture and Sculpture (1959)
  (b) The Greater Anglo-Saxon Churches: An Architectural–Historical
      Study (1962)
  (c) Anglo-Saxon Towers (Newton Abbot 1969)
Fleming, Lindsay. The Little Churches of Chichester [Chichester Papers,
  No 5] (Bognor Regis 1957) St Olave's ch, pp 7–10
Freeman, Rev Philip. 'On Some Antiquities lately Discovered in St Olave's
  Church, Chichester', SAC, v (1852), 213–38
Gentleman's Magazine.
  (a) 'Restoration of Old Shoreham Church, Sussex', NS, xv, pt 2 (1841),
      640–1
  (b) Ibid, NS, xxxvii (1852), 164; St Olave's Church, Chichester
  (c) Ibid, NS, xxxvii (1852), 272–3; St Olave's Church, Chichester

(d) Ibid, Rev W. Watkins. 'Roman Urns and Fresco Paintings at St Olave's Church, Chichester', pp 373–4

Godfrey, W. E. 'Old Shoreham Church', *Arch J*, cxvi (1959), 245

Godfrey, W. H.

(a) 'Axial Towers in Sussex Churches', SAC, lxxxi (1940), 97–120 [Kingston Buci, pp 112–13]

(b) 'The Parish Church of St Andrew, Bishopstone', SAC, lxxxvii (1948) 164–83

(c) *Guide to the Church of St Andrew, Bishopstone* (Oxford 1957)

(d) *Guide to the Church of Southease* (Eastbourne 1952)

(e) *Guide to the Church of St Margaret, Ditchling* (Oxford 1958)

(f) *Guide to the Church of St Nicholas, Worth* (Oxford 1962)

(g) *Notes on Lewes Castle, The Priory of St Pancras, Anne of Cleeves' Home, and other Ancient Buildings in Lewes* (2nd ed 1929, pub for Sussex Arch Soc)

(h) 'St Mary's and Priory College, Bramber', SAC, lxxxvi (1947) 102–17

(k) *Guide to the Church of St Mary, Sompting* (Oxford 1951)

(l) *Sussex Notes and Queries*, 3 (1930–1), Sussex Church Plans: No X, Singleton, p 81; No XIII, Clayton; No XV, Botolphs, p 718

(m) with L. F. Salzman (ed) *Sussex Views, Selected from The Burrell Collection* (Oxford 1951) [The Jubilee volume of the Sussex Record Society]

Grayling, Francis. 'Kingston-Buci Church', SAC, lxi (1920), 53–60

Green, A. R. 'Anglo-Saxon Sundials', *Ant J*, viii, 489–516

Hall, A. D. and Russell, E. J. *A Report on the Agriculture and Soils of Kent, Surrey and Sussex* (1911) (Min of Ag) especially ch V 'Building Stone and other Economic Products', pp 157–61

Hannah, I. C. 'West Hoathly, St Margaret's Church', SAC, lxxvi (1936) 201–11

Harmer, Florence. *Select English Historical Documents of the 9th and 10th Centuries* (Cambridge 1914)

Harrison, Frederic. *Notes on Sussex Churches* (4th ed, Hove 1920)

Hayward, R. L.

(a) *Storrington, The Parish Church and Village in Early Times* (Glos 1955)

(b) *Yesterday in Sullington: The Church, The Parish and the Manor* (nd)

Hills, A. M.

(a) 'The Church of Westhampnett, Sussex, chiefly in Reference to the Roman Remains', SAC, xxi (1869) 33–43 (reprinted from *J Br Arch Ass*, xxiv (1868), 209–18

(b) 'Earthenware Jars in Church Walls', *J Br Arch Ass*, xxxv (1879), 95–8

Hinckley, Helen. *Easebourne, its Church and Priory* (Hove 1919)

Hope, Sir W. St J. *Cowdray and Easebourne Priory* (1919)

Horsfield, Rev T. W.
  (a) *The History of Lewes and its Vicinity* (Lewes 1824)
  (b) *The History, Antiquities and Topography of the County of Sussex,* 2 vols (Lewes 1835)

Hurliman, Martin and Meyer, Peter. *English Cathedrals* (1950)

Hussey, Rev A.
  (a) *The Churches in the Counties of Kent, Surrey and Sussex mentioned in Domesday Book, and those of more Recent Date* (1852) [Sussex churches pp 171–311]
  (b) 'Rottingdean Church in 1855', SAC, ix (1857), 67–70

Hutchinson, T. 'Ditchling', SAC, xiii (1856), 240–61

Jackson, E. D. C. and Fletcher, E. G. M.
  (a) 'Further Notes on "Long and Short" Quoins in Saxon Churches', J Br Arch Ass, 3rd Ser, xii (1949), 1–18
  (b) 'Constructional Characteristics in Anglo-Saxon Churches', ibid, xiv, (1951), 11–26
  (c) 'The Saxon Church at Bradford-on-Avon', ibid, xvi (1953), 41–58
  (d) 'Porch and Porticus in Saxon Churches', ibid, xix (1956), 1–13 (See also under Fletcher and Jackson)

Jackson, Sir T. G. *Byzantine and Romanesque Architecture* (Cambridge 1920)

Johnston, P. M.
  (a) (1) 'The Low-Side Windows of Sussex Churches', SAC, xli (1898), 159–202; (2) ibid, xlii (1899), 117–79
  (b) 'Ford and its Church', SAC, xliii (1900), 105–57
  (c) 'Ford and its Church: Addenda and Corrigenda', SAC, xliv (1901), 306–8
  (d) 'Hardham Church, and its Early Paintings', SAC, xliv (1901), 73–115 (reprinted from Arch J, lviii, NS viii (1901), 12–92
  (e) 'Hardham Church', Arch J, xcii (1935), 417–19
  (f) 'Mural Paintings in Sussex Churches', SAC, xliv (1901), 204–6
  (g) 'The Church of Lyminster and the Chapel of Warning Camp', SAC, xlvi (1903), 195–230
  (h) 'A pre-Conquest Grave Slab at Bexhill', SAC, xlviii (1905), 153–5
  (j) 'A Supposed Pre-Norman Font at Waldron', SAC, xlix (1906), 126–7 (plate)
  (k) 'An Ancient Painting at Aldingbourne Church', SAC, xlix (1906), 157–8
  (l) 'Ecclesiastical Architecture', VCH II (1907), 327–79 details of churches up to AD 1120, pp 362–7; building materials, pp 333–8

(*m*) 'Mural Painting in Sussex' in *Memorials of Old Sussex* (1909), pp 242–82 (See also below under Mundy)

(*n*) 'Chithurst Church', SAC, lv (1912), 99–107

(*o*) 'Steyning Church', J Br Arch Ass, NS, xx (1914), 275–84

(*p*) 'Steyning: St Andrew's Church', SAC, lvii (1915), 149–61

(*q*) 'Clayton Church', J Br Arch Ass, NS, xxiii (1917), 154–57

(*r*) 'The Church of St John Sub-Castro, Lewes', J Br Arch Ass, NS, xxiii (1917), p 161–2

(*s*) 'Old Shoreham Church', J Br Arch Ass, NS, xxiii (1917), p 173

(*t*) 'Poling and the Knights Hospitalers: Part I, The Village and Church', SAC, lx (1919), 67–91

(*u*) 'Cocking and Its Church', Arch J, lxxviii, NS xxviii (1921), 174–204. [Has a note on Walberton, 187–8]

Kendrick, T. D. *Late Saxon and Viking Art* (1949)

Keyser, C. E.

(*a*) *List of Buildings having Mural Decoration* (1883)

(*b*) 'Description of the Mural Paintings at the Churches of Clayton and Rotherfield, Sussex', SAC, xl (1896), 211–21

(*c*) 'Mural Painting of the Doom in Patcham Church, Sussex', Arch J, xxxviii (1881), 80–95 (See also under Waller)

Levitt, Canon A. M. SAC, xlviii (1905), p 40–1, note criticising P. M. Johnston's views.

Legge, W. Heneage. 'The Villages and Churches of the Hundred of Willingdon', *The Reliquary*, vii (1901), pp 1–10 and 145–7

Lower, M. A.

(*a*) *A Compendious History of Sussex*, 2 vols (1870)

(*b*) *Sussex Parish Churches: Specimens of Church Architecture, including Doorways, Windows, Fonts, Effigies, etc. from original etchings by a local artist*: not published, folio (Brighton 1874) [Illustrations for Lower's History of Sussex]

Macdermott, K. H. *Bosham Church: Its History and Antiquities* (3rd ed, Chichester 1926)

Meade, W. E. 'The Ancient Churches of East Sussex', a series of articles published in the *Sussex Express*, weekly from Jan 1931 to 1938, 3 vols of cuttings in Library of Sussex Archaeological Society at Lewes.

Melland, Rev T. 'Notices of the Early History of Steyning and Its Church', SAC, v (1852), 111–26

Mitchell, H. 'On the Early Traditions of Bosham, and the Discovery of the Stone Coffin containing the Remains of a Daughter of King Canute in the Nave of Bosham Church', SAC, xviii (1866), 1–9

Mullens, W. H. *A Short History of Bexhill in the County of Sussex*, privately printed, (Bexhill 1927)

Mundy, P. D. (ed and part author). *Memorials of Old Sussex* (1909)

Neale, J. M. 'An Account of the Late Restoration in the Church of Old Shoreham, Sussex', *Camb Camden Soc*, pt I (1839–41), 28–34

Nibbs, R. H. *The Churches of Sussex*, etched by R. H. Nibbs, 1851; reissued in 1872 with history and architectural descriptions by M. A. Lower (Brighton 1872)

Page, W. 'Some Remarks on the Churches of the Domesday Surrey', *Arch*, lxvi, sec ser xvi (1914–15), pp 61–102 [Sussex churches, 79–82]

Parry, J. D. *Historical and Descriptive Account of the Coast of Sussex* (1833)

Peat, A. H. and Halsted, L. C. *Churches and other Antiquities of West Sussex* (Chichester 1912)

Peckham, W. D.
    (a) 'Up Marden', *SAC*, lxv (1924), p 261
    (b) 'The Parishes of the City of Chichester', *SAC*, lxxiv (1933), 65–97 [St Olave, 84–5]

Peers, C. R. Review of Baldwin Brown's *Anglo-Saxon Architecture*, *Ant J*, vi (1926), 209–12

Penny, R. J. 'Tarrant Rushton Church, Dorset', *Proc Dorset Nat Hist & Ant Field Club*, xviii (1897), 53–65 [Jars in wall, 59]

Poole, H. 'The Domesday Book Churches of Sussex', *SAC*, lxxxvii (1948), 29–76

Powell, C. E. 'Arlington Church', *SAC*, xxxviii (1892), 184–8

Ray, J. E. 'The Church of SS Peter and Paul, Bexhill', *SAC*, liii (1910), 61–108. [History and pre-Conquest, 61–6]

Rickert, Margaret. *Painting in Britain, The Middle Ages* (1954)

Rickman, T. *An Attempt to Discriminate the Styles of Architecture in England*, (5th ed 1848)

Round, J. H. 'The Early History of North and South Stoke', *SAC*, lix (1918), 1–24 (see also under Domesday Book)

Rouse, E. C.
    (a) 'Wall Paintings in Southease Church', *SAC*, lxxviii (1937), 3–12
    (b) 'Clayton: Church of St John the Baptist', *Arch J*, cxvi (1959), 233–4

Rush, H. J. 'Wivelsfield Church', *SAC*, xxii (1870), 50–6

Salzman, L. F.
    (a) 'Some Sussex Domesday Book Tenants: II, The Family of Dene', *SAC*, lviii (1916), 171–89
    (b) *Building in England to 1540* (Oxford 1952)
    (c) *The Chartulary of Sele Priory* (1923). (See also under Domesday Book, and under Godfrey and Salzman)

Sawyer, F. E. 'St Wilfrith's Life in Sussex and the Introduction of Christianity', *SAC*, xxxiii (1883), 101–21

Searle, W. G. *Anglo-Saxon Bishops, Kings and Nobles* (Cambridge 1899)

Sharpe, Edgar. *Collection of Drawings by Henry Petrie, 1800–1820*, now in the Sussex Archaeological Society's Library at Lewes.

Simpson, F. S. W. *The Churches of St Nicholas, Old Shoreham, and St Mary de Haura, New Shoreham* (3rd ed, Glos 1958)

Sisson, Rosemary. *The Parish Church of St Mary Magdalene, Lyminster* (Littlehampton 1958, guide)

Speed, John. *The History of Gt Britaine* (1611)

Steer, F. W. *Guide to the Church of St Mary the Virgin, Burpham* (Chichester 1961)

Talbot-Rice, D. *English Art, 871–1100* (Oxford 1952)

Taylor, H. M. and J. *Anglo-Saxon Architecture* (Cambridge 1964)

Tristram, E. W.
  (a) *English Medieval Wall Painting, The Twelfth Century* (Oxford 1944)
  (b) *English Medieval Wall Painting, The Thirteenth Century*, 2 vols (Oxford 1950)

Turner, E.
  (a) 'On the Ancient Bridge discovered at Bramber in 1839', SAC, ii (1849), 63–77
  (b) 'The College of Benedictine Canons of South Malling', SAC, v (1852), 127–42

Turner, R. E. 'Fictile Vessel found in Buxted Church', SAC, xxi (1869), 202–6

Turner, T. R. 'Roman Pottery in Sutton, near Bignor, Church', SAC, xv (1863), 242–3

Vernon-Harcourt, L. 'The Mural Paintings recently Discovered at Stedham Church', SAC, iv (1851), 1–18

Victoria County Histories; Sussex, Vol I (1905); Vol II (1907); Vol III (1935); Vol IV (1953); Vol VII (1940); Vol IX (1937)

Walcott, M. E. C. 'The Bishops of Chichester from Stigand to Sherborne', SAC, xxviii (1878), 11–58 [Bishops of Selsey, p 13]

Walford, W. S. 'On the Church at Worth', SAC, viii (1856), 235–49

Waller, J. G. 'Notes on the Painting of the Doom at Patcham', Arch J, xxxviii (1881), 96–7 (See also above under C. E. Keyser (c))

Whitelock, Dorothy. *Anglo-Saxon Wills* translated, edited and annotated (Cambridge 1930)

Whitley, H. Michell. 'Primitive Sundials in West Sussex Churches', SAC, lx (1919), 126–40

Wynne, Rev A. E., Verey, Rev L. and Corrie, D. *The Story of the Parish Church of St Margaret, Rottingdean* (Glos 1953)

Acknowledgements

Thanks are due to a number of people for supplying photographs and for permission to publish copyright material; their names appear in the List of Illustrations at the front of this volume.

The Rev E. F. Taylor supplied much information about Hangleton church.

As with the author's earlier book (*Anglo-Saxon Towers*), special thanks are due to his publishers and their technical staff for careful editing and for converting his rather amateurish line drawings into a form suitable for publication.

Index

References to illustrations are printed in italic